CONCERN FOR THE OTHER

Edited by Svend Andersen
and Kees van Kooten Niekerk

CONCERN FOR THE OTHER

*Perspectives on
the Ethics of
K. E. Løgstrup*

University of Notre Dame Press
Notre Dame, Indiana

Designed by Wendy McMillen
Set in 10.6/13.6 Monotype Bell by Four Star Books

Library of Congress Cataloging-in-Publication Data

Concern for the other : perspectives on the ethics of K. E. Løgstrup /
edited by Svend Andersen and Kees van Kooten Niekerk.
     p.   cm.
  Includes bibliographical references and index.
  ISBN-13: 978-0-268-02031-6 (pbk. : alk. paper)
  ISBN-10: 0-268-02031-0 (pbk. : alk. paper)
  1. Løgstrup, K. E. (Knud Ejler), 1905–   2. Ethics.
I. Andersen, Svend, 1948–   II. Niekerk, Kees van Kooten, 1946–
  B4382.L64C66   2007
  170.92—dc22

                                                    2007033428

Contents

Preface

Knud E. Løgstrup is undoubtedly the most prominent philosopher-theologian Denmark has fostered since the days of Søren Kierkegaard. His book *The Ethical Demand* is a major work in twentieth-century Danish thinking. It reached an unusually broad audience when it was first published, and it still does. In his own lifetime Løgstrup had close contacts within German academic life, and many of his books and articles have been translated into German. His relation to the English-speaking world was different. Until recently, only the 1971 American edition of *The Ethical Demand* was available in English. The last two decades, however, have seen a growing interest in Løgstrup's ethics in the Anglo-American world. One testament to this interest is the fact that this ethics plays a prominent part in Zygmunt Bauman's well-known book *Postmodern Ethics*, from 1993, and another was the appearance in 1997 of a new edition of *The Ethical Demand* with an introduction by Hans Fink and Alasdair MacIntyre.

The Ethical Demand, however, mirrors only one phase of Løgstrup's ethical thinking. During the later decades of his life Løgstrup developed important new themes. It was therefore natural to make available to English-speaking readers a more comprehensive selection of Løgstrup's work in ethics. This consideration gave rise to the idea of translating texts and discussing them at an international workshop. Such a workshop, under the name "The Significance of K. E. Løgstrup's Ethics," was held in Denmark at the beautiful Sandbjerg Estate, the conference centre belonging to the University of Aarhus, from 8 May to 12 May 2002. The contributions from this workshop form the main content of the present volume. It is with great pleasure that we are now able to present this work and its companion *Beyond the*

Ethical Demand, a collection of texts by Løgstrup on ethics, newly translated into English.

The editors would first and foremost like to thank the Velux Foundation for generously funding the reconstruction of the Løgstrup Archive at the University of Aarhus and for making possible the Sandbjerg workshop. Our thanks are also extended to the contributors to this volume. Although Zygmunt Bauman was unable to participate, he wrote a contribution for the workshop material. Hans Fink, who was originally asked to comment on Bauman's paper, gave a general philosophical analysis of Løgstrup's ethics, which we gratefully include. Øjvind Larsen did not participate in the workshop, but his close relationship with Bauman made him an obvious respondent, and we appreciate his willingness to contribute.

The chapters by non-English-speaking authors have received a careful linguistic revision by Heidi Flegal, who also translated three of the Løgstrup texts in *Beyond the Ethical Demand.* Without her suggestions the language in this volume would not have been as fluent as we now find it to be.

Finally, we thank the publishers at the University of Notre Dame Press for their willingness to add two more Løgstrup volumes to complement *The Ethical Demand.* Our first principal contact was Jeffrey Gainey, who was succeeded by Chuck Van Hof and Rebecca DeBoer. They deserve special gratitude for their patience and professional handling of all problems.

Aarhus, Spring 2006
Svend Andersen
Kees van Kooten Niekerk

Abbreviations

Abbreviations refer to translations of K. E. Løgstrup in *Beyond the Ethical Demand* (Notre Dame: University of Notre Dame Press, 2007).

LI   Expressions of Life and Ideas (chapter 6 of *Beyond the Ethical Demand*)

NEL   Norm and Expressions of Life (chapter 4)

R   Rejoinder (chapter 1)

SEL   The Sovereign Expressions of Life (chapter 2)

SGCN Sovereign Expressions of Life, the Golden Rule, Character Traits, and Norms (chapter 3)

Introduction

Svend Andersen and Kees van Kooten Niekerk

Løgstrup's ethics of the *ethical demand* was formulated half a century ago. Nevertheless, it seems to be receiving renewed attention today. This might, in part, be a result of its tendency to reflect several important trends in contemporary moral thinking. Here one could think of the widespread skepticism towards "modern" efforts to give a purely rational foundation for claims about moral behavior. Løgstrup related himself to the modern project in its Kantian version. Against the idea of the rational agent he set up a description of the interrelatedness of human being. In his opinion, humans do not have to discover or decide about moral life—our life as such is ordered with ethics already "built in," so to speak. We cannot encounter others without being confronted with the radical demand to concern ourselves with their lives. Responsibility is a basic feature of human existence. This position lay close at hand for a Lutheran theologian, but Løgstrup developed and formulated it with the aid of phenomenological analysis. The appeal of his ethics therefore rests not so much on rational argument as on the careful descriptions of elementary features of interpersonal existence.

In his early work, Løgstrup put trust or self-exposure and the corresponding radical demand at the center of his ethical phenomenology. However, as can be seen from later texts, some of which are now collected in *Beyond the Ethical Demand*, important changes took place in his thinking. Most significant among these changes is the "appearance" of the concept or phenomenon of "sovereign expressions of life." These include phenomena such as trust, mercy, compassion, and openness of speech. Løgstrup originally regarded trust as the interpersonal feature out of which the ethical demand arises. But at this later stage he took it to be an ethical expression in its own right. Like the other expressions, trust is a spontaneous showing of regard for the other. Its sovereignty consists in the fact that we, as moral agents, do not have it under our control. We cannot produce trust by exercising our will. Rather, trust "takes us by surprise." Like trust, mercy is also an ethical phenomenon, both in the sense that it is a way of taking care of the other, and in the sense that it is a consummation of human life. As ways of taking care of others, the expressions of life fulfill the ethical demand—before the demand has even made itself felt. The sovereign expressions of life are therefore more fundamental ethical phenomena than the demand that derives from them.

The introduction of the sovereign expressions of life is related to a number of other changes and clarifications. First, it becomes clear in Løgstrup that ethics as such does not necessarily have a religious foundation: the expressions of life are "open to religious interpretation," but their ethical force is not dependent upon it. Second, even if Løgstrup still makes a clear distinction between what could be called "primary ethical phenomena" (such as the sovereign expressions of life and the ethical demand) and "ordinary" morality (consisting of norms, ideals, character traits, moral reasoning, and so on), the latter are granted a more prominent position. Besides drawing this distinction, Løgstrup proceeds to investigate the relationship between the two sets of phenomena. Thus, in some cases he regards norms as transformations of the expressions of life. Third, political ethics is given a more central place, and in the political domain, too, Løgstrup sees transformed expressions of life at work. The political-ethical ideal of helping those in need, for instance, can be seen as derived from mercy as an expression of life.

The contributions in the present volume deal with significant themes in Løgstrup's later ethical writing without losing sight of the argument in *The Ethical Demand*. Several authors consider Løgstrup's analysis of trust, which still plays an important role, now as one of the sovereign expressions of life. The analysis of trust is also discussed in several essays as an important instance of Løgstrup's thorough phenomenological description. Another recurring issue is the question of whether Løgstrup's ethics is defensible on purely philosophical grounds or rests on theological presuppositions.

The essays included here fall into two groups. The volume begins with three introductory interpretations by scholars associated with the university where Løgstrup held his professorship and who are familiar with his work in its Danish context. These are followed by four essays that discuss Løgstrup's ethics from an external perspective, thereby placing it in an international context. Each essay in the latter group is followed by a response from a Scandinavian scholar.

Hans Fink gives a loyal presentation of the main ideas of *The Ethical Demand* as read by a philosopher, offering a comprehensive answer to his own question, "Why should a philosopher like me, who is not a member of any church, be interested in studying Løgstrup's theologically motivated attempt to limit himself to the philosophical?" He makes a sharp distinction between the ethics of the demand—the radical requirement of taking care of the other—and "ordinary" morality. The one and only ethical demand arises from features of human life that must be accepted as given facts. Fink emphasizes, however, that life can be regarded as given and can be lived in humility without one imagining a giver. He agrees with Løgstrup that the radical nature of the demand can be convincingly demonstrated by purely philosophical—phenomenological—analysis. Only the demand deserves to be called "ethical," but if it "were the only demand we were under, life would be unbearable." The importance of the many moral demands equals that of the one and only ethical demand. Fink clarifies his point about Løgstrup's unusual approach to ethics by comparing Løgstrup with figures from traditional moral philosophy, such as Hume and Kant.

Svend Andersen follows up this line of thinking by reviewing the treatment Løgstrup himself gave to other moral philosophers. His aim is to help place Løgstrup within the landscape of moral philosophy. Løgstrup was not preoccupied with traditional moral philosophers—such as Aristotle and Aquinas—whereas we can regard Kant as his great adversary, and, on a par with Kant, Løgstrup's famous compatriot Søren Kierkegaard. Løgstrup's main inspiration was Martin Luther's idea of

4   humans as being placed in relationships of responsibility. Løgstrup, in various ways, tried to reformulate this so-called doctrine of creation ordinances from Luther using a philosophical vocabulary. He found his most convincing philosophical support in the all-but-forgotten German phenomenologist Hans Lipps. This contribution sketches the parts of Lipps's existential anthropology that were important for Løgstrup's ethics. As a link to Løgstrup, it also compares Lipps's analysis of the human face to that of Emmanuel Lévinas.

Kees van Kooten Niekerk's contribution aims at elucidating Løgstrup's view that morality is a substitute by tracing its genesis in the development of his ethical thought. In *Opgør med Kierkegaard* (Controverting Kierkegaard) Løgstrup regards acting out of duty or virtue as a substitute for the sovereign expressions of life: a substitute that is inferior to them, because the agent no longer draws the motivation from the intended benefit of the other, but draws it from his or her own sense of duty or virtue. According to Niekerk, Løgstrup's conception of the sovereign expressions of life has its background in the ideal of an immediate, pre-reflective preoccupation with the other, which he inherited partly from Luther and partly from a Danish type of philosophy of life. Under the influence of the Danish theological movement "Tidehverv" (Time on the Turn), Løgstrup came to contrast this ideal to morality as a reflective preoccupation with oneself, which, from a theological point of view, must be regarded as sin. However, in *Norm og spontaneitet* (Norm and Spontaneity) this rather negative view of morality is counterbalanced by a more positive view focusing on immediate moral action.

Brenda Almond once again deals with Løgstrup's position compared to twentieth-century British moral philosophy, a comparison that Løgstrup himself makes—at least partially—in *Norm og spontaneitet*. Løgstrup himself did not see much progress in the development from intuitionism to prescriptivism. And Almond to some extent agrees. She finds some similarity, however, between Løgstrup's "intuitionism of the situation" and H. A. Prichard's emphasis on the concrete situation in his rejection of the relevance of the question, "Why should I do my duty?" Almond's association of Løgstrup with intuitionism leads her to regard W. D. Ross's theory of prima facie duties as similar in many respects to Løgstrup's ethical thought. She also points out connections between Løgstrup's ethics and recent theories such as the feminist ethics of care.

Basically, Almond regards Løgstrup as a defender of an "ethics of agape" and hence as a Christian ethicist. Philosophically speaking, she defends the caution inherent in her English-speaking tradition "about foregoing the hard core of morality that is represented by concepts like rights, duties, and obligations." She agrees with Løgstrup, however, that our initial moral responses should be "responses to the facts of situations rather than the initiation of a chain of theoretical reflection."

In her response to Almond, *Anne Marie Pahuus* gives a more extensive treatment of the concept of "situation," which Løgstrup adopted to a substantial degree from Hans Lipps. Pahuus emphasizes the role of "imaginative understanding" in Løgstrup. But she critically argues in favor of the necessity of a self-reflective process in moral life.

Zygmunt Bauman is one of the principal authors who have made Løgstrup the ethicist known in the English-speaking world. He considers Løgstrup—as he does Lévinas—an important voice in postmodern (or "liquid modern") society, where traditional moral philosophy, with its relatedness to law, has ceased to be convincing. Løgstrup's ethics of the radical but silent demand shows that there is no security in ethics. Yet Bauman questions the fundamental phenomenon of trust. He speculates that in promoting this phenomenon, Løgstrup's course may have been determined by the social conditions in Denmark during his earlier years. But, he asks, is trust a realistic option in a modern society of "pure relationships" (to borrow a term of Anthony Giddens)? Is the world of today not "conspiring against trust"? In spite of this critical questioning, Bauman claims that the only hope for moral life is pre-reflective spontaneity. However—and this is a lesson Bauman learnt from Løgstrup—this hope is unavoidably connected with uncertainty. Bauman, too, points out the problems for moral action brought by globalization. How is it possible, he asks, to act on immediate sovereign expressions of life when the target of our action is far removed from our space of proximity? He concludes his essay by hinting at a possible connection between the much-needed global instruments of political action and Løgstrup's ethics.

In his response to Bauman, *Øjvind Larsen* points out that Bauman's enthusiasm for Løgstrup's ethics is based on the fact that Løgstrup advocates a sort of unconditional responsibility that is sorely needed in a cynical, postmodern society. Larsen takes a critical approach to Bauman's attempt to apply Løgstrup's conception of responsibility to a global

6   perspective and argues that it involves an unlimited, "metaphysical" guilt for circumstances that lie beyond our personal sphere of causal influence. He emphasizes that in Løgstrup's ethics, in contrast, responsibility and guilt are linked to personal relations between human beings in concrete situations. Larsen assesses Bauman's juxtaposition of Løgstrup's silent demand and the traditional "legislative forms of ethics." He finds this label too broad, and he does not share Bauman's conviction that Løgstrup's ethics of the demand can be transmuted to accommodate a postmodern, globalized situation completely unlike that of Løgstrup's day and age.

Alasdair MacIntyre also deserves credit for having introduced Løgstrup to the Anglo-American discussion of moral philosophy. In his contribution he looks at Løgstrup from a Thomist perspective, that is, from within a tradition that continually discusses questions with other schools of thought. For modern Thomism, one such important school is phenomenology. And, according to MacIntyre, it is from Løgstrup the phenomenologist that Thomists can learn something. Not surprisingly, though, MacIntyre does not find Løgstrup's dismissive remarks on virtues convincing. This difference is rooted in a more fundamental disagreement about teleology. Løgstrup did not deal with teleology in the Thomistic sense, in which humans are directed towards their good in the context of natural law. Virtues for MacIntyre differ from what Løgstrup calls "character traits" in that they are habits directed towards goods. MacIntyre is also critical of Løgstrup's analysis of trust, and he defends Aquinas's claim that we can have reasons for trusting others. Leaning on psychological insights from D. W. Winnicott, he also points out the necessity of "cultivating discriminating suspicion." Against Løgstrup's thesis that spontaneity excludes reflection, MacIntyre claims that the spontaneity of the good has to be acquired through learning. According to Thomists, the virtuous agent has integrated reflection to such a degree that he or she responds spontaneously to ethical situations. Finally, MacIntyre returns to the ethical demand and argues that Løgstrup's idea that the demand is unfulfillable is flawed. The demand is fulfilled by those who have advanced in virtue, especially the saints. This is a point on which the division between Thomists and Løgstrup turns out to coincide with the division between Catholics and Lutherans. So in the end, MacIntyre, too, draws attention to Løgstrup's Lutheran heritage.

In his response to MacIntyre, *Svein Aage Christoffersen* profits from his comprehensive reading of Løgstrup's work in Danish. He points to the very important distinction Løgstrup makes between the sovereign expression of life and the act in which it is embodied. The latter is always shaped by the situation and the society in which the agent is placed. Løgstrup would presumably be quick to grant reflection its place in relation to the sovereign expressions of life, namely, the actions to which they give rise.

The contribution from *Hans Reinders* explicitly presents Løgstrup as a Christian ethicist. Reinders takes seriously Løgstrup's language of life as a gift. Reinders reminds us that Løgstrup himself regarded "understanding life as a gift" as a necessary precondition if the one-sidedness of the ethical demand was to make sense. But understanding one's life as a gift is a religious belief, even if (according to Løgstrup) it is not a specifically Christian one. Løgstrup's argument cannot be understood as purely philosophical, for, as Reinders observes, "proceeding from a religious perspective is not what philosophical ethics does." In an illuminating way, Reinders places Løgstrup's language in the context of the contemporary discussions of "gift" as carried out by Bauman, Pierre Bourdieu, Jacques Derrida, and John Milbank. He interprets Løgstrup's analysis of the sovereign expressions of life as an answer to Derrida's claim that a "true gift" is not possible. The expressions of life are part of God's expansive giving of life itself. In thus claiming that the expressions of life can only be understood within language dealing with God's creation and grace, Reinders is well aware that he goes far beyond what Løgstrup himself would have found acceptable.

Jakob Wolf, in his response to Reinders, rejects Reinders's interpretation. He admits that Løgstrup's distinction between philosophy and theology is of Lutheran origin, but in his view this should not be understood in a confessional sense. Løgstrup's ethics admittedly has religious grounds, but grounds that are accessible to phenomenological analysis.

The contributions in this volume demonstrate that Løgstrup's ethical thought contains valuable insights for contemporary ethical discussion. This applies first and foremost to his phenomenological approach,

8   which bases ethics on acute analyses of what is going on in human living together. More specifically, one could think of his elucidations of the moral importance of human interdependence and the role of spontaneity in human life. Løgstrup's phenomenological approach was also the central subject of discussions during the Sandbjerg workshop. One of the principal topics of these discussions was the question, provoked by the different positions of Fink and Reinders, of whether Løgstrup's ethics is convincing on purely philosophical grounds or can be accepted only on the basis of theological presuppositions. Another important theme was the scope of phenomenology. Is the notion that life is a gift (*donum*), for example, implied in a phenomenological description of the experience of gratitude, or does it involve a religious or theological interpretation that transcends such a description? Obviously, these two topics are connected insofar as a view of the reach of phenomenology affects the question of whether Løgstrup's ethics can be considered philosophically plausible. There was general agreement among the workshop participants that these issues, as well as a number of others, deserve further research.

CHAPTER ONE

The Conception of Ethics and the Ethical in K. E. Løgstrup's *The Ethical Demand*

Hans Fink

The Ethical Demand is the most important work of moral philosophy written in Danish in the twentieth century, and it remains the central work by its author, K. E. Løgstrup. *The Ethical Demand* is not an easy book to read, and a university education in moral philosophy is no guarantee that the task will be any easier. In this work Løgstrup seeks to explicate a fact about human life, a fact that he takes to underlie everything ethical, and that he claims is so elementary that it tends to be systematically overlooked in ordinary schools of moral inquiry, whether they focus on philosophy or theology, and whether they are rooted in Anglo-American or Continental traditions. Løgstrup seeks to articulate a conception of the ethical that is unlike any other I know of, being at once extremely simple and extremely complex. I believe he is after something quite important that deserves to be taken into account and discussed by moral philosophers in general. In this essay I shall try to defend this claim, organizing my discussion into five sections. In the first four sections I extract what I consider to be the main argument of the book. In the fifth and final section I place Løgstrup's conception of ethics and the ethical in a wider perspective by comparing it with other, better known, conceptions, and by trying to spell out what it is I believe we could all learn from Løgstrup, even if we may not agree with him.

ETHICS, RELIGION, AND PHILOSOPHY

Løgstrup was educated as a theologian, and before becoming a professor of ethics and philosophy of religion he worked for a time as a pastor in the Lutheran Church of Denmark. There is no doubt about his Christian commitment. But Løgstrup was also a philosopher, and well aware that philosophy should not be dogmatically committed. In *The Ethical Demand* he makes an attempt "to give a definition in strictly human terms of the relation to the other person which is contained in the religious proclamation of Jesus of Nazareth" (Løgstrup 1997, 1). This task is clearly set within a theological framework, but the task is equally clearly presented in such a form that it must be performed in purely secular and philosophically acceptable terms.

Why should a Christian theologian be interested in setting himself this purely philosophical task? Løgstrup offers two reasons. First, if we want to understand the proclamation of Jesus of Nazareth, it is necessary that we understand what it is saying in strictly human terms, since no other form of understanding is open to human beings. And "faith without understanding is not faith but coercion" (ibid., 2). Second, the believer needs a purely secular understanding in order to understand why and how the proclamation is more than a mere philosophy of life, to understand why and how Jesus of Nazareth for the Christian believer is to be taken to be more than a moral reformer like Socrates. I believe we can rely on Løgstrup when he says he is trying to argue as a philosopher, and that he himself would regard it as a failure if his argument could be shown to hinge on his religious commitments.[1] On the other hand, he also makes it quite clear that he is confident the readers who have followed his philosophical argument will feel invited, though not logically forced, to step beyond philosophy and into the realm of faith.

Why should a philosopher like me, who is not a member of any church, be interested in studying Løgstrup's theologically motivated attempt to limit himself to the philosophical? Ever since my student days I have been impressed by Løgstrup's seriousness and deeply personal way of thinking, and I am convinced that his philosophical argument can, in fact, stand on its own without any specifically Christian presuppositions, and that it is quite possible to accept its central tenets without being forced or inclined to embrace any views that go beyond what should be perfectly acceptable in philosophical terms—which is, of course, not the same as being accepted by all philosophers. And so, no matter how Løgstrup himself may have regarded the connections between his philosophy and his theology, I shall try in this paper to interpret his argument in strictly human terms and for purely philosophical purposes. (I thus disagree with Hans Reinders, whose contribution to this volume insists that Løgstrup's ethics is essentially a Christian ethics. But even if he were right in this conclusion, I believe that a purely philosophical reconstruction of Løgstrup's argument would be of interest to non-Christian philosophers.) Løgstrup the philosopher was trained in the phenomenological tradition, whereas I was educated within the analytical tradition. I believe the elements in Løgstrup's philosophy that I am interested in here can be expressed in terms that should be acceptable to both these traditions.

Løgstrup follows the Lutheran theologian Friedrich Gogarten in claiming that the central point in the religious proclamation of Jesus of Nazareth is that "the individual's relation to God is determined wholly at the point of his relation to the neighbor" (ibid., 4). In strictly human terms this could be taken to mean that the relation to the other person is what holds the highest importance in our life. What will matter most on our dying day is how our life has been in relation to others. Failing others is an important aspect of failing ourselves. According to Løgstrup, Gogarten's understanding of the proclamation has an important implication: "If my relation to the other person is the place where my relation to God is determined, then it must at the same time be the place where that person's existence is so totally at stake that to fail him is to fail him irreparably" (ibid., 5). If the relations to other people are what hold the highest importance in my life, something highly important must also be at stake for other people in their relations with me. If my failure in relation to another person may be something that matters crucially on my dying day, this is because my failure may be something that has mattered crucially in that other person's life. How should we conceive of human life in strictly human terms if person-to-person relationships are thus of the utmost importance in human life? This is the question I take Løgstrup to be addressing.

12   ELEMENTARY PHILOSOPHICAL ANTHROPOLOGY

In most modern philosophy, and indeed in most of our everyday life, we simply take the individuality of human beings for granted. It is just obviously true that we each have a birth, a life, and a death of our own. This is not to be denied. Yet according to Løgstrup it needs to be stressed that our life is not first solitary, and then, as if by accident, lived together with other human beings. Who we are and how we live is, to an unfathomable extent, dependent upon our involvement with others. Human life is communal living. In *Dependent Rational Animals*, Alasdair MacIntyre emphasizes the fact that in philosophy we often forget our obvious dependence on others in childhood, old age, and times of weakness.[2] The dependency that Løgstrup is interested in, however, goes much deeper and is far more extensive. It includes the dependencies that even the strongest and most independent practical reasoners have on others at all times. We are dependent animals in that our lives are seamlessly interwoven with the lives of others. We are who we are in virtue of our relations to parents, siblings, friends, lovers, colleagues, enemies, children, grandchildren, and strangers of all kinds. We can withdraw into an inner world of our own for shorter or longer periods, but even that world is made up of what others have done to us, and for us. All this should, in one sense, be too obvious for words, but we nevertheless keep thinking as though our lives could somehow be disentangled from the lives of others. "We have the curious idea that a person constitutes his own world, and that the rest of us have no part in it but only touch upon it now and then. . . . This is really a curious idea, an idea no less curious because we take it for granted. The fact is, however, that it is completely wrong because we do indeed constitute one another's world and destiny" (Løgstrup 1997, 16).

This crucial fact is easily overlooked, and it may be quite convenient for us that this is so. "It is a common observation that the most elementary phenomena of our existence are the ones we are least aware of. It should be added that the phenomenon we are discussing here is highly disquieting. For the sake of our own peace of mind it is perhaps fortunate that we are not more aware of the extent to which, by what we were or said or did in our relationship with them, we have actually determined other people's joy or pain in living, their sincerity or duplicity" (ibid., 16). Løgstrup uses the Lutheran metaphor that we are "daily bread" in the life of one another. In your life, other people provide the most important "sustenance" that you digest and live on mentally, just as you provide material for their mental metabolism. Or to use a different set of metaphors: other people contribute to the "atmosphere" you breathe, just as you make some difference to the "climate" they live in; they form part of the situation you are in, just as you are part of the situation in which they find themselves, however good or bad the "chemistry" between you may be. We make a difference in each other's lives by our direct actions, but also by our way of being, say, open, or aloof, or cautious towards them. "By our very attitude to one another we help to shape one another's world. By our attitude to the other person we help to determine the scope and hue of his or her world; we make it large or small, bright or drab, rich or dull, threatening or secure" (ibid., 18).

One way of coming to see how deeply our lives are mutually dependent is through understanding the basic and pervasive role trust plays in our social life. What Løgstrup is talking about here is once again something highly elementary. An analogy may help: In the life of a garden snail there is a clear difference between coiling up inside one's shell and coming out into the open. Coming out is necessary for many reasons, but it always involves exposing soft spots and taking all sorts of risks. There would be no blessings in the life of a garden snail if it did not instinctively trust the world to be a place where one can risk sticking out one's feelers. Of course, the life of a garden snail can be infinitely cruel; many a garden snail lives too short a life to learn exactly how dangerous life out in the open can be. Nevertheless, the life of a garden snail would be impaired and the creature would wither away if it remained coiled up within its protective shell—which does not even provide protection against all dangers. There is a similar logic in the social life of human beings. Communication involves self-exposure. In addressing others, you inevitably leave yourself vulnerable to attack or indifference. There would be no blessings in your life if you did not risk coming out to meet others, but doing so is like putting something of yourself at the mercy of those others, trusting them without any guarantee that they will take good care of what was put in their keeping. "Regardless of how varied the communication between persons may be, it always involves the risk of one person daring to lay him or herself open to the other in

14 the hope of a response. This is the essence of communication and it is the fundamental phenomenon of ethical life" (ibid., 17).

As a matter of fact, distrust is quite widespread, and there can even be a general climate of distrust within an entire society for a long period of time. People may shield themselves against each other in all kinds of ways, and it may be quite rational for them to do so. Social life can be infinitely cruel as well. And yet: "Initially we believe one another's word; initially we trust one another. This may indeed seem strange, but it is a part of what it means to be human. Human life could hardly exist if it were otherwise. We would simply not be able to live; our life would be impaired and wither away if we were in advance to distrust one another, if we were to suspect the other of thievery and falsehood from the very outset" (ibid., 8–9). There is nothing naive, optimistic, sentimental, or idyllic about this view. It is thus quite wrong when Zygmunt Bauman, in his contribution to this volume, suggests that Løgstrup's understanding of trust was more at home in his parish in the countryside in prewar times than it was in the university town of Aarhus under Nazi occupation, or than it is today in a Big Brother society. It is precisely when trust is lacking that we can come to realize what a basic and pervasive role it has in life. Løgstrup is not preaching that we must cultivate trust. He is the first to admit that we have to teach our children to not simply trust any stranger (R, 6). Nevertheless, there is an asymmetry between trust and distrust, openness and reserve. Distrust is something that has to be learned; trust is openness to the world and is presupposed by the more or less severe reservations we normally place on it. If we did succeed in holding our trust back completely, remaining consistently coiled up within our self-built defenses, our lives would indeed be impaired and wither away. Of course, occasionally something like that does happen. Some people do actually seal themselves off from others almost completely, but their fate only provides more evidence that trust is more basic than distrust.

To trust is to lay oneself open, to deliver something of oneself into the hands of another, thereby vesting the other person with some power over oneself. We cannot help being, to some extent, at the mercy of others. The other side of the coin is that others cannot help vesting us with power over them, and thus putting themselves, to some extent, at our mercy. "A person never has something to do with another person without having some degree of control over him or her. It may be a very small matter, involving only a passing mood, a dampening or quickening of spirit, a deepening or removal of some dislike. But it may also be a matter of tremendous scope, such as can determine if the life of the other flourishes or not" (Løgstrup 1997, 15–16). Personal relations are relations of interdependency; they are relations of power through and through. Along with our undeniable power over others comes an undeniable responsibility for how we use that power. This is the source of the specifically ethical form of normativity arising out of the other person's openness towards us.

THE ONE AND ONLY ETHICAL DEMAND

It is a fact that we have power over the life committed to us in trust. To have this power is to be faced with the choice between either taking care of the life thus placed at our mercy, or destroying it. There is no third and neutral option, and the responsibility for what we choose is our own. This choice is made under the implicit, prima facie demand that we do take care of that which it is within our power to take care of in the life of the other. "To accept the fact without listening to the demand is to be indifferent to the question whether life is to be promoted or ruined" (ibid., 18 n. 6). If we take advantage of the trust of others and use it against them for our selfish purposes, we shall have failed them. We may have all kinds of excuses, and even good moral reasons for acting the way we did, but if we failed someone we failed them, and we did so while under the implicit demand that we should have done what would serve them best instead of failing them. We may be under other explicit or implicit demands, such as doing what would benefit ourselves in the long term, what would benefit our company, what would benefit our nation, what would benefit mankind, or what would most greatly benefit all those concerned. All these demands can be real and important, but Løgstrup uses the term "ethical" exclusively to refer to the demand to act unselfishly for the best of each of the other persons who trust in us. If what is most important in our life is how we act towards each and every person that we have power over, and if the ethical is regarded as a matter of judging our actions in the light of what is most important in our life, then unselfishly

16   caring for this particular other is almost by definition what is ethically demanded of us in the given situation. Love of one's neighbor, according to Løgstrup, is the one and only ethical demand. Objectively speaking and in terms of its content, the demand is that we use our power to the greatest benefit of the other. Subjectively speaking and in terms of its motive, the demand is that we do so unselfishly. If you want to know what is ethically demanded of you, the question you have to ask is: "How can I use the power I have over the life of this person to benefit him or her the most?" There are many other questions you could also ask when determining what to do, but for Løgstrup this stands out as the ethical question. The ethical point of view is the point of view of that which, in the life of another, is in your hand. The ethical demand is a prima facie demand, but it remains standing as the ethical demand, no matter what other demands we may be under and may eventually follow. You may let the ethical demand be overruled by other demands or temptations, but then you are ethically at fault. The ethical demand is thus singled out and distinguished from all other demands, even moral demands, in a somewhat unusual way. Løgstrup tries to explain what is at stake by claiming that the ethical demand can be characterized as being silent, radical, one-sided, and unfulfillable, whereas conventional moral demands are articulated, relative, mutual, and fulfillable. So, what is involved in drawing a distinction between the ethical and the moral in this way?

The ethical demand is silent in that it is unspoken, unarticulated, and merely implicit. The ethical demand is not identical with any demand that the other person may make on you. What is demanded of you is not what the other person wishes for or wants from you; what is demanded is that you do what will, to the best of your knowledge, most greatly benefit that other person. In certain cases what is ethically demanded of you is that you go directly against what the other person asks from you; "what we are speaking of is a demand for love, not for indulgence" (ibid., 21). It is your own responsibility to find out for yourself what, on this occasion, will benefit this other person, making use of such insight, imagination, and understanding as you may possess. Furthermore, the ethical demand is not expressed by the law of the country or by conventional morality. In certain cases what is ethically demanded of you is that you go directly against that which is legally or conventionally demanded of you if that will clearly benefit the other most. The demand is also silent in the sense that it is anonymous. No one can speak on its behalf or spell out its contents. It is the demand of the situation, or the demand of life itself; it is a demand that arises from the choice that is being forced upon you by the trust of the other: the choice between either taking care of that which is given into your trust, or not taking care of it. The demand is additionally silent in the rather dramatic sense that any formulation of it as an explicit demand is unavoidably a misrepresentation of it. "What is demanded is that the demand should not have been necessary" (ibid., 146). What is demanded is that you should already have acted to benefit the other without having to be reminded of this by any explicit demand—not even by talk of the implicit ethical demand. If a demand is felt or expressed, it is because there is something that could have gone better. And in a sense, the demand always comes too late. You should act unselfishly for the sake of the other and not for the sake of fulfilling this or that demand. An articulated demand may be called for, yet in a way it can provide nothing but substitute motives for substitute actions.[3]

The ethical demand is radical in that it is unconditional, or absolute. You should act unselfishly for the benefit of the other no matter who that other person is, and no matter what your relationship to that person is. You are ethically bound to take care of the other no matter how he or she has acted towards you. You are not very likely to do so in any case, and naturally even less likely to do so if the other is your enemy and someone you have every reason to dislike, but the demand is not there to please you, or to support your cause, however rational. It is here and now you must act unselfishly and to the benefit of the other, and not somewhere else or at some other time when it might be more convenient for you. The demand is also radical in that it is without any special cultural preconditions; it is eternal, or part of the natural makeup of human life. People were under the demand to act responsibly towards others long before and quite independent of Christianity, and they will remain under this demand no matter how social conditions evolve. Jesus of Nazareth pointed to this demand because it is the ethical demand; it is not his pointing it out that makes it the ethical demand. The ethical demand is an implicit standard of behavior that is unaffected by the fact that it may be widely, and almost systematically, disregarded in ordinary life. If you failed someone, you failed them, and thereby failed something important in yourself. This is the basic distinction between good and evil; this is the ethical "up and down," as it were, of human life, whether anyone notices or not. You may or may not be motivated by your concern for the other, but the ethical demand is a reminder that you could have been motivated by it, and that there is something destructive involved in acting against it. There is a robust ethical realism in this claim. It is a highly elemental issue whether the trust of another is being taken care of, neglected, or crushed; moral maturity is not least a matter of not having one's natural sensitivity to this issue undermined by one's equally natural sensitivity to other obvious issues in the situation.

The ethical demand is one-sided. It is a demand on you, and you alone. There is no bargain or agreement involved. The ethical is not up for negotiation between you and the other. It is not a matter of mutual back-scratching. Nor is it a matter of a social contract of any kind. It is prior to any convention. The point of the ethical demand is not to strike a reasonable balance between your natural concern for the other and your natural selfishness. The ethical demand is that your concern should be for the other, and thereby for your relation to the other. You end up making a compromise with your selfishness, of course, but what is ethically demanded is that which you thereby compromise, not the result of your compromising. The ethical demand has its source in the fact of our mutual dependency, but ethically speaking the demand isolates you; the responsibility is yours. Our lives cannot help being, to some extent, symbiotic; the ethical demand forces our individuality upon us.

Finally, the ethical demand is unfulfillable. You must unselfishly do what will benefit the other person most, but you cannot will yourself to do this. In a way it is the easiest thing in the world just to care for the other. We have all received and given care like that; yet as soon as we direct our attention to the task of trying to care unselfishly, all kinds of doubts about the results of our actions and the purity of our motives set in. You can never know that you did, in fact, act unselfishly—or rather, if you ask yourself the question, you can know that you did not act unselfishly. The ethical demand is never less than a demand for doing the very best for the other, which makes it a so-called *supererogatory* demand, a demand that goes beyond conventional duties. You must always act as best you can by your own lights, but there is no guarantee that what you did was ethically right. And anyway, that is not what you should be concerned about; you should be concerned about the other, not about your own moral standing. As soon as we take an evaluative or normative stance and begin judging our own actions, it creates a kind of alienation. The ethical is prior to all moralizing.

The characteristics mentioned do indeed make the ethical demand rather peculiar, and even quite harsh and unhelpful at that. The ethical demand is basic, but if this were the only demand we were under, life would be unbearable. It would be unbearable for the other person because the ethical demand provides no protection whatsoever. There are people who simply disregard the demand they are under, and here the demand is powerless. It lies in the essence of the ethical demand that it could have no sword to back it up. The demand leaves it entirely up to me to do what is best for you, and chances are I will be more concerned with my own business, or even actively engaged in doing you harm. There is nothing to stop me from disregarding both you and the ethical demand completely. So in that respect you are entirely at my mercy, just as I am entirely at your mercy. And even if I should wish to live in accordance with the ethical demand, my own situation is almost impossible. I shall never be able to claim that I did the right thing. The situation is almost as grim as in a Hobbesian state of nature, in spite of everyone being under the ethical demand. If there were no other normativity in our life than what the ethical demand provides, humankind would really be in a terrible predicament. The ethical demand is an expression of the difference between good and evil inherent in human life as such, and prior to and independent of all our activities and interactions. It is a natural or pre-conventional normativity, so to speak. But there are and must be other sources of normativity. The ethical demand applies to us along with a whole array of conventional, cultural, and social normativity of another order. The important thing for Løgstrup is that both forms of normativity are needed, and that one should not be mistaken for the other.

THE MANY MORAL DEMANDS

The ethical demand can stand on its own, but it cannot stand alone. Our lives together are always mediated by all manner of objective issues and

20   purposes. These provide us with a sense of shared purpose and thereby give our personal relations content and context beyond the relationship itself. We meet, not just for the sake of being together, but also for the sake of doing something together, something that creates mutually agreed necessities and some kind of order of importance putting us on equal ground. We give, and have always already given, form to our life beyond the form provided by the ethical demand. This is so both on the personal level and on the social level, where all kinds of norms, conventions, laws, rules, values, and ideals are in force. The power we have over each other is thus not wielded in a moral vacuum but within a rich field of practical tasks and social institutions that are constantly demanding something of us. Such demands have all the opposite characteristics of the ethical demand; they are or can be formulated, they have more or less well-defined conditions of application, they have evolved historically, their validity is often limited to a particular culture, they are often reciprocal in character, and they are by and large fulfillable. They can protect the interests of people because they are more or less efficiently backed up by social force, and we can know when we have done what is expected of us. Most traditional moral philosophy has been concerned with giving reasons for such demands in terms of aspects like their contribution to social stability, their contribution to the greatest happiness of the greatest number, or their conformity with principles that are fit to be universally valid principles.

The relation between the ethical demand and the moral conventions is quite complex. The social norms give form to our lives, thereby greatly facilitating our relationships with one another, yet at the same time they reduce both the trust we show and the demand that we take care of the other person's life. The moral conventions help protect us from psychological exposure. They help define the horizon of expectations within which the other person lives, and they tell us what counts as specific goods and evils in the social world in which that person is living. They thereby guide us in finding out what would actually be in his or her best interest. All of this makes our life easier, but it also threatens to make it more superficial. In ordinary social situations, at least in certain northwestern European cultures, even others who are close to us are generally quite satisfied, as long as we refrain from breaking any laws and behave politely towards them. They expect us to do no more for them than that, and might even resent it if we were to go out of our way to do something for their benefit. Their trust in us is reserved within conventional limits, and we are therefore relieved of being under the demand of their unreserved trust. "Instead of allowing convention to give needed form to our life, we use it as a means for keeping aloof from one another and for insulating ourselves" (ibid., 20). We create a kind of joint system of protective shells within which we can remain more or less coiled up, avoiding the risks, but also renouncing the blessings of being deeply involved with each other. Thereby the moral conventions also provide obvious evidence "for the curious idea that a person constitutes his own world, and that the rest of us have no part in it but only touch upon it now and then" (ibid., 16). Perhaps because he emphasizes this negative aspect so strongly, Løgstrup has very little to say on the traditional questions of how norms can be justified or criticized.

Unlike the ethical demand, the moral demands are always articulated on a historically and culturally specific level. That is what makes them more determinate than the ethical demand. Løgstrup is anxious to point out, however, that this cultural relativity does not entail any form of relativism. "Generally speaking, the difference between what is good and what is evil in my relation to the other person is and remains absolute, regardless of how relative the norms may be which determine what is good and what is evil. In the other person's life as well as in my own the norms which, historically speaking, are relative are absolute in the sense that we are unable to replace them. The historical knowledge that what is good today was evil two hundred years ago does not make the good today one iota less imperative for us" (ibid., 102). There is one condition for this, though: "It is of course presupposed that it makes no sense to speak of the changeable character of the radical demand. Its distinction between good and evil is assumed to be fixed: eternal, metaphysical, or however one may wish to express it" (ibid., 103).

For Løgstrup the ethical demand is an aspect of the created order of life. In the final analysis he believes that life thus ordered should be received as if it were a gift (*donum*) from a Creator. My claim is that it is sufficient support for his argument that the order of life be accepted as something which is clearly not of our own making, and thus something given (*datum*) understood in strictly human terms. It would be quite appropriate if our attitude to life were one of humility and gratitude, but

22   it is through our practical actions towards others that we show we have this attitude, not by any professed beliefs in a giver. The ethical demand is a factual or empirical aspect of the natural order of things that needs no further justification.

The distinction Løgstrup draws between the ethical demand and the moral and legal norms is in some ways a version of the traditional distinction between natural and positive law. The function of the ethical demand in relation to the positive moral and legal norms is, however, mainly negative. The ethical demand provides no, or very minimal, guidance for setting up a system of positive law, and it can never be used to justify any specific rule of positive law. It is largely a matter of reminding us to ask ourselves what impact our action has on the other person. It provides an implicit understanding of what should be the spirit of the law, a normative background that allows us to insist that there is always an open ethical question about what impact we actually had on another person, even when all questions regarding an action's conformity with legal or moral rules have been answered. There is more to the ethical than rule-following, however important rule-following may be in our social lives.

CONCEPTIONS OF ETHICS AND THE ETHICAL

If we take "ethics" to be the name of a philosophical discipline, we could say that a central part of Løgstrup's ethics is his account of the relation between the ethical demand and the conventional moral demands, or simply between the ethical and the moral in human life. His ethics differs from the ethics of other philosophers in the way he conceives of the ethical in its relation to the moral within what I call the entire field of practical normativity in human life. His ethics further differs from the ethics of other philosophers in the way he conceives of ethics—in what he takes to be the task of the moral philosopher. Let me try to shed some light on both these conceptions by comparing them with some of the conceptions we find in the work of other, better known, philosophers.

Some moral philosophers use the terms "ethical" and "moral" interchangeably. Others use only one term. The Greeks, with good reason, had to make do with *ethikos*; most Latin authors used only *moralis*, though many of them knew *ethice* to be an imported noun used to denote a branch of philosophy; most British moralists of the eighteenth century used only "moral," "morals," and "morality." The last twenty years have seen a remarkable swing away from the terms derived from Latin (the "M-words") and towards the terms derived from Greek (the "E-words") both in philosophy and in ordinary language. In the preface to his anthology *Ethics*, Peter Singer announces that he will use only E-words, given that the M-words have been so thoroughly corrupted by Christianity and Victorian sexual narrow-mindedness (Singer 1994, 4–5). Bernard Williams' attack on morality in the name of a less demanding ethics[4] and the almost exclusive use of E-words in the names of all the modern institutions of practical ethics provide further evidence of this change. The philosophers who use both sets of terms and try to differentiate between them can muster very little agreement on how the terms should be used (and little consistency in their actual usage). In ordinary language, the most reliable difference seems to be that E-words more often relate to the philosophical, theoretical, and abstract, and that M-words relate more to the ordinary, practical, and actual. The ethics of Spinoza is expressed in his book and his teachings; the morals of Spinoza are expressed in the quality of his actual behavior towards other people and the consistency between his views and his practice. The German tradition has had a tendency to follow Kant in inverting this usage, using M-words for the abstract and universal principles and E-words for the more concrete and particularistic. This trend is clear (although with some variation) both in Hegel and in Habermas. Bernard Williams seems to be most in line with the German tradition. Zygmunt Bauman, in his *Postmodern Ethics*, takes the E-words to relate to social rules and the M-words to relate to personal responsibility.[5] I find it difficult to discern much order in all of this.

Løgstrup, in *The Ethical Demand*, seems to use the terms "ethical" and "moral" to mark a distinction between what relates to our concern for the other person and what relates to a subspecies of our other conventional, normative concerns. I do not think this should be taken as a terminological recommendation (and Løgstrup is not completely consistent in his usage, either), but I do consider it to be a way of highlighting what he thinks is involved if one accepts that person-to-person relationships are what is most important in a human life.

24   The ethical demand is not a demand for mere altruism; it is not a matter of how we should treat all others. Løgstrup wants us to focus narrowly on what is the best thing for this particular other on this occasion in our unique relationship with him or her. We should not let this concern be drowned by, or subsumed under, some of our many other relevant concerns, including our conventional moral concerns. If we fail another person, our failure is not justified by being useful in some respect, by being the normal thing to do in our culture, or even by being inevitable. It remains a fact that we failed another person, and we should not forget it. One simple, factual question—what will best serve the other— is taken to be the crucial question. Other questions are important and relevant in all kinds of ways, but they do not answer this question. As things are, we are quite likely to disregard the question, but this is wrong in an elemental sense, no matter what. I believe it is the single-mindedness with which this essential question is kept in focus that makes *The Ethical Demand* a valuable, albeit problematic, contribution to ethics. It may be instructive to compare Løgstrup to Kant at this stage.

Much of Løgstrup's thinking is highly critical of Kant. There are nevertheless a number of striking similarities. The Kantian categorical imperative, like the ethical demand, is an attempt to focus our attention on the one and only question it is crucial for us to ask when deciding what to do—a question that cannot be answered by answering any other questions, however important and relevant they may seem. Like the ethical demand, the categorical imperative points to a pre-conventional normativity that is in a category all its own, and which must be sharply distinguished from that of the ordinary, hypothetical, and heteronomous norms, conventions, values, and ideals. (Kant's terminology, however, differs from Løgstrup's in that Kant uses the terms "moral" and "morality" to single out the rational and therefore highest and most pure part of the subject matter of ethics which he takes in a broader sense to include all the empirical considerations of what he calls "practical anthropology") (Kant 1785, Preface).

The categorical imperative even shares all the peculiarities of the Løgstrupian ethical demand in that it, too, is silent, radical, one-sided, and unfulfillable. The categorical imperative is silent in that it does not tell us what to do in a given situation. It provides a principle for testing the ideas we may come up with, but it is up to us to suggest possible concrete actions with such insight, imagination, and understanding as we may possess. The categorical imperative is radical in its being categorical, unconditional, absolute, eternal, and an aspect of rationality as such. The categorical imperative is also one-sided; it is addressed to each individual, and its force is not dependent on what others may or may not do. Finally, the categorical imperative is unfulfillable. We cannot know for sure that any one action is really done in accordance with the moral law and out of nothing but respect for that law. We can never cite an example of a morally good action.

According to Kant, we ought to act in each situation as legislators for the whole of humankind. No set of virtuous habits, no set of already formulated conventional norms can carry the burden of that task for us. According to Løgstrup, we ought to act in each situation as supporters of the person whose life is in our hand. No set of virtuous habits, no set of conventional norms can carry the burden of that task for us. Both Kant and Løgstrup operate with a strongly marked duality within the field of practical normativity, but whereas this duality amounts to an ontological and epistemic dualism in Kant's case, it is a duality without such dualisms in Løgstrup's case. Like the ethical demand, the categorical imperative has both an objective and a subjective side. Objectively the categorical imperative demands that we act in accordance with the one necessary and universal moral law, and subjectively the imperative demands that we act with no other motive but respect (*Achtung*) for the moral law. Here, the differences between Kant and Løgstrup stand out clearly. On the objective level the ethical demand is that we act to the greatest benefit of the other person. Løgstrup is not concerned with the rationality, universalizability, or law-likeness of the ethical. He has no conception of a practical reason, either in a Kantian or in an Aristotelian form. Deliberation is important in finding out what is best for the other person, and one may even have to remind oneself of many rules in doing so, but the method or form of deliberation is not what qualifies an action as ethically demanded. On the subjective level the difference is perhaps even clearer. Here the ethical demand is that we act unselfishly and for the sake of the other. To act out of respect for moral law or for our own rational nature is ethically speaking quite beside the point. (This is a rather traditional and perhaps unfair criticism of Kant, but if unfair, it is because Kant can be shown not to hold this view; it is not wrong, however, to criticize it).

There is a somewhat surprising affinity here between Løgstrup's conception of the ethical and an element in David Hume's conception of the natural virtues. In *A Treatise of Human Nature,* Hume argues that it may be established as an undoubted maxim "that no action can be virtuous, or morally good, unless there be in human nature some motive to produce it, distinct from the sense of its morality" (Hume 1738, Book III, Part II, Section I). I believe Løgstrup would agree completely. The will to care for someone for his or her own sake is one possible motive in human nature; this motive and the actions it leads to are good or virtuous on a basic level, prior to and independently of any ethical or moral considerations. It is ethically demanded that we act on this motive because it is good; it is not good because it is ethically demanded. If it is commonly recognized that this virtuous motive is what is ethically demanded, one may indeed act with the motive of following the demand, thereby attempting to become virtuous, but this motive is not, or at least not in the same way, a virtuous motive. "When any virtuous motive or principle is common in human nature, a person, who feels his heart devoid of that motive, may hate himself upon that account, and may perform the action without the motive, from a certain sense of duty, in order to acquire by practice, that virtuous principle, or at least to disguise to himself, as much as possible, his want of it" (ibid., III, II, II). This is a clear description of what Løgstrup refers to as "having a substitute motive for a substitute action." It is better than acting viciously or carelessly, but there is something missing. For Hume there are many virtuous motives in human nature, both self-regarding and other-regarding. He discusses generosity and benevolence at length, but, unlike Løgstrup, he does not place the motive of caring for a particular other for his or her own sake in any special category.

Løgstrup uses the term "ontological" to characterize his own form of ethics and to distinguish it from both teleological and deontological forms of ethics. However, I am not convinced that this is a particularly illuminating way of presenting what is special about it. I believe that his account of the ethical demand is quite clearly a form of deontology, and that his account of the many forms of conventional norms would have to involve strong elements of teleology if he were to unfold it. His reason for calling his ethics ontological is, of course, his emphasis on the ethical demand being not of our own making, but a preexisting aspect of the order of things. I believe that Plato, Aristotle, Hobbes, Spinoza, Kant, and Bentham could all similarly claim to have pointed to ontological, preexisting aspects of the order of things with normative implications for our way of ordering our affairs. The term "ontological" is perhaps more appropriate in drawing a distinction between Løgstrup and all the traditional forms of teleology and deontology on the one hand, and modern positivistic or existentialist forms of anti-realism on the other. But even A. J. Ayer, J. L. Mackie, Simon Blackburn, and Jean-Paul Sartre would each claim that the great advantage of their account is that it gives a better explanation of the ontology of the ethical than do realist theories, Løgstrup's included.

The Ethical Demand is an unusual work of moral philosophy, not only because it contains an unusual conception of the ethical, but also because it practices moral philosophy in a rather unusual fashion. It is not an edifying work. It does not allow the virtuous to congratulate themselves on their virtue; it rather reminds us of the limitations and temptations of even the most virtuous. Løgstrup can be almost Pharisaic in his anti-Pharisaism. The Ethical Demand is a descriptive work within the phenomenological tradition, but in spite of its use of literary examples I do not think its strength lies in giving close and detailed attention to concrete situations. It is rather a work of phenomenology in and by its attempt to avoid the vocabulary of the traditional philosophical schools of thought and other preconceived theoretical categories and distinctions. Instead it invents its own new and often striking metaphors. The advantage for the open-minded reader is that this allows one to see the ethical in human life afresh, in spite of all the customary ethics, whether religious or philosophical. The disadvantage is that it can give the impression of being homespun and out of touch with the most widely discussed issues. (In some quarters in Scandinavia the advantage may even seem to be lost, in that Løgstrup's metaphors have become so dominant that reciting them can come to substitute for independent thought, and hence today it may actually demand a new phenomenological effort to see the ethical in life afresh, in spite of Løgstrup's ethics).

Let me conclude by briefly mentioning one aspect of Løgstrup's conception of ethics that I find particularly appealing, but which may also point to a place beyond his conception of the ethical. This aspect is the way his work demonstrates that ethics can be a completely descriptive endeavor that becomes normative just at the point where it describes that which is there to be seen, and which we should therefore not overlook, disregard, or actively suppress, no matter how strong our tendency to do so may be. I believe this is precisely the way to avoid first creating an

28 unbridgeable gap between fact and value, or fact and norm, and then being faced with endless problems when the gap must somehow be bridged after all. There is no gap; there is no special ontology, epistemology, or semantics for ethics. To me this suggests another account of the specificity of the ethical, one that goes beyond Løgstrup's in claiming that the concern for the other is not the ethical concern, simply by being the concern for the other. The ethical concern is the concern for that which is overlooked, disregarded, or suppressed. More often than not, this is our concern for the other person, but it may happen that our own real needs are what we are about to overlook, disregard, or suppress—needs which thereby, and behind our backs, so to speak, become the actual ethical concern in the given situation.

NOTES

1. He does so quite clearly (Løgstrup 1997, 207–209).
2. See MacIntyre 1999, especially ch. 1, "Vulnerability, Dependence, Animality."
3. See SEL, 69 and 77–79, and also the very thorough discussion of this whole theme by Kees van Kooten Niekerk in his essay in this volume.
4. See Williams 1985, especially ch. 10, "Morality, the Peculiar Institution."
5. See Bauman 1993, especially the section "Postmodernity: Morality without Ethical Code," 31–36.

REFERENCES

Bauman, Zygmunt. 1993. *Postmodern Ethics*. Oxford: Blackwell.
Kant, Immanuel. 1785. *Grundlegung zur Metaphysik der Sitten*. Berlin.
Hume, David. 1738. *A Treatise of Human Nature*. London.
Løgstrup, K. E. (Knud Ejler). 1997. *The Ethical Demand*. Notre Dame: University of Notre Dame Press.
———. 2007. *Beyond the Ethical Demand*. Notre Dame: University of Notre Dame Press.
MacIntyre, Alasdair. 1999. *Dependent Rational Animals*. London: Duckworth.
Singer, Peter, ed. 1994. *Ethics*. Oxford and New York: Oxford University Press.
Williams, Bernard. 1985. *Ethics and the Limits of Philosophy*. London: Fontana.

CHAPTER TWO

In the Eyes of a Lutheran Philosopher

How Løgstrup Treated Moral Thinkers

Svend Andersen

Løgstrup regarded himself as both a Christian theologian and a philosopher. Accordingly, his ethics is dual in nature. Here I deal with his philosophical ethics. As the reader will discover, however, the thought of Martin Luther plays a decisive role in Løgstrup's philosophical ethics. In fact, Løgstrup, in working out his ethics, shows himself to be a Lutheran philosopher. I seek to substantiate this claim by considering Løgstrup's ethics in relation to that of other prominent classical and contemporary philosophers. The reader should be aware of my approach from the outset: I do not give my own interpretation of the various moral philosophers, but I stick to what Løgstrup himself said of them and how he positioned himself in relation to them. I deviate from this approach in only one instance: the German philosopher Hans Lipps. This contemporary of Heidegger is all but unknown in the Anglo-Saxon world, and consequently I have given my own presentation of those parts of Lipps's phenomenology on which Løgstrup builds his ethics. The following overview also supports the claim that Løgstrup's ethics are a reformulation of Luther's idea of natural law, achieved by the application of existential phenomenology.

30   One reason why Løgstrup never gave a comprehensive treatment of moral philosophers is that he never wrote a textbook on ethics. (He was, in fact, skeptical of the "institution" of the textbook.) However, there does exist at least one textbook-like treatise of his on the subject of ethics—"Ethik und Ontologie" (1960)—in which he presents theories of ethics using the distinction between teleological, deontological, and ontological ethics.[1] I follow this structure in my presentation of the moral philosophers discussed by Løgstrup.

TELEOLOGICAL ETHICS

Under the heading of teleological ethics—he did not use the term "consequentialism"—Løgstrup deals primarily with three types of theories, which we can call the ethics of antiquity, ideal consequentialism, and utilitarianism.

Aristotle

Løgstrup deals with the ethics of antiquity in a strictly descriptive manner, and of the little he writes, most is devoted to Aristotle. He mentions the concept of virtue but provides no deeper discussion. This is not because he lacked interest in the relation between Aristotle's ethics and his own. On the contrary, he was aware of possible similarities between his concept of the sovereign expressions of life and Aristotle's concept of virtues. He also hoped that some of his students would investigate the potential connection, but unfortunately none of them did so.[2] Under the heading of teleological ethics, Løgstrup also mentions the traditional positions of Plato and Thomas Aquinas.[3]

Max Scheler

By "ideal consequentialism" I mean theories that define the good to be promoted in moral action as a kind of ideal entity. In "Ethik und Ontologie," Løgstrup mentions two German philosophers from the early twentieth century, Max Scheler and Nicolai Hartmann. In Løgstrup's context the most important is Scheler; Scheler's so-called *materiale Wertethik* was made the topic of a prize paper in a competition announced by the University of Copenhagen, for which Løgstrup submitted an essay in 1932. This essay—which was awarded a gold medal—is important because it is Løgstrup's first academic work on phenomenology, the tradition of contemporary philosophy in which he is situated.

According to Scheler, a human act is morally good (or right) if it realizes a value. Moral values are ideal, and hence moral insight has the character of intuition (*Anschauung*).[4] Epistemologically, Scheler can be called an intuitionist, which in his case means that he represents a Husserlian kind of phenomenology. A "phenomenon," in this view, is an ideal unity of meaning that is given in an immediate intuition. Ontologically speaking, Scheler is, of course, a realist, and the values to be realized in moral acts are ordered in hierarchies. Scheler argues, against Kant, that the most basic feature of moral life is not obligation (*Pflicht*) but rather virtues, in the sense of positive moral capabilities. Although clearly Scheler does not deny the existence of obligations, he regards them as secondary in relation to the insight into a value that is to be realized. An obligation can be connected with a demand made by another person, but the obligation to obey a command or an imperative is, in turn, based on an insight into the existence of some value. Christian ethics, in Scheler's philosophical interpretation, is an ethics of love, and love is the affirmation of the value of another person. The command of neighborly love is to be understood not as an imperative but rather as an invitation to imitation.

In the essay he submitted in 1932, Løgstrup advances a critique of Scheler that can be summarized in four points. First, ethics has to be deontological, as the basic phenomenon of moral life is an "ought." Løgstrup does not reject the terminology of values, but he claims that no obligation follows from mere insight into a value. Rather, the "ought" is to be understood in terms of the relation of command and obedience. But Løgstrup finds Scheler unable to give a correct account of this relation because Scheler conceives of it in terms of a static intuition of values. By way of contrast, Løgstrup claims that the relation must be understood as a personal one. We are confronted with the good not in intuition but in choice. Second, ethics is based on divine command. The "ought" that defines moral goodness can have its origin only in a "superhuman command," that is, in the command of a divine creator. This explains the "ought"-like nature of moral values: the "ought" is not inherent in the content of the values; rather, it derives from the fact that the values are created and upheld by God in his fight against evil. Therefore the relation of human beings to moral values does not consist in realizing intuitions but in being situated in a conflict-laden reality. Love of our neighbor does not belong to moral philosophy. This is because love of our neighbor is not a humanly possible act. The command to love our neighbor presupposes the proclamation of Jesus. Hearing this word, the individual sees the concrete neighbor as one for whom he or she has responsibility, but also recognizes his or her own evil. In this tension-filled situation, God creates love of neighbor in the individual by an act of grace. Løgstrup's alternative to Scheler's ethics is, then, explicitly a Christian ethics. More specifically, it is a Christian ethics of a Protestant, Lutheran kind.

Fourth, ideal phenomenology is not an adequate method to apply to ethics. As already indicated, moral knowledge, according to Løgstrup, cannot be merely a static intuition of values. It has to be dynamic knowledge: knowledge of "really existing individuals, participating in the real conflict of the real world of values." Løgstrup is looking for an ethics in the sense of "the study of actual human beings." I think it is fair to say that he found this kind of study in the phenomenology of Martin Heidegger and Hans Lipps, which we can call "existential phenomenology."

Utilitarianism

In *The Ethical Demand,* Løgstrup mentions utilitarianism as an example of a theory according to which moral reflection in the concrete situation consists merely in applying a preconceived theory. A special problem with utilitarianism is the fact that the result of the utilitarian calculation can go against the interests of the agent. Løgstrup is not interested in analyzing this any further "here" (Løgstrup 1997, 118 n. 3).

The most comprehensive treatment of utilitarianism is found in Løgstrup's "Ethik und Ontologie," mentioned above. To understand Løgstrup's discussion of utilitarianism, it is important to realize that he was writing primarily for Danish and German readers who were acquainted with so-called Continental philosophy. Løgstrup was convinced that Anglo-American (analytical) philosophy contained important insights that had to be taken into account. This is also true concerning his view of moral philosophy, and one of the reasons why he discussed utilitarianism.

Løgstrup did not choose as representatives of utilitarianism the classic thinkers such as Jeremy Bentham and J. S. Mill. Rather, he deals chiefly with Bertrand Russell and P. H. Nowell-Smith. In his view they represent, respectively, a psychology-of-need approach and a logico-linguistic approach to utilitarianism.

In this kind of utilitarianism—to which Løgstrup also assigns Jørgen Jørgensen, the main Danish representative of logical positivism—the good is simply defined as the satisfaction of need. The moral dimension comes in because there is also a need to promote the satisfaction of other people's needs as well as the agent's own. In turning this "altruistic" need into an obligation, the need is strengthened. The logico-linguistic part of the argument—which Løgstrup primarily finds in Nowell-Smith—is to the effect that teleological "pro-words" such as "good," "desire," and "aim" are a necessary condition for the meaningfulness of the deontological "pro-words" such as "ought" and "right."

Løgstrup's critique of this kind of utilitarianism is that its way of picturing moral life is not convincing. Morality or ethics appears simply as a partial aspect of praxis (not practice), in the sense of the pursuit of one's own interests. In other words, utilitarianism regards moral reason as part of technical, goal-oriented rationality. The problem in Løgstrup's view is that the significance of *the world* is thereby downplayed: the world is reduced to the set of circumstances under which we humans seek to reach our goals. As far as I can tell, by "world" Løgstrup means the world of human interpersonal and social life, in particular the features that are somehow independent of human production or construction. The world is something given.

Hence Løgstrup can formulate his alternative as the claim that moral life is constituted by the fact that we human beings are confronted with calls or demands that issue from "the world and its orders." By the world's orders Løgstrup means structures of human existence such as the exposure of the other to the power of the agent. This line of thought leads to the further claim that there is a similarity between moral life and the worldview of *art*. In a work of art, according to Løgstrup, a world is brought forward, a world that is different from the social and cultural world that is produced by ourselves. To summarize, Løgstrup formulates

34 his alternative thesis by saying that ethics is a backlight flowing from the relations in which we find ourselves and from the basic conditions under which we exist. This is what he means by the *ontological foundation* of ethics. I shall return to this central claim and its philosophical roots later.

There is an aspect of moral epistemology in this critique. Moral knowledge, Løgstrup says, is not subordinated to a goal of action; that would reduce moral knowledge to rational knowledge in the technical sense. It is the other way round: moral knowledge determines the goals for our moral actions. Basically, utilitarianism attributes to moral knowledge the character of a subjective worldview (*Weltanschauung*). This, in a positivist manner, is regarded as the only alternative to scientific knowledge. Against this view, Løgstrup emphasizes the interpretation inherent in ordinary, natural language. Here, "interpretation" is a semantic concept, designating one important way in which words "see" the world, so to speak. As an example Løgstrup mentions the word "trust": in his view it is part of the word's meaning that trust is something intrinsically good. A linguistic interpretation of this kind is directed towards human life not as mere biology, nor as subjective feelings, but rather as *human nature*. As to the "method" of moral philosophy, it consists in construal (*Auslegung*) of the linguistic interpretation. The target of construction is not a subjective reflection but *"the phenomenon in itself."*

In the course of his critical argument, Løgstrup uses the expressions *Miteinandersein* (being-with-others) and *Miteinanderschaffen* (creating-with-others). I think it is reasonable to see them as echoes of the terminology of Heidegger's *Sein und Zeit*. Generally speaking, the philosophical background for Løgstrup's rejection of utilitarianism is existential phenomenology.

DEONTOLOGICAL ETHICS

Kant

The main representative of deontological ethics for Løgstrup is, needless to say, Immanuel Kant. Generally speaking, Kant plays a very important role in Løgstrup's thinking—a role that could be described as a "love-hate relationship." In one of his very rare passages of an autobiographical nature, Løgstrup recalls:

> During my first year of high school I still played with tin soldiers with one of my classmates. He later became a general, whereas I, without much transition, went from tin soldiers to philosophy. Thinking back, I realize that I must have been incredibly captivated by philosophy, as it did not weaken my interest that I did not understand any of it—and that I knew I did not understand any of it. For years. Or, to be accurate, for four years, two in school and two at the University of Copenhagen. What it meant to read and work carefully, this I only discovered in my third year of study. At that stage I had attended Frithiof Brandt's course on *Critique of Pure Reason* for two semesters (it lasted four), and I had to concede that I had not understood the slightest bit. Then I got stubborn, started anew, swearing that regardless of how long it would take, I wanted to understand it, wanted to get to the bottom of it. If I have learned to work thoroughly, I owe it to Kant, to his scholastic conceptual world and his unreasonable syntax. (Løgstrup 1987, 158)

This acquaintance with Kant's thinking later resulted in three monographs by Løgstrup on Kant's philosophy, one of which contains a textbook-like presentation of Kant's ethics (Løgstrup 1952). Løgstrup's most important work on Kant's ethics, however, is a rather early (Danish) article on the anthropology in Kant's ethics (Løgstrup 1947).

In this article, Løgstrup points out that in Kant's examples of ethical conflict there are no conflicts between incompatible obligations. The only conflict is that between obligation and temptation. This, according to Løgstrup, is explicable in light of Kant's concept of obligation (*Pflicht*). Kant defines obligation on the basis of the concept of necessity, and he analyzes the latter with the aid of his theory of knowledge. Hence, the concept of obligation, according to Kant, is marked by the contrast between empirical and pure. Kant assumes from his theory of knowledge that necessity can only be explained on the basis of pure reason. Moral obligation must therefore be understood as pure practical reason determining the will. In contrast, empirical knowledge deals solely with contingent data. The result is that the actual, empirical world in Kant's ethics only plays

36   the role of the contingent circumstances relevant to the determination of the will by pure practical reason. Thus, Løgstrup claimed—as he also did against utilitarianism—that Kant gravely misrepresents the features of moral life.

Besides this main criticism, Løgstrup makes a number of critical comments on Kant's idea of the moral law of practical reason. In this law and in the emphasis on rules (maxims), he sees a mentality of "stubbornness," a mentality of principle that tries to obtain firmness in life but is only a surrogate for involving oneself in life. Furthermore, Kant's epistemological model of moral life causes him to ignore the relatedness of human beings and to picture them exclusively as isolated individuals. And finally, Løgstrup criticizes Kant's definition of the place of reason in ethics. In Kant, he says, reason is not merely an instrument but is a self-sufficient source of moral knowledge. According to Løgstrup's conception of ethics, however, moral reason is instrumental in the sense that it is not, in and of itself, the source of moral insight. Our knowledge of moral law has a different source, and reason has its role in discerning which course of action is the most appropriate in the given situation.[5]

Here, too, Løgstrup's criticism is based on his alternative conception of moral law, described as follows: "the law manifests itself in the relationships of responsibility that constitute life within the orders" (Løgstrup 1947, 154). This is once again a formulation of what Løgstrup later labeled his "ontological ethics."

Kierkegaard

Søren Kierkegaard plays a role in Løgstrup's thinking somewhat similar to that of Kant, and here we could also speak of a "love-hate relationship." Løgstrup's sharp criticisms of Kierkegaard are most clearly formulated in the chapter entitled "Polemical Epilogue" of *The Ethical Demand* and in *Opgør med Kierkegaard* (Controverting Kierkegaard), the latter being a rejection of what Løgstrup takes to be the essence of Kierkegaard's understanding of Christianity. Given his criticisms, Løgstrup's relationship to Kierkegaard is sometimes interpreted as one of pure opposition. I think that this is mistaken. In my view there is no doubt that Løgstrup in many respects adopted important elements of his thought from Kierkegaard. In this section, however, I will consider only Løgstrup's critique of Kierkegaard as a representative of deontological ethics.

Løgstrup deals in his critique not only with Kierkegaard but also with "Kierkegaardian theologians." Although his theological argument proper is not important in our context, it does contain some points relevant to moral philosophy. The main critique of Kierkegaard (seen as a deontological moral philosopher) is that in his ethics the features of human existence do not contribute to the content of the demand with which humans are confronted. Actual existence, according to Kierkegaard, only consists of relative goals and ends. According to Løgstrup, this can be explained by Kierkegaard's "rejection of any mediation" (Løgstrup 1960, 387; Løgstrup 1997, 290). Here "mediation" means mediation between the absolute/divine and the relative/worldly. The consequence of this view is that the demand is basically without content. What is demanded is that the individual should be responsible, but the demand does not say anything about what this responsibility consists in. A further consequence of this line of thinking has to do with moral knowledge. Kierkegaard—and Kierkegaardian theologians—seem to think that if the demand has to be respected as divine and absolute, there is no place for knowledge or understanding. Obedience must be blind. But this, Løgstrup says, means that the Kierkegaardians are actually dealing with a *command* and not a *demand*. A shared feature of the two is that they require obedience as a response, but the difference between them is crucial: the requirement of obedience to a command is based solely on the authority of the commander, whereas obedience to a demand is based on "the fact that we owe something" (Løgstrup 1960, 389; Løgstrup 1997, 291). Of the latter fact—of the demand—we have knowledge and understanding.[6]

In the context of his critique of Kierkegaard's deontologism, Løgstrup reiterates his own alternative: "an ethical demand takes its content from the unshakable fact that the existence of human beings is intertwined with each other" (Løgstrup 1960, 387; Løgstrup 1997, 290).

ONTOLOGICAL ETHICS

The philosophers who inspired Løgstrup while he was developing his ontological ethics, as indicated above, are within the tradition of existential phenomenology. However, it is also necessary to take into account another thinker whom we would not normally consider a moral philosopher.

38   Luther

A general claim in Løgstrup is that there are important philosophical elements in Martin Luther's thinking. He makes this claim most clearly in the context of philosophy of religion, which plays an important role in Christian theology because Christian belief comprehends a "universal" aspect. "Universal" beliefs are ones contained in common human experience and insight. In Luther's thought, Løgstrup mainly finds them in relation to our natural knowledge of God (Løgstrup 1995, 57–61).

In his ethical discussions, Løgstrup explicitly mentions Luther in connection with his critique of Kant. In his early article on the anthropology of Kant's ethics, Løgstrup refers to two quite different ethical conceptions and calls Kant's ethics the "prototype" of one of these two. The other conception has Luther as its prototype, and its basic claim is "that the human being, due to the fact that its nature as created is an ordered nature, is, from the outset, obliged to live its life within orders, with and against the others, so that in these relations of responsibility humans hear the law, which is material as *lex naturalis*" (Løgstrup 1947, 154).

Løgstrup refers here to Luther's concept of "creation ordinances." The idea is that the createdness of human life manifests itself in the existence of a number of basic structures. As examples, Luther mentions marriage and family life. Humans are created as sexual and procreative beings. As a framework for realizing these features, God has given the structures of marriage and parent-child relations. In modern terminology we would say that "creation ordinances" is a theological concept describing both biological facts and social institutions. What Løgstrup emphasizes in this theological concept is, first, the fact that human beings are "from the outset" placed in these relations with others, and, second, the concept of natural law as an imperative that originates from these relations.

In the early article on Kant, Løgstrup formulates the Lutheran conception of ethics in non-theological language:

> [H]uman nature is an ordered nature, and its orders are orders for our lives with and against each other, so that we are closed in on each other in relations of responsibility. In this case the individual, whether he or she likes it or not, is placed in the choice for or against

the other (or others). And here the law is not a formal principle, it is rather material; it is the law of responsibility saying that the neighbor is to be served. (Ibid.)

This Lutheran conception forms the basis of Løgstrup's critique of two kinds of ethics, the teleological and the deontological. We have seen that, according to Løgstrup, both misrepresent the "world" and the place of human beings in it. Both positions "level" the world: utilitarians, by emphasizing the individual's pursuing of its own interests, hence reducing the world to a set of circumstances; deontologists, by emphasizing the pure rational or absolute (divine) origin of the imperative, hence reducing the world to contingent data. Against this, Løgstrup claims that the world of human existence possesses structure (order) independently of human effort or construction. This structure is basically connected with the interrelatedness of human life. And it is from this given structure that the basic ethical appeal arises as a "backlight."

I now turn to the kind of philosophy—"existential phenomenology"—that gave Løgstrup the tools to analyze this conception from his Lutheran theological tradition and translate it into contemporary philosophical terminology.

Heidegger

The importance of Martin Heidegger for Løgstrup's philosophical thinking is indicated by the fact that Heidegger is the only philosopher besides Kant about whom Løgstrup wrote a monograph for teaching purposes.[7] In many of Løgstrup's works, moreover, Heidegger occurs as a discussion partner. To Løgstrup, the significance of Heidegger—particularly his analyses in *Sein und Zeit*—mainly lies in his rejection of the view of human beings as isolated individuals, distanced from both other human beings and the external world. This means that, to Løgstrup, the idea of human being (*Dasein*) as a being-in-the-world (*In-der-Welt-Sein*) and a being-with-others (*Mit-Sein*) is of the utmost importance, ethically and otherwise.

As is well known, Heidegger himself did not establish an ethics as part of his analytics of existence. It has been widely debated why this is so, and whether it is possible to make Heidegger's "ontology of human nature" the "ground of ethics," as it is called in a recent book (Olafson 1998; cf. also Gethmann-Siefert and Pöggeler 1987). In calling his own ethics "ontological," Løgstrup places himself, beyond any doubt, in a Heideggerian context. "Ontological" thus has to be understood as "belonging to the structures and traits of human being." In formulating an ontological *ethics*, Løgstrup positions himself, so to speak, among the philosophers who stand in the Heideggerian tradition and who try to formulate an ethics within its framework. We may count authors such as Emmanuel Lévinas and Hans Jonas in this group.

The main text in which Løgstrup deals with Heidegger's relevance to ethics is the 1950 work *Kierkegaards und Heideggers Existenzanalyse und ihr Verhältnis zur Verkündigung* (Kierkegaard's and Heidegger's Analyses of Existence and Their Relation to the Proclamation). In this we can see how, on the one hand, the idea of "ordered human nature" is reformulated in Heideggerian terminology, and, on the other, this terminology becomes ethically enriched with the help of Kierkegaard.

As for Heidegger, Løgstrup remarks that his concept of the constitutive feature of human being—*Sorge (cura)*—is of a pre-ethical nature. He mentions Heidegger's distinction between ontological guilt and guilt in the vulgar sense of the transgression of concrete norms. Løgstrup seems to interpret the absence of ethics in Heidegger as a result of the assumption that ethics amounts to measuring human existence against some normative standard. In this way, ethics would turn the state of human being into something purely "ontic."

Against this latter assumption Løgstrup mobilizes Kierkegaard's concept of an *infinite demand*. According to Kierkegaard (in Løgstrup's reading), human existence is marked by infinity. This is not to be understood in the sense of human beings' having infinity as a property or essence. Rather, infinity presents itself to humans in the shape of an infinite and unconditional demand. These latter qualifications of the demand express the fact that it is not something finite that is demanded, say, a concrete act. What is demanded is the individual as a self. Therefore the demand cannot be regarded as a business to be finished. It requires an act that has the character of repeatedly making decisions in relation to the future.

Now this kind of demand is not something objective, like given norms. In the terminology of Heidegger, belief in such a demand would not turn human existence into something *Vorhandenes* (present-to-hand). On the contrary, Løgstrup claims that such an unconditional demand is compatible with the ontological traits of human existence that Heidegger describes. So far, Løgstrup adopts Kierkegaard's idea of the connection between human existence and the infinite demand. However, there is one important point on which he cannot follow Kierkegaard, and that is the claim that being confronted by the infinite demand requires abstracting infinitely from concrete existence. Against this Løgstrup says that we meet the demand in our concrete existence and, more specifically, that we meet it in our responsibility. In this context, Løgstrup uses the terminology we know from his critique of Kant: the demand originates from our "ordered nature" and its relations of responsibility. The demand has the character of a universal and material law. "Material" here, of course, stands in contrast to Kantian "formalism" and means that the demand has a content. What is demanded is that all we do must be for the sake of the other.

The adoption of Kierkegaard's concept of the infinite demand leads to a remarkable duality in Løgstrup's ethics. From the fact that we live in relations of responsibility, he says, two kinds of demand arise. The first consists of the demands inherent in social norms, morality, and legal rules. These demands are rooted in the "order of things" as a product of human nature in a biological sense and as cultural shaping. Hence these (finite) demands are changeable. The second kind is the infinite demand that is not rooted in the "order of things." It is of a purely personal nature. Løgstrup's line of reasoning seems to be this: the given biological-social orders are the concrete framework within which the relations of responsibility are located. The infinite demand is not rooted in this framework, but rather in the very fact of one individual being responsible for the other.[8]

This duality also has a consequence for the nature of ethical decision-making. There is, on the one hand, an "inward" decision as to whether the individual agent is willing to serve the other. On the other hand, there is an "outward" decision as to which acts and omissions are to make manifest the inward decision. This duality implies that there is an essential fervor in ethical decision: ethics is not merely about the relation between the individual and the other. It is also about the invisible relation between the individual and the demand itself.

42   Hans Lipps

The philosopher who had the greatest influence on Løgstrup's ethics was undoubtedly Hans Lipps (1889–1941). Both Lipps and Heidegger were students of Husserl, and both undertook an existential transformation of phenomenology, but unlike Heidegger, Lipps is largely unknown outside Germany. This is due partly to his early death and partly to his style of writing, which is difficult to access. Løgstrup stayed with Lipps in Göttingen during 1931 and 1932. It would be misleading to call Lipps a moral philosopher, since ethics has basically no role in his thought; what influenced Løgstrup was Lipps's conception of human existence and of philosophical analysis.

The two main areas of Lipps's philosophical inquiries were the philosophy of language and philosophical anthropology. His anthropology is the most relevant to ethics, and below I seek to sketch its most important characteristics based on his book *Die menschliche Natur* (Human Nature), first published in 1941.

Lipps does not view philosophy as a scientific occupation in an objective sense. Philosophy is a part of the human being's understanding of its own existential conditions. A philosophical analysis of the human being therefore cannot be carried out from a detached viewpoint, but, on the contrary, presupposes participation. Philosophical anthropology inquires into what is at issue in human existence. In this way it is distinguishable from conventional scientific psychology, for instance, which, according to Lipps, presupposes a scientific concept of consciousness. This concept includes a separation between the soul, which is a kind of inwardness, and its external bodily expression. By means of a series of analyses (which are apparently lumped together without any systematic link), Lipps shows that this scientific way of approaching the human being is misconstrued. His point of departure is the phenomenon of embarrassment. Embarrassment reveals itself externally—blushing, awkwardness, and so on—but it is wrong to say that these externals "express" an "inward" state of embarrassment. Embarrassment is something one finds oneself "in the spell of." A situation can cause one to be embarrassed, but so can the reactions of others. To put it metaphorically, embarrassment means losing one's footing, and the one who is embarrassed is therefore concerned with regaining a firm foothold. In this way embarrassment expresses a decisive trait in the human being's existence. What is at stake is always coming to one's self, existing with oneself as the point of departure or as subject. In contrast to the traditional philosophy of subjectivity, Lipps does not presuppose that the human being has "a" self in the sense of a firm point of departure. On the contrary, the human being has the ongoing task of becoming or finding itself.

Lipps may be described as "anti-foundationalist," but he retains a residue of the philosophy of subjectivity by holding on to the task of becoming a self. The task of becoming a self lies in the human being's character as *existing*. But embarrassment shows that the human being is also bodily or *natural*. The task of becoming a self arises at this point because it leads one out of simply responding to affects. The foregrounding of the indissoluble unity of existence and nature can be said to be the chief point on which Lipps's existential phenomenology differs from Heidegger's. Like the latter, Lipps understands the human being as situated in a world, and he understands the world-relationship as determined by the existential task. But he is not content, as is Heidegger, to point to the *Zuhandenheit* (readiness-to-hand) of things. He also speaks of *in-die-Hand-bekommen des Empfundenen* (getting-into-hand the perceived), meaning that he points to the bodily and sensuous dimension of the human being's relation to the world. Things are received not only as meaningfully useful, but also as sensibly material. Although the human being's existential task can be said to be individual—only I can become a self—for Lipps it is closely connected with relationality and sociality. This can be seen both on the level of knowledge and on the level of action.

Knowledge, according to Lipps, means conceiving of things in a definite way. And this conception is closely connected with coming to one's self or becoming a self. Knowledge means creating a distanced, free relation to the world and the things in it. This already occurs at the level of the senses, not least of the sense of sight, but it is most prominent in language. But precisely the case of language shows that the individual lives in a world that he or she shares with others as *seinesgleichen* (the likes of him/her). As a knower, the human being relates to the world in a situation of reciprocal intersubjectivity.

A similar situation is found on the level of action or, better still, on the interpersonal level. Human beings are visible to one another: others make an impression on one, have an effect on one, that is, one is attuned

44 to others. One can be infected by other people's moods. The meeting with the other is always a meeting with one that has the same basic task in life—to be continually concerned about becoming clearly aware of the challenge that existence is.

This might suggest that interpersonality would provide Lipps with the point of departure for a moral philosophy. That is not immediately the case. Morality and ethics are certainly not systematically absent, but Lipps only touches on the phenomena associated with them. One of the few occasions on which the word "moral" is used is in connection with his discussion of the phenomenon of stupidity: "An obdurate lack of freedom, self-satisfied complacency, well-meaning ignorance are called stupidity. There is something moral in it" (Lipps 1977, 40). Lipps emphasizes that stupidity is not a simple lack of knowledge. His characterization shows that stupidity has something to do with the way in which a human being demonstrates such a lack. Lipps must have a reason for saying that there is "something moral" about it. This phrase occurs one more time, namely, in connection with respect and contempt, both of which Lipps calls "moral feelings." He interprets respect as an attitude that a human being can simply demand. Contempt, on the other hand, must have a reason; it is synonymous with turning away from the other person to completely overlook him or her (ibid., 127).

The concepts of virtue and vice also appear in Lipps's analyses. In connection with the adventurer and his challenge to the bourgeois way of life, he mentions courage and *Kühnheit* (audaciousness), which both mean "the measure of a person, their virtue" (ibid., 121). Meanness, on the other hand, is a vice that indicates "the crippling of the person" (115).

The conventional approach that treats love and hate as opposites is rejected by Lipps. Not hate but lovelessness is the opposite of love. Another pair of opposites is unselfishness and egoism. These concern the way in which one is involved in some matter, whether one thinks about oneself or has regard for the other. It is worth mentioning that Lipps briefly discusses phenomena that play a role in Løgstrup's thought. Concerning compassion, Lipps says that it is not directed at an other as a definite self, but has a general character that is then showed to a person in some definite situation. Regarding contempt, he says that it has a "*sovereign*" quality that hate lacks (ibid., 127, emphasis added).

The references to ethics found in this series of descriptions of phenomena can scarcely be said to amount to a coherent moral philosophy.
If one wants to find anything like that in Lipps's anthropology, one might
do so via the idea of existential perfectionism. There is no doubt that
Lipps's foregrounding of the connection between nature and existence
is inspired by the Aristotelian definition of the human being as *zoon logon
echon*. But for Lipps, *logos* is not a clearly defined intellectual capacity. It
is rooted in the manner of one's existence, in the task of becoming a self.
And it shows itself in knowledge, in the free relation to things that comes
to expression in intersubjective discourse. The basis for talking about
perfectionism in Lipps lies, among other things, in his notion of human
"measure" (*das Mass eines Menschen*). There is a measure to being human—
not in the form of some determinate potential that has to be realized,
but in the very task of continually becoming one's self in relation to the
world and to others. It is this purpose that determines how one individual encounters another. As previously stated, Lipps specifically discusses respect as a moral attitude; the other demands respect in the sense
of being recognized as one who has the same fundamental task in life as
I myself have. In Lipps's anthropology, human beings encounter one another as beings of equal worth. Contrary to this, solicitude and related
phenomena play no apparent role. Only at one point does he mention the
human being's vulnerability: "the soul is vulnerable" (ibid., 191). Yet Lipps
does not consider what kind of response might ultimately be made to this
vulnerability.

According to Lipps, the soul reveals itself in "the look." I shall, in
conclusion, take up this idea of the look as a way of approaching his analysis of "the face," briefly comparing his treatment of the face with that
of Lévinas. This comparison will then be extended so as to indicate how
Løgstrup uses Lipps's philosophy in his own ethics.

Lipps finds two decisive attributes of "the face" in the German word
Gesicht. One is the attribute of the look with which a human being looks
out on the world. This is synonymous with the human being's being visible to others—visible in terms of the way in which one relates to the
world, the direction one takes towards it. It is also the look that determines the characteristics of the face, not in the morphological sense but
spiritually. The look is free; it hits the mark when it looks at something.
"The face" means taking a "frontal approach to the world." The way in

which one looks out at the world, as found in one's look, is what makes a person a self. One sees the other's self in his or her look. It is pointless to try to imitate a look, as opposed to a person's walk or gestures. The look can, however, be understood and translated. A person is thus a self in his or her face in a different way than in his or her body. The body can be clothed or naked, but the face cannot. One can hide one's face—in shame, for example—but this means that one is avoiding the look of another. It is precisely in the look that one meets the other. A look cannot be seen or evaluated from an external standpoint. Looks meet and cross one another, people can exchange looks. A necessary reciprocity is connected with being able to look another person in the face. This is why communication belongs, in an essential way, to looking a person in the face. The peculiarity of the look shows itself in the fact that, strictly speaking, one cannot meet one's own look, or look oneself in the face. Also related to the face is the voice: one senses the other in his or her voice. For this reason the voice, like the face, is a decisive trait of inter-personality: in apprehending the other self, one apprehends someone who is similarly situated (*meines gleichen*). According to Lipps, there is no contradiction between apprehending the other as similarly situated and as inexchangeably other: "For exactly as 'my own kind' is he plainly 'another'" (Denn gerade als 'meinesgleichen' ist er schlechthin 'ein anderer') (ibid., 143).

Let us now turn to Lévinas, whose analysis of the face is explicitly ethical. At the same time it also holds a much wider significance, in that ethics is the basis for a critique of conventional philosophy and metaphysics. Lévinas condenses the latter into the concept of "totality." Over against totality, the face represents "infinity." The orientation towards totality shows itself, for instance, in the way we usually approach the world of things visually. This approach has the character of an exercise of power, and by the way in which we gain access to things, we make sure of maintaining our grounding in the realm of "the same." But the face of the other refuses to be comprehended in such an approach. The other shows himself or herself in the face as infinitely strange, in that the face expresses transcendence. The relation to the other's face is fundamentally ethical. The face contradicts our habitual way of exercising power, not by eliminating power but by modifying it. In relation to the other I do not have the power to "take" (that is, to use), but only to kill. The face

thus finds expression in the basic word "Thou shalt not kill." To summarize: the infinite shines forth "in the face of the Other, in the total nudity of the defenceless eyes, in the nudity of the absolute openness of the
Transcendent" (Lévinas 1999, 198).

The ethical relationship is *asymmetrical*. The encounter with the other
puts a question mark against the "I." Consciousness of duty is, essentially,
not a consciousness at all, since the meeting with the other destroys consciousness by subordinating it to the other. It should nevertheless be added
that the ethical relationship also comprises equality and brotherhood
between human beings.

Overall, one can say of Lévinas's ethical reflections that the face manifests the other as a complete break with the conventional way of relating
to the world. In its nakedness the face shows the other's powerlessness,
and thus the possibility of murder. At the same time the face binds the
ethical agent to a one-sided responsibility for the other. In comparison
with Lipps, the asymmetry in the relation is especially worthy of note.
Methodologically, it is striking that Lévinas does not carry out a particularly subtle phenomenological analysis of the face, whereas Lipps's analysis is both more detailed and more convincing.

Returning to Løgstrup, it is, up to a point, justifiable to say that he
finds himself between Lipps and Lévinas. With the latter he shares the
notion that the encounter with the other is "born" as ethical: that to meet
another is synonymous with having power over his or her life. This assertion also comprises another trait in relation to which Løgstrup is in
agreement with Lévinas: there is an asymmetry in the relationship in the
sense that interpersonality is characterized by the situation of being-
delivered-over-to. And this being-delivered-over-to is, so to speak, asymmetrical at every point, so that reciprocity and equality are thereby con-
temporaneous features of interpersonality. With Lipps, Løgstrup could
say that one meets the other as *seinesgleichen*, in the sense that the other,
too, is a human being who has responsibility. Thus Løgstrup emphasizes
that the responsibility of the one can never involve removing responsibility from the other. The decisive point on which Løgstrup differs from
Lipps, however, is his underlining of being-delivered-over-to, and thereby
becoming vulnerable. For Løgstrup this is the central element of ethics,
and his ethics makes a fundamental demand that we be unselfishly solici-
tous in respect of the other's life.

48   Ontological ethics, then, is a conception that Løgstrup develops in dialogue with Luther, Kierkegaard, and the existential phenomenologists Heidegger and Lipps.[9] Whereas the philosophies of Heidegger and Lipps play a constitutive role in Løgstrup's development of ontological ethics, other figures in the tradition of existential philosophy play more subordinate roles.

Sartre

Løgstrup dealt with Sartre not so much on the basis of his philosophical works as on the basis of his plays. (See also the introductory comments to the extracts from *Opgør med Kierkegaard* in chapter 2 of *Beyond the Ethical Demand*.) According to Løgstrup, the "moving forces" of these plays are ethical problems; they are expressions of ethical subjectivism. A basic idea in existentialism is that the world is devoid of meaning and hence cannot ground morality. Human acts are marked by absurdity, and it is up to humans themselves to give meaning to their acts.

In *Norm og spontaneitet*, Løgstrup presents some ethically relevant themes in Sartre's play *Les séquestres d'Altona*, set during the Nazi period. The main characters are members of a German industrial family. The father sells some of his land to the Nazis, who want to build a concentration camp. After the camp has been established, a Jewish prisoner escapes and the son of the family, Frantz, finds and helps him. The Jew, however, is caught by the Gestapo and executed in front of Frantz, whose father plays an active role in this course of events. The play shows, according to Løgstrup, that power is a key phenomenon in ethics. Frantz has the power to help, and that is what places him in an ethical situation. The intervention of his father puts him in a position of powerlessness, however, and this, together with the irretrievability of his failure, ruins his life. The irretrievability is an expression of a basic feature of our world of action: the irreversibility of time makes our acts irrevocable. If we have failed, our guilt becomes irrevocable. Time makes what is irrevocable eternal. One of the existentialist motifs in the play, as Løgstrup presents it, is Frantz's will to make the irrevocable guilt his own, to be faithful to it. Because of this he is unwilling to recognize the other side of time's ethical significance. Time, Løgstrup says, gives renewal to life. It continually places us in new situations with new demands. Yet for Frantz, recognizing this would seem like being unfaithful to his guilt and would take all gravity out of life.

Karl Jaspers is often regarded as the second great existential philosopher, after Heidegger. Løgstrup did not share this assessment. His estimation of Jaspers's contribution to the analysis of human existence was not high. Even so, Løgstrup had one thing in common with Jaspers—and not with Heidegger or Lipps—in that both he and Jaspers treated questions in political ethics.[10]

In *Norm og spontaneitet*, Løgstrup discusses Jaspers in connection with his considerations on the politico-ethical problems of nuclear war. Løgstrup's position is clear: there is no ethical justification for such a war. One of the arguments he considers runs along these lines: starting a nuclear war, with the risk of annihilating all of humankind, would be justifiable because the ensuing total destruction is preferable to surrendering to a totalitarian regime. Løgstrup finds a religious version of this argument in Jaspers. According to Jaspers, the sacrifice of nuclear annihilation might be necessary because of human beings' relation to transcendence. To preserve life at all costs would be the same as distorting it into inhumanity. Løgstrup counters this by arguing that it is the relation to transcendence that gives meaning to the sacrifice of life. But, he explains, a sacrifice does not take place for the sake of transcendence, but rather for the sake of life. A sacrifice of life must, at the same time, be an affirmation of life.

OTHER PHILOSOPHERS

As indicated earlier, I do not seek to give a complete account of the roles played by other thinkers in Løgstrup's ethics, but I would like to mention two additional, main figures in ethical thinking who do not fit into Løgstrup's tripartite division of ethical conceptions.

Hegel

It appears that among Hegel's writings, Løgstrup read only his lectures on aesthetics. Hegel does, in fact, touch on ethics in these lectures, and Løgstrup briefly discusses this in *Opgør med Kierkegaard* (Controverting Kierkegaard). The issue is what Løgstrup calls "the disappearance of popular ethos." For Hegel, the significance of Kant is his realization that

50   when customary ethos—taking norms for granted—loses its power of
conviction, then moral reflection and the readiness to act out of pure obligation become necessary. A reduplication takes place: the question is
whether there is an obligation to be obliged. Morality acquires the character of spirituality (*Geist*) through reduplication. Løgstrup recognizes
that the disappearance of popular ethos has become a permanent condition. But he does not agree with Hegel's approval of Kant's solution. As an
alternative to the morality of reflection, Løgstrup points to the sovereign
expressions of life. Interestingly, and characteristically, Løgstrup does
not discuss what is normally regarded as the most significant contribution to ethics by Hegel: the concept of *Sittlichkeit*.

Nietzsche

Løgstrup has commented on one text by Nietzsche: Aphorism 133 in
Morgenröte. The subject is pity, or rather, the claim that when we help an
unknown person in need, we do it out of pity (*Mitleid*). Nietzsche has an
altogether different explanation: we help because we want to avoid some
possible reactions to our not helping. Thus, if we remained passive, we
would show our powerlessness, and so on. Løgstrup accepts Nietzsche's
unmasking of our motives to a certain point. He does not deny that when
we feel an impulse to help, all kinds of selfish motives appear. But Løgstrup wants to preserve a distinction between the impulse of pity as a sovereign expression of life, on the one hand, and our betrayal of it through
our selfish motives, on the other. Nietzsche goes too far in his unmasking: he expresses not only a disdainful attitude towards human beings,
but also disdain for human life. Løgstrup does not follow Nietzsche in the
claim that trust and love are "interpretations of our life that have the character of illusions and have never been anything else but illusions" (Løgstrup 1996, 30). According to Løgstrup, Nietzsche's process of unmasking does not stop at any point. It does not "serve a truth of ontological
character" (31).

CONCLUSION

One could perhaps say that, in Løgstrup's view, teleological and deontological ethics pretend to be alternatives to Nietzsche, but the only actual

alternative is an ontological ethics. As we have seen, the concept "ontological" is to be understood here in terms of Heidegger's analysis of existence. It signifies the fundamental structures concerning the human being's way of being in the world with others. The work of Hans Lipps teaches Løgstrup the finely shaded analysis of the concrete phenomena in human existence. For Løgstrup, an ethically decisive aspect of our existential structures is interdependence, the mutual relationship of being-delivered-over-to and power. He regards this relationship as "the fundamental phenomenon of ethical life" (Løgstrup 1997, 53). The rise of the radical ethical demand from the conrete relation of being-delivered-over-to is Løgstrup's correcting hypothesis against Kierkegaard and Kant. But the circumstance that ethics is a constituent part of the given human world also justifies a critique of utilitarianism as being an abstract calculation aimed to optimize the fulfillment of our needs. Ultimately, the idea of the demand and responsibility being justified in interdependency is one that Løgstrup takes from Luther's idea of the creation ordinances. "The ethical demand" is Løgstrup's term for Luther's version of natural law. What we are dealing with is a universal ethics formulated by a Lutheran philosopher.

NOTES

1. The original version of this classification is, as far as I can see, Løgstrup 1960. An abridged version of this article appears in Løgstrup 1996, and the original text is included as an appendix in the 1997 English edition of *The Ethical Demand*. When referring to Løgstrup 1960, I also provide the pages in the 1997 English version.

2. There is still work to be done here. A search for the word "Aristotle" in Løgstrup's manuscripts yields more than one hundred finds. One occasion on which Løgstrup may have done some studies on Aristotle was in the early 1950s, while carrying out the duties of the vacant philosophy chair at his university. These included giving the general introductory lecture in the history of philosophy (*studium philosophicum*).

3. Løgstrup expends even fewer words on Aquinas than on Aristotle. In Løgstrup 1996 we find two sentences, whose main point is that for Thomas Aquinas the relation to the good served to help human beings actualize their own possibilities. I think it is fair to assume that Løgstrup, unlike his colleagues Johannes Sløk and Regin Prenter, never read Aquinas.

4. Scheler himself sometimes describes his own position as "emotionaler Intuitionismus" (Scheler 1954, 14).

5. This is not the place to assess the adequacy of Løgstrup's criticism of Kant. However, it might be useful to notice that Løgstrup (like many other of Kant's critics) does not include *Die Metaphysik der Sitten*. Also, he does not reflect on the political dimension of Kant's ethics.

6. There seems to be a significant development here. In the 1932 prize essay, one of Løgstrup's theses against Scheler is about the essence of "ought": "Imperative ought is founded in a command. The *authoritative command . . .*" (Løgstrup 1932, 119, emphasis added).

7. In Løgstrup's lifetime, his monograph on Heidegger's *Sein und Zeit* was circulated as a stenciled manuscript.

8. In *The Ethical Demand* we find the duality in the distinction between "the social norms" and "the radical demand."

9. In Andersen 2001, I present Løgstrup's ontological ethics from a theological point of view. I regard it as a philosophical reconstruction of a natural-law theory.

10. It is, of course, not true that problems of politics are absent from Heidegger and Lipps, but in both cases the involvement was marked by a controversial relationship to Nazism.

REFERENCES

Andersen, S. 2001. "Theological Ethics, Moral Philosophy, and Natural Law." *Ethical Theory and Moral Practice* 4, no. 4: 349–364.

Gethmann-Seifert, A., and O. Pöggler, eds. 1987. *Heidegger und die praktische Philosophie*. Frankfurt am Main.

Lévinas, Emmanuel. 1999. *Totality and Infinity. An Essay on Exteriority*. Translated by Alphonso Lingis. Dordrecht, Boston, London.

Lipps, H. 1977. *Die menschliche Natur*. Werke III. Frankfurt am Main.

Løgstrup, K. E. 1932. [Written in 1931.] *Besvarelse af Universitetets Prisopgave: Teologi B. En Fremstilling og Vurdering af Max Scheler's "Der Formalismus in der Ethik und die materiale Wertethik."* University of Copenhagen (submitted prize essay on Scheler's ethics).

———. 1947. "Antropologien i Kants Etik." In *Festskrift til Jens Nørregaard*. Copenhagen.

———. 1950. *Kierkegaards und Heideggers Existenzanalyse und ihr Verhältnis zur Verkündigung* [Kierkegaard's and Heidegger's Analyses of Existence and Their Relation to the Proclamation]. Berlin.

———. 1952. *Kants filosofi I*. Copenhagen.

———. 1960. "Ethik und Ontologie." *Zeitschrift für Theologie und Kirche* 57: 357–391.

————. 1972. *Norm og spontaneitet. Etik og politik mellem teknokrati og dilettan-tokrati* [Norm and Spontaneity: Ethics and Politics between Technocracy and Dilettantocracy]. Copenhagen.

————. 1987. *Solidaritet og kærlighed og andre essays* [Solidarity and Love, and Other Essays]. Copenhagen.

————. 1995. *Metaphysics.* Vol. 1. Milwaukee.

————. 1996. *Etiske begreber og problemer* [Ethical Concepts and Problems]. Copenhagen.

————. 1997. *The Ethical Demand.* Notre Dame.

————. 2007. *Beyond the Ethical Demand.* Notre Dame.

Olafson, F. A. 1998. *Heidegger and the Ground of Ethics: A Study of Mitsein.* Cambridge.

Scheler, M. 1954. *Der Formalismus in der Ethik und die materiale Wertethik, Neuer Versuch der Grundlegung eines ethischen Personalismus.* Bern.

CHAPTER THREE

The Genesis of K. E. Løgstrup's View of Morality as a Substitute

Kees van Kooten Niekerk

In his book *Opgør med Kierkegaard* (Controverting Kierkegaard) Løgstrup presents a Kantian transformation of the biblical story of the Good Samaritan. According to him, the original story tells us how the Samaritan, moved by mercy, spontaneously took charge of the victim of assault, his thoughts occupied by the victim's needs and the question of how best to come to his aid. But we can imagine, Løgstrup continues, that the Samaritan was tempted to pass by and leave the victim to his fate. In that case he could have come to realize that it was his duty to aid the victim, and this realization could have made him take charge of the victim nevertheless. If so, he would not have acted out of mercy, but out of duty. His act would have been a *moral* act. As such it would have been a *substitute* for acting out of mercy. Løgstrup recognizes, of course, that this is better than brutality or indifference. However, at the same time he emphasizes that the Kantian Samaritan's act, being a substitute, is *inferior* to the biblical Samaritan's acting spontaneously out of mercy (SEL, 76).

Løgstrup substantiates this claim by comparing the role of motivation in acts of mercy and corresponding acts of duty. In acts of mercy, the agent is motivated by the need of another person and by the intended result of his or her action, consisting in the removal of obstacles to the other's flourishing. The

56   agent is completely engaged in caring for the other. In corresponding acts of duty, on the other hand, engagement and its inherent motivation have been disrupted. Now, duty—that is, the sense of the rightness of the action—is resorted to as a fresh motive. This motive, however, is only a substitute for the motivation inherent in the original engagement. The same applies to virtue, which Løgstrup describes as a disposition to act motivated by "the thought and the sense of the rightness of the action," that is, as a disposition to act out of duty. He concludes: "Just as duty is a substitute motive, virtue is a substitute disposition" (SEL, 78).

According to Løgstrup the problem with these substitutes is that the engagement with the other and the world is loosened. "[T]he thought of and sense of the rightness of the act are given independent status and are interposed. . . . [T]he motive is no longer drawn from the consequences that the action will have for the lives of others and for society, but is sought in the individual himself." The individual is thrown back upon himself or herself. Therefore, "[d]uty and virtue are moral introversions." And Løgstrup adds that the thought of the rightness of the action involved in duty and virtue naturally evokes a "rapture at one's own righteousness" (SEL, 78–79).

The above quotations about duty and virtue as substitutes and introversions suggest that Løgstrup is making a general point. Indeed, he uses the example of the Good Samaritan to say something about morality in general. The Samaritan's mercy is an instance of what he calls the "sovereign expressions of life." These are, roughly, spontaneous, other-regarding impulses or modes of conduct such as trust, mercy, and sincerity. What Løgstrup claims is that morality is secondary and inferior to the sovereign expressions of life. In his own words: "Morality exists to deliver substitute motives to substitute actions because the sovereign and spontaneous expressions of life, with their attachment to what the act is intended to achieve, either fail to materialize or are stifled" (SEL, 78).

It is not so easy to make out what Løgstrup, in the present context, means by "morality." In any case, as secondary and inferior to the sovereign expressions of life, morality must be distinguished from them. Indeed, Løgstrup characterizes the sovereign expressions of life as "premoral" (SEL, 77). In the section of *Opgør med Kierkegaard* that ends with the example of the Good Samaritan (SEL, 72–76), he uses "morality" (Danish: *moral*) first as a designation of customary ethics. However, he

also uses the word later as the designation of a Kantian type of morality.
This type of morality "is distinguished by reflection," that is, reflection on
what is right, and on the question of why one should do what is right.
The answer to that question is: because it is your duty to do so. Kantian
morality is thus "a determinate consciousness of what duty requires and
action based on that consciousness, which accordingly precedes it" (SEL,
73–74; quotations, 74).[1] Løgstrup's transformation of the Good Samaritan into a Kantian Samaritan and his consequent contrast between acts of
duty and acts of mercy suggest that he is thinking of this Kantian type of
morality. Furthermore, in the course of his argument, Løgstrup extends
his concept of morality to a morality of virtue as a disposition to act out
of duty. I therefore think it is fairly safe to conclude that morality for Løgstrup in the present context is a phenomenon that, in contradistinction
to the spontaneous sovereign expressions of life, is characterized by reflection and acting out of duty, which kind of action may, or may not, have
been habitualized in virtue.

I think many readers will be puzzled at Løgstrup's rather negative
appraisal of the moralities of duty and virtue. Is it not unambiguously
positive when people do things that are right for the sake of their rightness, or when they act out of virtue? It may be difficult to see why such
actions should be inferior to the sovereign expressions of life. In the following I will try to clarify Løgstrup's view of morality as a substitute by
pointing to some of the theological and philosophical ideas that have
influenced it. This does not mean, however, that I subscribe to this view.
To indicate why I do not, I will conclude this essay by asking some critical questions.

MARTIN LUTHER

Løgstrup's view that the sovereign expressions of life are superior to
moral acts of duty has a theological background in Luther's conception
of the works of love as fruits of faith. In his treatise *The Freedom of a
Christian,* Luther refers to the word of Jesus that says a good tree cannot
bear bad fruit, nor a bad tree good fruit (Mt 7:18) and uses it to support
his claim that human beings can do good works only by virtue of justification through faith (Luther 1962a, 69 ff.). He explains the relationship

58 between faith and the works of love as follows: "Behold, from faith thus
flow forth love and joy in the Lord, and from love a joyful, willing, and
free mind that serves one's neighbor willingly" (ibid., 75–76).

In his treatise *Secular Authority*, Luther relates this view of good
works to the concept of the law. He quotes the biblical statement that
the law is not given for the righteous but for the unrighteous (1 Tim 1:9),
and asks why this is so. He answers: "Because the righteous does of himself all and more than all that all the laws demand. But the unrighteous
do nothing that the law demands, therefore they need the law to instruct,
constrain, and compel them to do what is good" (Luther 1962c, 369). In
other words, the Christians, insofar as they are true believers, do not need
the law; they do good works of themselves, without the law. The law has
been given for the nonbelievers, to instruct them and compel them to
do the good works they do not do of themselves.

This should not be misunderstood. Luther does not intend to say
that nonbelievers can do good works in the proper sense of the word.
True, they can do the works that are demanded by the law. But, according to Luther, the law, being God's law, demands more than that. It demands that those works are done with all one's heart and with love. By
themselves human beings cannot achieve that. If they do the works of
the law at all, they do them owing to fear of punishment or hope of reward, not with all their hearts. Therefore, they cannot fulfill the law. As
Luther puts it in his *Preface to the Epistle of St Paul to the Romans:* "To
fulfil the law, we must meet its requirement gladly and lovingly; live virtuous and upright lives without the constraint of the law, and as if neither the law nor its penalties existed"—and this is only possible in faith
(Luther 1962b, 19–22; quotation, 21). According to Luther, this means
that only the good works of faith are genuine good works. This they are
because they are done with all one's heart. Good works constrained by
the law are good works only in an external, improper sense.

I think Luther's contrast between the works of faith and the works
of the law lies at the root of Løgstrup's view that the sovereign expressions of life are superior to the performance of acts of duty. This is not
only a natural idea, considering the fact that Løgstrup was a Lutheran
theologian. It can also be supported with reference to Løgstrup's writings. Later in this essay we will see how Løgstrup's view of morality is
dependent on Luther's view of the law. Here I focus on the relationship

between Luther's view of the works of faith and Løgstrup's conception **59** of the sovereign expressions of life.

In one of his earliest publications, long before he developed his conception of the sovereign expressions of life, Løgstrup explicitly subscribes to Luther's view of good works as the fruits of faith. This is not particularly remarkable for a Lutheran theologian, of course. What is remarkable, however, is how Løgstrup interprets that view. He explains it by saying that "the branch bears the fruit before it is aware of it, without making an effort and only because it is on the tree, so that the fruit is there before thought" (Løgstrup 1936a, 140; my translation). This explanation shows that Løgstrup understands Luther's idea of the fruits of faith in terms of what we normally consider as spontaneous acts, namely, as acts that happen of themselves, without our thinking about them and making an effort. It is not difficult to understand why Løgstrup does not actually use the word "spontaneous" here. The reason must be that in everyday language we use that word only to designate natural human acts, not acts that flow forth from faith. But this does not alter the fact that there is a *substantive* similarity between what we normally call spontaneous acts and the acts of faith as Løgstrup describes them.[2]

It should be clear, however, that there is also an important difference between Løgstrup's conception of the sovereign expressions of life and Luther's view of the works of love. Whereas Luther's works of love are fruits of *faith*, the sovereign expressions of life are *natural* human phenomena. I will explain what brought about this difference later. For the moment I restrict myself to noting the substantive similarity between Løgstrup's interpretation of Luther's works of love and his later conception of the sovereign expressions of life as *spontaneous* phenomena.

JAKOB KNUDSEN

Løgstrup's conception of the sovereign expressions of life has more than merely a theological background in Luther. It has also a philosophical background in what might be called "the ideal of living immediately," in the form in which it was propounded by the Danish theologian, philosopher, and writer Jakob Knudsen (1858–1917). This ideal consists in an engagement with the world, which has a "self-forgetful, immediate,

60   and unreflected nature" (Knudsen 1949, 47).[3] Knudsen contrasts this
ideal with self-contemplation, which he specifies as "the looking at yourself that kills . . . the tender, living moment" (ibid., 49). Moreover, he con-
nects it with the ideal of love when he writes: "The self's longing for and
commitment to another self is its own and proper function, it is *being oneself,* for it is the only *relation* entered by the self, which it cannot leave and
contemplate from the outside" (Knudsen 1948, 155, emphasis in original). In other words, it is precisely by virtue of the self-forgetfulness involved in the commitment to another person that a human being in love
attains the purpose of being oneself.

Løgstrup's thinking was strongly influenced by Knudsen.[4] His influence was already present in Løgstrup's first academic work, a prize-
winning dissertation on the ethics of Max Scheler (1931, unpublished).
Apart from references to Scheler's *Der Formalismus in der Ethik und die
materiale Wertethik* (Formalism in Ethics and Material Ethics of Value),
which is the main source used for the dissertation, it contains very few
references to other works. One of those, however, is a reference to a biography of Luther written by Knudsen. Here Løgstrup quotes Knudsen's
statement: "None of us should try to look at the back of our own neck,"
which he (Løgstrup) regards as an expression of "the destructivity, indeed, the pointlessness of self-contemplation" (Løgstrup 1931, 140).[5]

In *The Ethical Demand*, Løgstrup criticizes the condemnation of living immediately found in Kierkegaard's *Concluding Unscientific Postscript.*
According to Løgstrup, immediacy can mean two things: "a) It can mean
devotion: to devote oneself to one's work, to take pleasure in a carefree
manner in fellowship with others, to be spellbound in love, to be heart-
broken at the loss of somebody one cared for. And b) it can mean the
selfish form we give our devotion . . ." (Løgstrup 1997, 234). The trouble
with Kierkegaard is that he does not make this distinction, which has
the annoying consequence that he rejects living immediately because
of the selfishness it involves. Interestingly, Løgstrup associates the first,
positive, meaning of immediacy with Knudsen's concept of zest for life,
and he refers to the fact that Knudsen already distinguished between zest
for life and selfishness (ibid., 234–235).

In his *Opgør med Kierkegaard*, Løgstrup returns to Kierkegaard's
condemnation of living immediately in connection with his treatment of
the sovereign expressions of life. He opposes Kierkegaard's view that it is

our task to detach ourselves from immediacy through a reflection on the   61
infinite in ourselves. His argument is, once again, that immediacy is not
merely selfishness: "The immediacy with which the individual is bound
to the world through desire and pleasure is matched by the immediacy
with which he is bound to the world through . . . sovereign expressions
of life" (SEL, 70–71). This means that our task is not to detach ourselves
from immediacy, but rather to live the right kind of immediate life, that
is, giving way to the sovereign expressions of life (SEL, 71).

On the basis of these expositions, Løgstrup's positive conception of
living immediately can be described as living engaged in and absorbed
by the tasks and occurrences of life without stopping short to reflect upon
oneself. Moreover, in conjunction with Løgstrup's references to Knudsen,
they reveal a clear influence from the latter's ideal of self-forgetful commitment to the world and the other. Finally, the exposition from *Opgør med
Kierkegaard* shows that Løgstrup regarded the realization of the sovereign expressions of life as a part of living immediately. I therefore think it
is fair to say that, among other things, Løgstrup's emphasis on the agent's
engagement with the world and the other in the sovereign expressions
of life reflects Knudsen's ideal of living immediately.

This raises the question of how Løgstrup's concepts of immediacy
and spontaneity relate to one another. Immediate engagement in the world
and the other is the opposite of reflection. Spontaneity, on the other hand,
means that human action happens effortlessly and of its own accord.[6] The
relationship between these concepts is that spontaneous actions are normally immediate actions in which the agent is absorbed by the task at
hand. This does not mean, however, that all immediate actions are spontaneous actions. Making an effort to perform a difficult task may be referred
to as immediate action in the sense that the agent is completely absorbed
by the task, but it is certainly not spontaneous action happening effortlessly and of its own accord. However, the circumstance that spontaneous
actions are normally immediate actions explains why Løgstrup could
elaborate on Luther's notion of "spontaneous" love in terms of Knudsen's
ideal of living immediately.

Løgstrup's view of morality as a substitute must be understood in
relation to his conception of the sovereign expressions of life. Thus far
I have focused on the ideas that contributed to the formation of that
conception. Now it is time to consider Løgstrup's view of morality as a

62 substitute. For this view, too, it is possible to point to a source that exerted a substantial influence on the young Løgstrup, namely, the Danish theological movement known as "Tidehverv."

TIDEHVERV

Tidehverv (literally, "Time on the Turn") was a Danish movement parallel to Swiss-German dialectical theology. It arose in the 1920s out of an opposition to the prevalent understanding of Christian belief, which aimed at religious and moral development of one's personality oriented towards the person of Jesus as the ideal. Drawing upon Luther's view of sin as egocentrism, Tidehverv condemned this understanding as a selfish preoccupation with one's own perfection.[7] Instead, believers were to turn their attention away from themselves towards their neighbors, to serve them in love.

Upon becoming a vicar in the Danish Church (1936), Løgstrup joined Tidehverv. Prepared by Knudsen's criticism of self-contemplation, he adopted Tidehverv's condemnation of pious preoccupation with oneself.[8] This appears clearly in an article from 1936, in which Løgstrup asserts that "[h]uman life consists in wrapping everything into the cocoon of egocentrism so that everything—including piety—is used to elevate and secure oneself" (1936b, 429). This statement serves as a point of departure for an attack on the view, allegedly dominant in Christian ethics, that it is the attitude of mind that matters. According to Løgstrup, this view implies an interest in one's own attitude of mind, which makes any moral consideration egocentric and Pharisaic; Pharisaic, because "[t]he motor of the good works is the projected image of oneself as good. . . . With the emergence of the faintest consideration we no longer do good as a matter of course; we want to get something out of it." He concludes: *"Every moral thought entails an ulterior motive"* (ibid., 432, emphasis in original)—that is, the motive of being a good person.

In an article from 1938 Løgstrup applies this idea to Kant's ethics of duty. Here it is "the projected image of oneself as dutiful" that is the motor of acting rightly, which means that "[i]n the ethics of duty every moral thought entails an ulterior motive" (Løgstrup 1938, 215). Løgstrup sees this idea confirmed by the fact that Kant says that we should do our duty in order not to be unworthy in our own esteem (ibid., 212–213). Instead of living by duty, Løgstrup says, we should live in responsible commitment to the other: "*A human being can only become free of self-preoccupation by means of a fellow human being*" (ibid., 213, emphasis in original).

From these texts it appears that for Løgstrup, long before he developed his conception of the sovereign expressions of life, the fundamental disjunction was: either preoccupation with the other or preoccupation with oneself. Moreover, it appears that in Løgstrup's view, morality, at least the Christian morality of the attitude of mind and the Kantian morality of duty, belongs to the wrong side of the disjunction: preoccupation with oneself. The reason is that, according to Løgstrup, morality includes reflection on oneself as a moral agent, which results in the fact that the wish to be a good person becomes the ultimate motive for acting rightly. And, from a Tidehverv point of view, this kind of preoccupation with oneself is sin. As I see it, this association of moral self-reflection, moral motivation, and sin constitutes an important part of the background of Løgstrup's view of morality as a substitute.

VILHELM GRØNBECH

Above I claimed that Løgstrup's conception of the sovereign expressions of life was influenced by Luther's view of the works of faith. However, there is an important difference between Løgstrup and Luther in that Løgstrup's sovereign expressions of life, being natural human impulses or modes of conduct, are not dependent on Christian faith. This raises the question: What is the background of this difference?

The most general is the influence of the so-called *Lebensphilosophie* (Philosophy of Life), a type of thought associated with the ideas of Friedrich Nietzsche, Wilhelm Dilthey, and Henri Bergson that dominated German philosophy between 1880 and 1930. This is not the place to give an exposition of this type of philosophy. What is important in this context is that it cherished the ideal of living naturally, immediately, dynamically, and creatively.[9] Not only did this ideal of life mark German philosophy around 1900, it also found its way into Danish philosophy and theology. This is manifest in Knudsen's ideal of living immediately, of course, but Eduard Geismar, Løgstrup's teacher in ethics and theology at the Faculty of Theology in Copenhagen, was influenced by it as well.[10]

64   Løgstrup met the *Lebensphilosphie*'s ideal of life in Denmark in Geismar's and Knudsen's transformations, but also in more original forms during his studies in Germany and France after completing his theological education in Copenhagen.[11] However, this ideal became particularly influential for his theological and ethical thought through the book *Jesus, Menneskesønnen* (Jesus, The Son of Man, 1935), written by the Danish historian of religion Vilhelm Grønbech (1873–1948).

In this book Grønbech depicts Jesus as the champion of living immediately, both through his way of living and through his proclamation of the Kingdom of God. According to Grønbech, this proclamation claims that "true humanity consists in giving, always turning outwards, never thinking of the feelings and thoughts I have, but merely letting life break through and stream out freely into the world" (Grønbech 1935, 23–24). This quotation nicely expresses the spontaneous and anti-reflective nature of Grønbech's conception of living immediately. At the same time Grønbech's characterization of this way of living as giving shows that he regarded it as morally good. He elaborated on the notion of giving in connection with a discussion of the parable of the Good Samaritan by stating that giving is giving unconditionally, which includes forgiving unconditionally (ibid., 19–23). Grønbech contrasted such living with the regulated and purposive life of culture and morality: "Life does not recognize any commandment, any rule, he [Jesus] says, life itself is its only law" (ibid., 61).

In 1942 Løgstrup defended his doctoral dissertation, entitled *Den erkendelsesteoretiske Konflikt mellem den transcendentalfilosofiske Idealisme og Teologien* (The Epistemological Conflict between Transcendental Idealism and Theology). Among many other things, this thesis contained an interpretation of the life and proclamation of Jesus that was deeply influenced by Grønbech's ideas. Løgstrup states, for example, that Jesus "distinguished between cultural life, which is purposive and methodical and calculating, and life itself, the life of the moment, which is forgiving and giving and mercy, in which there is precisely no purpose, no plan, no task, because it is not culture" (Løgstrup 1942, 103). However, in contradistinction to Grønbech, Løgstrup gave a theological interpretation of 'life itself' as life such as God has created it: "In the belief of Israel and the proclamation of Jesus life in itself is . . . something definite, because it is created life" (ibid., 90).[12]

It is clear that at this stage Løgstrup, unlike Luther, considers "spontaneous" love of the neighbor as a natural human possibility. The difference between Løgstrup and Luther, however, should not be exaggerated. Løgstrup additionally states that love is never realized naturally because human beings always destroy their created life. Therefore, for Løgstrup as for Luther, its realization is dependent on God's justifying love. As Løgstrup puts it in dialectical-theological terms: The Kingdom of God consists in a personal relationship between a human being and God, and between one human being and another, "but it is God's Kingdom, because the word that creates it is God's word" (ibid., 150).

Løgstrup's adoption of Grønbech's *Lebensphilosophie* explains why, in his thesis, he came to consider spontaneous love of the neighbor as a natural human possibility. However, at least two questions remain. First, what made Løgstrup shift from denying to affirming the realization of natural love of the neighbor in the sovereign expressions of life? Second, how did he develop his previously negative view of morality into the view of morality as a substitute for the sovereign expressions of life? To find an answer to these questions we must begin by examining Løgstrup's conception of the ethical demand.

THE ETHICAL DEMAND

The outline of Løgstrup's conception of the ethical demand is already perceptible in his thesis. Here he asks how our created natural love of the neighbor is related to the biblical commandment of love, and he answers: "The particular nature of our human life as created life is separated from life itself and faces it as laws, because we have used the powers of our lives to destroy the particular, human, nature of our lives." Consequently, this particular nature "makes the law's unconditional demand to our lives" (Løgstrup 1942, 91). In other words, because we destroy created life, we meet its content in the form of a law that *demands* of us that we do that which we do not do spontaneously, or, as Løgstrup puts it in this context, in "paradisiacal unconscious naturalness" (ibid.). This does not mean for Løgstrup that we know by ourselves what is demanded of us. Our sin is so radical that it involves "a destruction of ethical-religious cognition." That is why the law had to be revealed to us by God (ibid., 93–94).[13]

According to Løgstrup, then, natural humans, being sinners, become acquainted with the morally good only in the form of a demand. In *The Ethical Demand*, he sets out to explain how this may happen. He does so first and foremost by means of a phenomenological analysis of the trust in which a person delivers something of his or her life over to the goodwill of another person. According to Løgstrup, from this "fact" the demand arises to take care of the person who has placed his or her trust in us. This argument is well known, and I do not intend to expand on it here.[14] What is important in the present context is that Løgstrup now has abandoned the idea, put forward in his thesis, that human beings cannot know the law on their own. His phenomenological argument is supposed to be acknowledgeable to everyone, Christians and non-Christians alike.[15]

In his account of the ethical demand, Løgstrup maintains the idea, as expressed in his thesis, that there is a correlation between created and demanded love. What is demanded from us is love of our neighbor. This appears from what Løgstrup calls the *radicalness* of the demand: the demand does not merely demand of us that we take care of the other, but also demands that we do so exclusively for the sake of the other (Løgstrup 1997, 44–46). By virtue of this radicalness, the demand can only be fulfilled in love, "[b]ecause love alone corresponds to the fact that something of the other person's life is delivered over to us" (ibid., 143). According to Løgstrup, the demanded love is the spontaneous love, the possibility of which has been given to us by God, the Creator: "[L]ove exists only in the individual's life as given to him or her. This constitutes love's immediacy."[16]

In *The Ethical Demand*, Løgstrup also sticks to the view that human beings naturally never realize the love that is demanded of them. Having set out that the demand can only be fulfilled in love, he states: "We do not possess such love" (ibid., 143). We can, of course, make an effort to do the deed that is demanded of us. Yet that is not the same as acting out of love: "Though we do not possess love, we do the deed which love would have us do, albeit for all sorts of other motives" (ibid.). Here, once again, we notice the influence of Luther, or more specifically, of his idea that nonbelievers can do the works of the law only in an external sense, out of improper motives. Showing acute insight into human motivation, Løgstrup lists many such motives, including fear, pride, self-righteousness, not wanting to be irresponsible, and faithfulness to one's outlook on life.

Acting out of these and similar motives is merely a "compromise with the demand" (ibid., 144), because it replaces the spontaneous love that is demanded.[17] And even though *we* might think well of the last two motives, it can hardly be doubted that Løgstrup associates them with sin — in the sense of preoccupation with oneself instead of the other. One place where this becomes evident is Løgstrup's comment that the individual who acts out of these motives is acting "for the sake of *his or her own* attitude or outlook of life" (ibid., 144, emphasis added) — and thus not for the sake of the other, as he or she should do.[18]

Løgstrup gives another reason why the ethical demand is never fulfilled. He points out that the demand, by demanding love (that is, the realization of the possibility of love that we have been given as creatures), actually tells us "that each of us is to live by continually receiving his life as a gift" (ibid., 146). As such the demand is opposed to any attempt to manage our lives apart from receiving our lives as a gift. As a consequence, the demand is also opposed to any attempt to obey it. In reality, any such attempt is the expression of our will to be sovereign in our own life. Løgstrup concludes: "By willing to be sovereign in our own life, by refusing to receive life as a gift, we place ourselves in a sharp contradiction: every attempt to obey the demand turns out to be an attempt at obedience *within the framework* of a more fundamental disobedience" (ibid.).

Here we meet Løgstrup's fundamental disjunction in an elaborated form. On the one hand, in a fusion of theological ideas and ideas derived from the *Lebensphilosophie,* there is the ideal of living spontaneously in receiving life as a gift from God. Such a life is a life in spontaneous love that fulfills the ethical demand, because the agent is completely preoccupied with the neighbor. On the other hand, there is our own, sovereign management of our lives, which includes our attempts to obey the demand. Again, *we* might think that such sovereign management is a good thing, especially when it serves the purpose of obedience to the demand. But for the Lutheran theologian Løgstrup, it is a form of sinful preoccupation with oneself, now in the sense that we let not God, the Creator, rule in our lives, but in haughty self-righteousness think that we are our own masters.[19]

This explains why, for Løgstrup, all motives of acting in conformity with the demand except love merely represent a compromise with the demand: as expressions of our own sovereignty they are fundamentally

68   selfish and thus sinful. Only in a spontaneous love, which precedes any awareness of the demand, is the demand fulfilled. When we become aware of the demand as a demand, this spontaneity has been broken. In this situation only conscious obedience remains, but precisely in such obedience the demand cannot be fulfilled, at least not in its radical sense of acting completely for the sake of the other. Thus the demand leads to the paradox that "what is demanded is that the demand should not have been necessary. This is the demand's radical character" (ibid., 146).

Løgstrup's claim that we cannot fulfill the demand must be understood against the background of the theological purpose of *The Ethical Demand*. This purpose is, generally speaking, to serve the proclamation of the gospel. As Løgstrup explains in the introduction, he pursues this purpose by giving a philosophical analysis of those aspects of human existence to which that proclamation relates. This analysis aims both to promote the understanding of the proclamation and to clarify its specific Christian nature (ibid., 1–3). Now, Løgstrup's account of the unfulfillability of the demand has the wider goal of making us realize our guilt.[20] This realization serves as a pre-understanding of the proclamation's speaking of sin, which at the same time points to God's remission of sins as the proclamation's specific Christian core. From a theological point of view, Løgstrup's account of the ethical demand can thus be said to be a reinterpretation of Luther's idea of the *usus theologicus* of the law, that is, of the law's leading us to Christ by showing us our sin. Seen against this background, it is natural that *The Ethical Demand* should conclude with a chapter on "the unfulfillability of the demand and the proclamation of Jesus."

Convincing us of guilt as a pre-understanding of the gospel is, however, not the only purpose of Løgstrup's discussion of the ethical demand. *The Ethical Demand* contains many considerations about how to shape the obedience to the demand in concrete life. Examples are Løgstrup's reflections about respect for the other's independence (ibid., 22–28), the role of the demand for meeting the social norms (ibid., 60–63), and the ethical decision (ibid., 148–163), but also his stressing of the Christian's secular responsibility with regard to the concretization of the demand (ibid., 108–114). These reflections show that Løgstrup's treatment of the demand has not only a theological purpose but also a practical one: to offer guidance for our lives with our fellow human beings in the world.

In this context obedience to the demand has a legitimate place. Just as Løgstrup's considerations about the unfulfillability of the demand can be regarded as his reinterpretation of Luther's idea of the *usus theologicus* of the law, his considerations about how to frame our obedience can be regarded as his concretization of Luther's idea of the *usus civilis* or *usus politicus* of the law, that is, its function as a guideline for our social lives.[21]

Løgstrup's twofold treatment of the ethical demand entails a problem. In the theological context he stresses that the demand cannot be fulfilled, because we never act out of unselfish love. In the practical context, on the other hand, he seems to assume that it is possible to fulfill the demand, as when he points to the importance of unselfish love in rearing one's children (ibid., 60–62). This raises questions as to whether Løgstrup's considerations are wholly consistent. It is a difficult issue, and one that I cannot discuss exhaustively here. I shall therefore confine myself to a few remarks.

We should begin by remembering that the unfulfillability of the demand concerns its *radicalness:* the demand cannot be fulfilled in the sense that we act *solely* out of love, that is, *solely* for the sake of the other. Our attempts to obey the demand always involve selfish, and thus sinful, motives. As a consequence, all of Løgstrup's practical considerations about how to obey the demand concern the sphere of the *compromise* with the demand. I understand these considerations to the effect that Løgstrup admits that unselfishness may play a part, for instance in the raising of our children. The decisive thing is, however, that we never act *solely* for the sake of the other. Our action will always include selfish motives. As Løgstrup puts it when dealing with what he calls the "refraction" of the demand by our selfish nature: "[A]t best all kinds of other motives have a way of getting mixed up with the will to obey the demand" (ibid., 107–108). This formulation allows for the possibility that unselfishness may play a part, but since it will always be mixed up with selfish motives, our obedience to the demand can never fulfill it in a *radical* sense. For this reason I do not think there is a contradiction between Løgstrup's theological claim that the demand cannot be fulfilled and his apparent reckoning with the possibility of unselfishness in a practical context.[22]

It is Løgstrup's conception of obedience as a compromise with the demand that sets the stage for his view of morality as a substitute. To be sure, in *The Ethical Demand* he does not mention duty as a possible motive for obedience, but, as conscious efforts to do what is demanded, acts of duty must belong to the sphere of the compromise with the demand. Moreover, the Kantian Samaritan's aid to the victim, which is Løgstrup's point of departure for his treatment of morality as a substitute, is precisely a conscious attempt to obey the demand. This partly answers my second question as to how Løgstrup moved from his negative understanding of morality in the 1930s to his view of morality as a substitute. In order to understand this view better we must now turn to my first question, the one concerning Løgstrup's shift from denial to affirmation of the realization of neighborly love as it appears in his conception of the sovereign expressions of life.

THE SOVEREIGN EXPRESSIONS OF LIFE

The principal reason behind Løgstrup's development of the conception of the sovereign expressions of life, in my opinion, is simply a phenomenological recognition of the existence of spontaneous other-regarding impulses or modes of conduct such as trust, mercy, and sincerity. In a sense this recognition is already present in his phenomenological analyses of trust and natural love in *The Ethical Demand*.[23] Consequently, as Ole Jensen has noted elsewhere, *The Ethical Demand* contains a contradiction between Løgstrup's speaking of "the realities of love and trust" and his theologically motivated treatment of love and trust as "imaginary entities" that are never realized.[24]

In a reply to Jensen appearing in *Opgør med Kierkegaard*, Løgstrup admits that Jensen is right. He certainly sticks to the view that the demand cannot be fulfilled in conscious obedience: "The demand is unfulfillable, the sovereign expression of life is not produced by the will's exerting itself to obey the demand" (SEL, 69). However, at this stage he acknowledges that the demand is fulfilled spontaneously in the sovereign expressions of life, "without being demanded" (SEL, 69). Only when the sovereign expression of life fails does the demand make itself felt, as a demand insisting that one do the deed that was not done spontaneously. Yet then, in a way, it is too late, since now the deed can only be performed in a willed obedience that cannot fulfill the demand in a radical sense. By way of conclusion, Løgstrup returns to the idea of *The Ethical Demand*, asserting that what is demanded is that the demand should not have been necessary. In his own words: "[T]he demand demands that it be itself superfluous" (SEL, 69).

The acknowledgement that the demand is fulfilled in the sovereign expressions of life does not make Løgstrup give up his Lutheran conviction of the gravity of sin that lay behind his view of the unfulfillability of the demand in *The Ethical Demand*. He still thinks sin adheres to the sovereign management of our lives, including our attempts to obey the demand. The difference is that here, unlike previously, Løgstrup recognizes that, thanks to the sovereign expressions of life, sin cannot completely destroy our communal life. This is not our own merit, however, but God the Creator's. The reason is that in the sovereign expressions of life "we live off something that we cannot credit to ourselves" (SEL, 67). Thus, Løgstrup's interpretation of the sovereign expressions of life as created by God enables him to recognize the presence of goodness in human life without abandoning the Lutheran doctrine of sin. As he puts it: "[T]here are no limits to our iniquity, but there are limits to the devastation it can effect; which limits are evidenced by our inability to prevent the sovereign expressions of life from forcing their way through and realizing themselves" (SEL, 69).

To clarify Løgstrup's view of morality as a substitute it is not necessary that I give a comprehensive account of his conception of the sovereign expressions of life. But one thing is important in this connection, namely, the fact that Løgstrup developed this conception in opposition to Kierkegaard.

For Kierkegaard, as Løgstrup interprets him, the task of a human being is to become detached from living immediately. Instead, in a reflection on ourselves, each of us should become aware that we are fundamentally related to eternity or God, in order to live consciously out of this relationship and thereby become true selves. In opposition to this view, Løgstrup claims that a human being is already a true self in the immediacy of the sovereign expressions of life. Here "the human person is—ipso facto—himself. He no longer has to reflect upon becoming an independent person, nor has he to reflect upon the task of becoming his true self; he has only to realize himself in the sovereign expression of life, and it is that expression of life—rather than reflection—that takes care of the person's selfhood" (SEL, 53–54).[25] As Løgstrup explains further, persons are themselves in the sovereign expressions of life by virtue of the fact that they identify with them—which must mean that they do not

72   experience their sovereign expressions of life "forcing their way through" as if being seized by a foreign power, but rather they experience them as the realization of (a part of) their true selves. This makes it comprehensible that Løgstrup can even venture to state that "the *freedom* of existence . . . consists in the sovereign expressions of life" (SEL, 67, emphasis added).[26]

For Løgstrup the theologian, self-realization in the sovereign expressions of life has a religious dimension. He does not deny Kierkegaard's view that human beings were created in order to live in relation to God. But according to Løgstrup, Kierkegaard failed to recognize that God "creates the self not only for eternity but for the neighbor too, by investing it with the sovereign expressions of life as possibilities that correspond to the claims in which eternity incarnates itself in the interpersonal situation" (SEL, 71). That is to say, in their self-realization in the sovereign expressions of life, human beings already live in the relation to God for which God created them, because God has endowed them with the sovereign expressions of life in order that they should fulfill God's ethical demand.

These considerations show that Løgstrup articulated his conception of the sovereign expressions of life in the context of a rejection of Kierkegaard's ideal of self-reflection. In contrast to this ideal, the sovereign expressions of life represent the ideal of living immediately that Løgstrup inherited from Knudsen. At the same time, the conflict between these two ideals is an expression of what I have designated "Løgstrup's fundamental disjunction" between preoccupation with oneself and preoccupation with the other. Moreover, this conflict has theological significance by virtue of the fact that for Løgstrup, the very nature of human relationship to God and self-realization are at stake. I think that awareness of this conflict helps to understand why Løgstrup, in his view that morality is merely a substitute for the sovereign expressions of life, focuses so strongly on the reflective aspects of morality.

LØGSTRUP'S VIEW OF MORALITY AS A SUBSTITUTE

The time has come to gather the various strands of Løgstrup's ethical thoughts as discussed above and see how they meet in his view of morality as a substitute.

From the beginning, Løgstrup's ideal of moral life was Luther's understanding of love of the neighbor as a fruit of faith, interpreted in terms of spontaneity. Under the influence of Grønbech, this ideal was naturalized as a possibility of life rooted in "life itself." Moreover, unlike Grønbech, Løgstrup interpreted the notion of life theologically as created life. These ideas converge in the conception of the sovereign expressions of life as spontaneous realizations of love of the neighbor.

Love of the neighbor is, of course, preoccupation with the other. Under the influence of Knudsen, Løgstrup interpreted this preoccupation in terms of the ideal of living immediately, that is, of living in self-forgetful commitment to the world and to the other. By virtue of this interpretation, love of the neighbor was opposed explicitly to preoccupation with oneself. For a man imbued with the spirit of Tidehverv, there was no way preoccupation with oneself could avoid being associated with sin. All of this means that the sovereign expressions of life constitute a complex fusion of what analytical moral philosophers would call "moral and nonmoral goodness." The sovereign expressions of life are morally good in the sense that they aim at caring for the neighbor. This moral goodness is underlined by the fact that, like preoccupation with the other, they are the opposite of "sinful" preoccupation with oneself. At the same time, their preoccupation with the other is a realization of the nonmoral good of living immediately. This nonmoral goodness is in turn underlined by the claim that the agents in the sovereign expressions of life are truly themselves and live in the relation to God for which they were created.

Against this background it is easy to understand why Løgstrup should treat morality (that is, the morality of duty and virtue) negatively as a mere substitute. The reason is that, in several respects, morality is the opposite of his ideal of the sovereign expressions of life. As involving conscious and sovereign action, it contrasts with the spontaneous action of the sovereign expressions of life. As involving reflection, it contrasts with the immediate preoccupation with the other that is the hallmark of the sovereign expressions of life. And whereas the sovereign expressions of life embody the presence of divine goodness in human life, morality, insofar as it involves preoccupation with oneself, is associated with sin and one's alienation from God.

This last statement calls for some elaboration. We have seen that the young Løgstrup made the association between morality and sin explicit by claiming that moral thinking inevitably leads to one's making the

74   projected image of oneself as a good, or dutiful, person the real motive of moral action. In *Opgør med Kierkegaard*, Løgstrup draws a more nuanced picture of morality: Morality is acting out of duty, which may or may not have been habitualized in virtue. As such it presupposes reflection on what is right and why I should do what is right. Acting out of duty is specified as acting motivated by the thought and the sense of the rightness of the action. Thus in morality the motive is not drawn from the expected benefit of the other, as it is in mercy, for example, but from something in the agent himself or herself. Therefore duty and virtue (which habitualizes acting out of a sense of duty) are "moral introversions."

That Løgstrup draws this new picture of the morality of duty and virtue does not mean, however, that he has abandoned his original association of morality with sin. To be sure, he no longer claims that the projected image of one's own goodness is the real motive of moral action, as he did in the 1930s. Now he points to the sense and thought of the rightness of the action—which seems to be a more adequate view, at least of the overt motive of acting morally. He immediately adds, however, that the thought of the rightness of the action hardly fails to evoke a rapture at one's own righteousness. Here the annoying preoccupation with oneself turns up again in the form of a satisfaction with one's own goodness. It is true that this satisfaction is presented not as a motivating force, but as a kind of side effect of planned or performed moral actions. Still, it is easy to imagine that the expectation of such satisfaction gains a motivational significance. At any rate, whatever its function, for a Lutheran theologian such satisfaction (called "haughtiness" or "self-righteousness") is the quintessence of sin. Løgstrup thus maintains the association of morality with sin, and it can hardly be doubted that this association was one of the reasons underlying his devaluation of morality as a substitute.

Now, we should not forget that Løgstrup, in his assessment of the Kantian Samaritan's taking charge of the victim, remarks that the Samaritan's act is better than brutality and indifference. Nevertheless, his characterization of morality as a substitute entails a more negative view of morality than the one we met in *The Ethical Demand*. I think that there are two reasons for this.

First, in *The Ethical Demand* Løgstrup's theological criticism of the selfishness involved in sovereign moral action was balanced by his practical moral considerations, which left that criticism out of consideration.

On the other hand, in *Opgør med Kierkegaard* he treats morality in the context of his dispute with Kierkegaard. In this dispute, which is mainly a theological one, Løgstrup controverts Kierkegaard's view of Christian faith. In this connection it is natural that, in his treatment of morality, he should elaborate *The Ethical Demand*'s theological criticism of moral action.

The second reason for Løgstrup's negative view of morality in *Opgør med Kierkegaard* lies, as far as I can see, in the fact that in *The Ethical Demand* moral action figured as the only realistic ideal for action, because Løgstrup denied that spontaneous love of the neighbor can ever be realized. Moreover, in this context the existential-theological ideal of responsible moral action played an important part, as an ideal born of necessity, so to speak.[27] In *Opgør med Kierkegaard*, on the other hand, the sovereign expressions of life have become a realistic alternative to moral action. It is therefore natural to assume that Løgstrup's recognition of this alternative has influenced his appraisal of moral action in a negative direction.

NON-REFLECTIVE MORALITY

Were we to stop at Løgstrup's view of morality as a mere substitute, we would be doing him an injustice. Concurrently with this view, Løgstrup's work contains reflections that undeniably provide a more positive account of morality. These reflections were first put forward in the article "Ethik und Ontologie" (Ethics and Ontology) from 1961 and appeared later, in an elaborated version, in *Norm og spontaneitet* (Norm and Spontaneity) from 1972.[28]

These reflections focus on the origins of morality. Approaching the problem in his characteristic phenomenological way, Løgstrup focuses on concrete daily life and the tasks and problems we encounter there. He claims: "Around every activity and every form of common life a set of moral rules crystallizes" (SGCN, 90). He exemplifies this claim with what he calls "the morality of the sea" as described in the tales of Joseph Conrad. The great commandment of this morality is that you should never abandon a person in a situation of peril to save your own skin. And Løgstrup characterizes Captain MacWhirr in the story "Typhoon" as "a decent enough fellow" because he obeys this morality, in spite of the fact that he is so foolish as to steer his ship into a typhoon (SGCN, 90).

According to Løgstrup, the same applies to character traits: "[A]c-tually, it is the task, the work, the life of the community that create both morality and the character that respects it" (SGCN, 91–92). Character traits must be distinguished from the sovereign expressions of life, from which they differ in that they can be produced by practice. Moreover, un-like the sovereign expressions of life, character traits can be used to serve harmful purposes. They can also converge with the sovereign expressions of life in the performance of a concrete task, however. Løgstrup exem-plifies this with the rescue of Jimmy, a black sailor, as described in one of Conrad's other stories, *The Nigger of the Narcissus* (SGCN, 92–93).

The positive account of morality found in these reflections applies both to moral action and to character traits, at least insofar as the latter serve beneficial purposes. The main reason is that Løgstrup at this point is dealing with what might be termed "non-reflective morality." This ap-pears in his comment that it is not necessary for us to be aware of the moral rules as rules in order to act in accordance with them—in oppo-sition to what he regards as "exaggerated conceptions of the role played by reflection on moral rules in our everyday actions and decisions" (SGCN, 90–91). It also appears in his claim that the moral person's character traits correspond to his or her morality "not, however, from love of mo-rality or reflection on its dictates, but rather through involvement in the enterprises and the life of the community out of which both morality and character are born" (SGCN, 92). Here, incidentally, we are given the reason why Løgstrup does not want to designate those character traits as virtues: in his opinion, this designation has become prejudiced by the idea that virtues should be acquired for their own sake—not for the sake of the tasks they are to serve.

Because of its non-reflective nature, Løgstrup interprets this type of morality in terms of Knudsen's ideal of living immediately: both moral action and morally supportive character traits develop from, and ex-press themselves in, a self-forgetful commitment to the tasks of commu-nal life. And because this type of morality does not involve the agent's reflection on himself or herself as a moral person, it does not entail the risk of evoking a sense of self-righteousness. This explains why Løgstrup treats moral action and character traits more positively, or at least in a more relaxed fashion, in *Norm og spontaneitet* than he does in *Opgør med Kierkegaard*.

This shift in Løgstrup's view of morality can, however, also be seen in a wider perspective. *Norm og spontaneitet* is wholly devoted to ethical questions, not least the practical moral problems of human life. It has no theological purpose, as *Opgør med Kierkegaard* had. Therefore Løgstrup is not interested here in the subtleties of human motivation. Whereas *Opgør med Kierkegaard* can be regarded as a continuation of the theological line of thought of *The Ethical Demand*, *Norm og spontaneitet* can be regarded as a continuation of its practical line of thought. Consequently, the overarching subject in the latter work is not the human relationship to God, but the human moral life in the world. And this subject is discussed from a purely philosophical point of view, which leaves aside the problem of sin. From this perspective, it is only natural that in *Norm og spontaneitet* Løgstrup should be more positive, or at least less worried, about moral action, much as he is in the practically oriented sections of *The Ethical Demand*.

SOME CRITICAL QUESTIONS

In my introductory discussion I remarked that understanding Løgstrup's view of morality as a substitute is not the same as subscribing to it. It is not my purpose here to begin a critical discussion of that view. Even so, in order to indicate why I do not subscribe to it I will conclude this essay by posing some critical questions.

My account of the ideas that contributed to the formation of Løgstrup's view of morality as a substitute does not entail the claim that this view was a mere product of those ideas, constructed out of them, so to speak. Rather, these ideas functioned as a *context of discovery* of this view. Løgstrup's view itself was, to a substantial degree, based on phenomenological analyses of phenomena such as trust, mercy, and human motivation, analyses which were made more or less independently of the above-mentioned ideas.[29] Nevertheless, the context of discovery inevitably codetermined Løgstrup's interpretation of those phenomena. And it is here that questions arise as to the phenomenological adequacy of some aspects of Løgstrup's view of the sovereign expressions of life and morality that resulted from his interpretation.

As for the sovereign expressions of life, we have seen that Løgstrup's application of the concept of sovereignty has a theological background in the fact that it serves to oppose these expressions to human sovereignty, on the one hand, and connect them with God's sovereignty, on the other. It is therefore hardly accidental that it is in a theological context that Løgstrup stresses the sovereignty of the sovereign expressions of life, to the effect that we cannot prevent them from forcing their way through and being fulfilled. The question arises, however, of whether this statement is consistent with Løgstrup's claim that the Kantian Samaritan's temptation to pass by the injured traveler prevented him from acting out of mercy. Løgstrup's former statement may apply fairly well to trust because trust is a natural attitude of which we are normally not aware. But it certainly does not apply to mercy, which, as a consciously felt incitement to action, easily evokes resistance because it conflicts with our self-interest. This raises the more general question of whether the concept of sovereignty, by which Løgstrup interprets these phenomena, is not too general or unspecific a concept, and one which therefore cannot do justice to the phenomenological differences between, for example, trust and mercy.

Similar questions arise with regard to Løgstrup's view of morality as a substitute. Løgstrup's rather negative judgment of morality in *Opgør med Kierkegaard* is clearly marked by the fact that he opposes it to the ideals of spontaneity and immediacy, which he finds embodied in the sovereign expressions of life. As we have seen, this judgment is also connected with Løgstrup's negative view of preoccupation with oneself. Here we may ask, however, whether moral self-reflection and acting out of duty necessarily lead to a "sinful" rapture at one's own righteousness.[30] Is it not possible to do something just because we consider it morally right, without thinking of, or aiming at, our own goodness? Moreover, should we not distinguish more clearly than Løgstrup does between situations of moral reflection and situations of moral action? If we do so, it would seem that acts of duty and acts of virtue, although they may ultimately stem from moral reflection, can, in the moment of their performance, be of a similar immediate nature as the non-reflective moral acts that Løgstrup discusses in *Norm og spontaneitet*. And if that is the case, should such moral acts still be regarded as expressions of a sinful preoccupation with oneself? Perhaps a Kantian Samaritan, or a Thomistic Samaritan, could be a Good Samaritan too.

NOTES

1. This characterization of Kantian morality is admittedly not Løgstrup's own, but Hegel's, as described by Løgstrup. But since Løgstrup introduces it as Hegel's "free and admirable rendering of Kant" (SEL, 74), we may assume that he subscribes to it.

2. Interestingly, Eduard Geismar, Løgstrup's teacher in ethics and the philosophy of religion, indeed used the word "spontaneous" in connection with love of the neighbor. In his textbook of the philosophy of religion (published in 1924), Geismar remarks that any secular ethics that recognizes the ideal of love is faced with the antinomy that "[a]cts of duty have to come forth spontaneously" (my translation). According to Geismar, this problem can be solved only through a relationship to God, which brings about the right attitude of the mind. In this context he refers to Luther's idea of the good tree that bears good fruits (Geismar 1924, 312–320; quotation, 316). Geismar's connection of Christian love with spontaneity may well have influenced the young Løgstrup.

3. This and the following quotations from Danish works that have not been translated into English are my own translations.

4. This is not the place to document Knudsen's influence. I limit myself to a statement made by Løgstrup in 1956: "In my opinion Jakob Knudsen is one of the most important theologians Denmark has produced" (Løgstrup 1956, 51 note).

5. In the biography, the quoted words are spoken by Staupitz to Luther, yet from the context and from our knowledge of Knudsen's ideas it is clear that they express his own view. At any rate, Løgstrup quotes them in this vein.

6. Cf. Løgstrup's statement in *Norm og spontaneitet* (Norm and Spontaneity) that "spontaneous" means that "what persons do, they do in accordance with the nature of things and of their own accord" (SGCN, 85).

7. Luther characterized the natural (non-Christian) human being as "so turned in on himself that he uses not only physical but even spiritual goods for his own purposes and in all things seeks only himself" (Luther 1972, 345).

8. It may be worth noting that Knudsen was an important source of inspiration for Tidehverv.

9. Cf. Bollnow 1958 and Schnädelbach 1983, 172–196.

10. Though generally critical of Nietzsche, Geismar praised Nietzsche's criticism of utilitarianism, which stated that it lacks "the abundance and spontaneity that leads to what he [Nietzsche] calls 'die schenkende Tugend', which does good out of richness" (Geismar 1924, 178; "die schenkende Tugend" can be rendered as "the giving virtue").

11. Løgstrup attended lectures given by Bergson and was especially influenced by Hans Lipps, whose existential philosophy integrated elements of the *Lebensphilosophie*. Cf. Hans Fink and Alasdair MacIntyre's introduction to *The Ethical Demand*, Løgstrup 1997, xvi–xix.

12. It should be noted that "life" in the *Lebensphilosophie* is a wide concept encompassing both human nature (or parts of it) and the process or activity of living. This ambiguity makes it difficult to form a clear idea of what Løgstrup understands by "life (in) itself." It seems to me, though, that the expression "life (in) itself" primarily refers to aspects of *human nature*, indeed those aspects that manifest themselves in acts like giving and forgiving. This interpretation matches Løgstrup's later talk of phenomena such as trust, sincerity, and mercy as expressions *of*—and thus distinguished from—life.

13. The general background of this argument is, of course, the idea (which we met above in Luther) that law presupposes sin. Løgstrup seems to have derived the correlation between the law and created life from the German theologian Friedrich Gogarten. At any rate, he subscribes to Gogarten's statement in *Politische Ethik* (1932) that in the fulfillment of the law it becomes manifest "how God has created human beings; *how*, in what way, God has given them life" (Løgstrup 1942, 101 n. 1). Cf. Gogarten 1932, 72.

14. For a short account of the main ideas of *The Ethical Demand*, see Niekerk 1999, 416–418.

15. It is Løgstrup's aim in *The Ethical Demand* "to give a definition in strictly human terms of the relationship to the other person which is contained within the religious proclamation of Jesus of Nazareth" (Løgstrup 1997, 1).

16. Here I give my own translation because the translation of Løgstrup 1997 is incorrect. The latter reads "[L]ove exists only in a life which is acknowledged to be given. This constitutes love's spontaneity" (146–147). I would contend that (1) Løgstrup does not have "acknowledged" and does not make the existence of love dependent on our *acknowledgement* of the fact that life has been given to us; (2) the Danish concept of *umiddelbarhed* (immediacy) is not quite the same as the concept of spontaneity, as we have seen above.

17. Alasdair MacIntyre argues in a similar way when he writes that "[t]o act towards another as the virtue of just generosity requires is . . . to act from attentive and affectionate regard for that other. . . . When we are so required, not to act from inclination is always a sign of moral inadequacy" (MacIntyre 1999, 122). The main difference is that MacIntyre's argument does not concern natural, spontaneous love, as it does for Løgstrup, but concerns generosity as a virtue, which can be cultivated. For more on this difference, see MacIntyre's contribution to this volume.

18. Cf. Løgstrup 1997, 164: "The impossibility of [fulfilling] the demand manifests itself most strikingly precisely in the attempt to fulfill it, when a person does what he or she believes love would do, whether out of fear or out of a self-righteous concern for what he or she may get out of the deed which is supposed to have been done unselfishly." I have substituted "impossibility of fulfilling the demand" for "impossibility of the demand," because this is a more precise rendering of the Danish *uopfyldeligheden*.

19. Cf. Løgstrup's definition of sin in an encyclopedia article from 1940: "Sin does not consist in . . . isolated bad deeds, but in the fact that a human being lives as his own and his fellow human being's master and thereby denies that God alone is the Lord. Therefore, the essence of sin is unbelief and haughtiness" (Løgstrup 1940, 401). For the background in Luther, see Jan Taeke Bakker's statement that *superbia* (haughtiness) for Luther is "the worst sin, . . . because it is essentially identical with the unbelief in which a human being refuses to surrender himself to God" (Bakker 1956, 88; my translation from Dutch).

20. Put more precisely, Løgstrup's argument is that our existence confronts us with a contradiction. On the one hand, by virtue of our recognition that the other has been delivered over to us and that our life is a gift, we must acknowledge the demand, which implies its fulfillability. On the other hand, we must admit that, due to our selfishness, we are not able to fulfill it. This contradiction can only be solved practically or existentially, by our accepting the unfulfillability of the demand as our guilt (Løgstrup 1997, 164–167).

21. Cf. the following passage from *Opgør med Kierkegaard*: "The political prompting of the law and its accusation are co-ordinate functions, and this is manifest in the fact that the self-centered and self-righteous attitude of mind with which the deeds are done, and which makes them the individual's own evil deeds, does not alter the fact that they are good deeds for the neighbor. For God the deed is at once evil and good, for God heeds both the agent's attitude of mind and the neighbor's benefit. God wishes the law to be used in both ways, and it happens that the neighbor reaps great benefit and joy from deeds which have been done in a dubious attitude of mind" (Løgstrup 1968, 61–62).

22. I do not wish to contend that this interpretation solves all problems. Løgstrup's apparent reckoning with the possibility of unselfishness in practical contexts seems to be at odds with the fact that, in connection with his discussion of the unfulfillability of the demand, the only alternative to spontaneous love seems to be obedience out of selfish motives. However, this may be explained by the consideration that the topic of unfulfillability naturally involves focusing on selfish motives.

23. By "natural love" Løgstrup does not mean love of one's neighbor, but affective love that is biologically, psychologically, or sociologically conditioned. See Løgstrup 1997, 124, 134, and 142. On the relationship between Løgstrup's conceptions of natural love and love of the neighbor, see Niekerk 1999, 422–424.

24. Jensen 1994, 23–24. The article by Jensen was originally published in 1967. Jensen refers to the opening chapter of *The Ethical Demand* and to pp. 138–141.

25. The inspiration from Jakob Knudsen's idea, mentioned above, that a human being is himself or herself in a loving commitment to another human being is obvious—and even more so when we realize that Knudsen formulated this idea in contrast to self-contemplation.

26. Cf. Løgstrup's remark with regard to the sovereign expressions of life (which occurred in the very context where he speaks of their "forcing their way through") that we are without excuses when we go on living in insulation, "precisely because . . . we . . . have *experienced* their freedom" (SEL, 69, emphasis added).

27. Cf. Niekerk 1999, 418–422.

28. "Ethik und Ontologie" has been included, translated into English, as an appendix in the 1997 edition of *The Ethical Demand* (Løgstrup 1997, 265–293). The relevant account of morality can be found on 273–276.

29. This is why I do not agree with Hans Hauge when he speaks of "opfindelsen af de suveræne livsytringer" (the invention of the sovereign expressions of life) (Hauge 1992, 349).

30. Cf. the remark made by Paul Tillich in connection with a discussion of self-affirmation: "It is time to end the bad theological usage of jumping with moral indignation on every word in which the syllable 'self' appears" (Tillich 1973, 90).

REFERENCES

Bakker, Jan Taeke. 1956. *Coram Deo. Bijdrage tot het onderzoek naar de struktuur van Luthers theologie.* Kampen: Kok.

Bollnow, Otto Friedrich. 1958. *Die Lebensphilosophie.* Berlin: Springer.

Dillenberger, John, ed. 1962. *Martin Luther: Selections from His Writings.* New York: Doubleday.

Geismar, Eduard. 1924. *Religionsfilosofi. En Undersøgelse af Religionens og Kristendommens Væsen.* Copenhagen: Gad.

Gogarten, Friedrich. 1932. *Politische Ethik.* Jena: Eugen Diederich.

Grønbech, Vilhelm. 1935. *Jesus. Menneskesønnen.* Copenhagen: Povl Branner.

Hauge, Hans. 1992. *K.E. Løgstrup. En moderne profet.* Copenhagen: Spektrum.

Jensen, Ole. 1994. *Sårbar usårlighed.* Copenhagen: Gyldendal.

Knudsen, Jakob. 1948 [1908]. *Livsfilosofi. Spredte Betragtninger.* Copenhagen: Gyldendal.

———. 1949. *Idé og Erindring.* Edited by J. Jensen and Th. Krøgholt. Copenhagen: Gyldendal.

Løgstrup, K. E. 1931. "Max Schelers *Der Formalismus in der Ethik un die materiale Wertethik.*" Unpublished manuscript. (University of Copenhagen 1932 prize essay.)

———. 1936a. "Retfærdiggørelse af tro." *Ungdomsarbejderen. Tidsskrift for kristeligt Ungdomsarbejde* 19: 139–143.

———. 1936b. "Enhver moralsk Tanke er en Bagtanke." *Menighedsbladet. Kirkeligt Samfunds Blad* 18: 429–438.

————. 1938. "Pligt eller ansvar." *Kirken og* Tiden 14: 206–217.

————. 1940. "Synd." In *Den lille Salmonsen*. Copenhagen, 1937–1940 (XI), 401.

————. 1942. *Den erkendelsesteoretiske Konflikt mellem den transcendentalfilosofiske Idealisme og Teologien*. Copenhagen: Samleren.

————. 1956. "Eksistensteologien og dens skelnen mellem tro og verdensanskuelse." In *Acta Societatis Theologicae Uppsaliensis, 1951–1955*. Uppsala, 33–54.

————. 1968. *Opgør med Kierkegaard*. Copenhagen: Gyldendal.

————. 1972. *Norm og spontaneitet*. Copenhagen: Gyldendal.

————. 1997. *The Ethical Demand*. Notre Dame: University of Notre Dame Press. [Danish original: *Den etiske fordring*. 1956. Copenhagen: Gyldendal.]

————. 2007. *Beyond the Ethical Demand*. Notre Dame: University of Notre Dame Press.

Luther, Martin. 1962a. *The Freedom of a Christian*. In Dillenberger 1962, 42–85.

————. 1962b. *Preface to the Epistle of St Paul to the Romans*. In Dillenberger 1962, 19–34.

————. 1962c. *Secular Authority: To What Extent It Should Be Obeyed*. In Dillenberger 1962, 363–402.

————. 1972. *Lectures on Romans*. In *Luther's Works*, vol. 25, edited by Hilton C. Oswald. Saint Louis: Concordia.

MacIntyre, Alasdair. 1999. *Dependent Rational Animals: Why Human Beings Need the Virtues*. London: Duckworth.

Niekerk, Kees van Kooten. 1999. "Review Article" [on K. E. Løgstrup, *The Ethical Demand*]. *Ethical Theory and Moral Practice* 2: 415–426.

Schnädelbach, Herbert. 1983. *Philosophie in Deutschland 1831–1933*. Frankfurt am Main: Suhrkamp.

Tillich, Paul. 1973 [1952]. *The Courage To Be*. London and Glasgow: Collins.

CHAPTER FOUR

Principles and Situations

K. E. Løgstrup and British Moral Philosophy of the Twentieth Century

Brenda Almond

INTRODUCTORY REMARKS: THE PHILOSOPHICAL CONTEXT OF LØGSTRUP'S WRITING

The year that Løgstrup's *The Ethical Demand* was published, 1956, was, as it happens, the year in which I began my own philosophical studies in England, and Løgstrup's remarks on British moral philosophy strike many familiar notes. The writers he is interested in were the ones who provided the focus for undergraduate courses in British universities at the time, and these were very much in the analytic, empiricist, indeed logical positivist tradition. The moral philosophers studied and on whom Løgstrup also comments included Bertrand Russell, G. E. Moore, C. L. Stevenson, and P. H. Nowell-Smith, but there was little interest in England at the time in the philosophers who had influenced Løgstrup's own early philosophical studies—existentialists and phenomenologists. Theology, too, was very much a separate study, detached from philosophy, apart from some—mainly skeptical—discussion of the historical proofs of the existence of God. But despite these differences between Løgstrup and those teaching and writing on the subject in British universities, Løgstrup saw a certain unity of purpose in English and Scandinavian approaches on the one hand, as contrasted with German and French traditions on the other. He writes: "Each of these philosophical traditions has its own world and lives in it as if the other did not exist." But he goes on to say: "One of the most pressing philosophical tasks is thus to connect these two philosophical worlds" (Løgstrup 1997, 281). In pursuing this goal, he hoped that his own work might be a mediating influence, and this is indeed the way in which his remarks on British philosophy are best construed.

Nevertheless, in many ways, the philosophical world as Løgstrup saw it does provide a contrast to the way in which moral philosophy was viewed from England at that time. In its richness and in its constant references to human needs and experience, Løgstrup's writing contrasts with the somewhat arid approach of mid-twentieth-century English, and more particularly Oxford, philosophy. And, although in *The Ethical Demand*, as Kees van Kooten Niekerk points out, Løgstrup does indeed offer a philosophical ethic rather than a religious or theological one, since the ethical demand is to be understood in terms of *agape*—"love of neighbor"—it remains an essentially Christian ethic (see Niekerk 1999, 415–426). To my mind, it is also suggestive of some more recent trends in moral philosophy, especially the so-called feminist ethic of care, for Løgstrup's interpretation of neighbor-love in terms of care and responsibility for particular others who are dependent on us—who are, in a sense, in our power—remarkably anticipates the theories developed as a consequence of Carol Gilligan's empirical findings about the way in which many women approach morality in terms of context and personal responsibility for particular others (see Gilligan 1993).

It is worth noting, too, that Løgstrup is also very much an applied philosopher, in today's terminology. He writes on human love and relationships, on sexuality, war, politics, economics, and science. He is also disposed to appeal to literature and to illustrate his views by reference to literary examples such as incidents from Joseph Conrad's *The Nigger of the Narcissus*, E. M. Forster's *Howards End*, or the plays and novels of Sartre.

All this is a world away from British philosophy of the 1950s, so it is not surprising that references to British philosophers in *The Ethical Demand* are few and fleeting. We meet Russell, Moore, Nowell-Smith, and the American emotivist C. L. Stevenson (for the latter, Løgstrup 1997, 168 n. 1). However, in his later work *Norm und Spontaneität* (Løgstrup

1989), the cast is expanded and Løgstrup describes the course of British twentieth-century moral philosophy in more detail. He sees it as beginning with a revolt against naturalism and, following Blegvad (1959), identifies the stages it passed through as the following:

Stage 1: moral intuitionism. For Løgstrup, this was represented by G. E. Moore (1903), but, as will be argued later, there were other important exponents.

Stage 2: emotivism. For Løgstrup, this was represented by the American philosopher C. L. Stevenson (1944), but from the point of view of British philosophy, it is perhaps better represented by A. J. Ayer's *Language, Truth and Logic* (1936).

Stage 3: prescriptivism. Løgstrup refers to R. M. Hare's *The Language of Morals* (1952) and *Freedom and Reason* (1963). Hare's *Moral Thinking* (1981) was published too late, of course, to feature in Løgstrup's writings. Løgstrup also discusses Stephen Toulmin (1950), seeing Toulmin's views as contrasting in important ways with those of Hare.[1]

Stage 4: ordinary language philosophy and the analysis of meaning as use. This understanding of the function of language is nowadays, of course, particularly associated with the philosophy of the later Wittgenstein, but the idea that moral language should be interpreted like this can be traced back to other writers in the first decades of the twentieth century, including C. K. Ogden and I. A. Richards (1923) in the United States and A. Hägerström in Sweden.[2] The moral philosopher whom Løgstrup discusses in this category is P. H. Nowell-Smith, whose *Ethics* (1954) was designed to study the purposes for which moral language is used: making decisions, advising, warning, and so on.

But behind these named figures hover (for me) some ghosts, whether or not they were significant for Løgstrup: G. E. M. Anscombe (in connection with her 1958 article "Modern Moral Philosophy" in the journal *Philosophy*) and the early Alasdair MacIntyre (his 1957 article "What Morality Is Not" in *Philosophy*). There are also other figures, unconnected with Løgstrup, but pursuing lines of thought which have echoes and resemblances to his own. These might include, for example, John Macmurray, the Scottish philosopher whose Christian communitarian and socialist philosophy was the acknowledged inspiration of the British Prime Minister Tony Blair and hence at least an influence on what became known as Third Way or (in Britain) New Labour politics (see Tony Blair's

88   introduction in MacMurray 1996). And in terms of reflection on moral epistemology one might also detect a sympathetic note in the work of the American theologian, Joseph Fletcher, author of *Situation Ethics* (1997).

THE REJECTION OF MORALISM

Before pursuing these connections further, it will be helpful to turn to the starting-point for reflection that Løgstrup himself provided in *Norm und Spontaneität*. His foreword to this book contrasts Cervantes' *Don Quixote* with E. T. A. Hoffman's *Klein Zaches*. Don Quixote, Løgstrup says, is irrational in a world which is itself fundamentally rational; Hoffman's characters, in contrast, are rational beings whose world is bewitched and topsy-turvy. Which, he asks, is the correct representation of the world? Humans have a deep instinct and desire to cling to the idea of the essential rationality of the world, and they link this to a belief that the world is also fundamentally good. Is this so, he asks, and is the evil we encounter in the world attributable to the evil acts of human beings? Or are some bad things beyond human agency? This is the way in which Løgstrup poses the question, and, while acknowledging that such problems as poverty, infant mortality, and overpopulation may be beyond easy human control, he finds much to blame in a besetting tendency to moralism—something he sharply differentiates from morality.

As far as ethical theory is concerned, this moralism is very much connected to thinking of morality in terms of norms or principles— understood by Løgstrup as moral rules of universal application. As he puts it, "they are obligatory not merely in this or that situation . . . they oblige, whomever, wherever, and whenever" (Løgstrup 1997, 280). Later, Løgstrup was to write: "If we believe that part of moral experience consists in reflection on a general principle, and believe further that moral reasoning includes the appeal to a general principle that is logically implied by experience and reasoning, both the experience and the reasoning become moralistic" (SGCN, 105).

Adherence to inflexible principles is, of course, an approach preeminently associated with Kant's deontological ethic, and Løgstrup identifies a non-metaphysical form of the Kantian assumptions in much English moral philosophy (Løgstrup 1997, 280). Perhaps surprisingly, Løgstrup finds utilitarianism, too, to be guilty of moralism since that system, because it depends just as much as Kantianism on a logical and rational approach, also ends by finding rigid and universalizable answers to moral questions.

If we are to avoid moralism, Løgstrup believes, we must renounce the search for universal principles, as well as any idea that there can be indisputable conclusions to moral controversies. Avoidance of the moralism charge may take the theoretical shape of existentialism (in Continental philosophy) or of emotivism (in British and American philosophy). In both contexts, one consequence of the rejection of universalism is that the issues of fanaticism and heroism become matters for debate, for both stand as non-universalizable moral positions. Hence Sartre's student, torn between responding to his mother's needs and the claims of patriotism, and Captain Oates, sacrificing himself for the possibility of saving the other members of Scott's Antarctic expedition, feature in many discussions of universalizability in British philosophy at this time, the first as exemplifying the position that there are no right answers to moral dilemmas, the second that there may be duties of supererogation—that a person may be morally admirable for doing something, but not morally condemnable for not doing it.

One way to describe this contrast in approaches to ethics is to say that it turns on a difference of opinion about what should be the focus of morality: principles or situations. Reason may be the route to recognizing the first; feeling is a natural response to the second. But while Løgstrup certainly wishes to turn the focus away from principles and towards the situations people confront in moral life, this does not mean that he believes that reason has no part to play in reacting to situations, nor does it mean that ethical judgments are bound to be subjective. But he does say that "[t]here are situations of ethical choice of such weighty uniqueness that it is simply impermissible to turn them into principles" (Løgstrup 1997, 281).

ONTOLOGICAL ETHICS: THE SOVEREIGN EXPRESSION OF LIFE

To understand Løgstrup's position more fully, then, it would be useful to look more closely at his reasons for rejecting both deontological and

90   teleological ethics, and at the alternative—ontological ethics—that he proposes. What the two rejected views have in common, Løgstrup says, is their propagation of empty moral concepts. The charge against Kant is that he has introduced into moral thinking a notion of "ought" and "duty" which is devoid of content. Løgstrup writes: "Duty runs the risk of losing all content. . . . Kant saves himself by turning the universality of the law into its content" (Løgstrup 1997, 289). Here Løgstrup is following Kant's many critics in saying that the Kantian "ought" does not unambiguously tell us what we should do. As far as teleological systems, such as utilitarianism, are concerned, the charge is that they, too, depend on a moral concept that is devoid of content—in this case the notion of "good." "'Good,'" he writes, "does indeed have a descriptive meaning but it is dependent on context, in the absence of which its descriptive meaning is nil" (SGCN, 120).

So what does have content? The answer, according to Løgstrup, is what he calls "the sovereign expressions of life," i.e., certain phenomena that cannot be described in abstraction from their goodness: love, mercy, trust, fidelity, sincerity. These have an intrinsic claim on us. He writes: "Principles, precepts, and maxims are applied. The expression of life cannot be applied, but can only be realized, as I realize myself in it. . . . It does not rigidify the situation but frees it up, transforms it" (SEL, 53). It is in engaging with a situation in this direct and personal way, according to Løgstrup, that a person becomes himself—achieves or realizes his own identity. Mere conformity to rules drowns this personal engagement and assertion of selfhood and individuality. As he puts it in the appendix to *The Ethical Demand*: "What human beings do out of duty, they do because they are forced to; they have no free choice" (Løgstrup 1997, 288). So to what can we look for an alternative? Løgstrup's answer is that we must look to the notion of spontaneity. The Samaritan, for example, just *sees* the need of the victim at the roadside and then acts accordingly. He does not reflect about the requirements of moral rules or norms (SEL, 76). Nor does he try to separate out different facets of his response such as motive or outcome, but he acts according to stand-alone moral concepts like "merciful," which Løgstrup calls "an ethically descriptive phenomenon." He writes: "There is no point in asking whether a merciful act is good in itself without considering its outcomes. Such separation is impossible: a term like 'merciful' is at once a characterization both of the attitude of mind and of the intention informing the act" (SEL, 77).

So Løgstrup rejects the old morality of rigid or laid-down conventions. As he puts it, "moral rules are safety features that we turn to when the immediate relation is not sufficient" (Løgstrup 1997, 278). Such taboos, customs, and requirements were vouched for in the past, he says, by society and religion but, eroded by the awareness of cultural differences, by social change, and by recognition of the possibility of clashes amongst the principles themselves, morality is now something for the individual to determine—not arbitrarily, however, but with regard to a specific context and within a specific community. This is not, then, just a matter of producing some new rules to replace the old ones. On the contrary, Løgstrup goes on to pose a radical challenge to the very idea of rule-following, which he sums up in Hegel's question: Have I a duty towards duty? His inclination to answer this in the negative is based on his belief that duty gives an independent status to the rightness of an act, and so forestalls the natural spontaneity of an individual's response to another person's needs.

LØGSTRUP'S PERSPECTIVE ON HIS BRITISH CONTEMPORARIES

The fact that Løgstrup poses the question in this way is interesting from the point of view of his perspective on twentieth-century British moral philosophy, since it could well have provided an alternative starting point for his reflections on this subject. This very question was raised by the Oxford philosopher H. A. Prichard in an influential paper published in the journal *Mind* in 1912 under the title "Does Moral Philosophy Rest on a Mistake?" (Prichard 1949). The "mistake" that Prichard identified in this paper was precisely the willingness of moral philosophers to ask the question that Prichard, like Løgstrup, deemed unanswerable: Why should I do my duty? And Prichard commented on this in a way that in some respects anticipates Løgstrup's own thoughts on the subject: "suppose that we come genuinely to doubt whether we ought, for example, to pay our debts. . . . The only remedy lies in actually getting into a situation which occasions the obligation, or—if our imagination be strong enough—in imagining ourselves in that situation, and then letting our moral capacities of thinking do their work" (ibid., 16–17). It is tempting to compare this passage from Prichard with Løgstrup's assertion that "a moral attitude is strongest when the demand is completely incorporated in a concrete situation and the situation is so immediate that there is no time or attention for reflection on the moral rules . . ." (Løgstrup 1997, 274).

However, Prichard's appeal to situations leads him in a direction diametrically opposed to that of Løgstrup. For Prichard, the reason it is wrong to ask the question "Why should I do my duty?" is that it is self-evident that I *should* do my duty. Hence, Prichard's reflections lead him immediately and directly to recognizing a rule—in this case, that one ought to pay one's debts. Løgstrup, on the other hand, believes that "[m]oral philosophers, no matter what their orientation, almost always entertain exaggerated conceptions of the role played by reflection on moral rules in our everyday actions and decisions" (SGCN, 90–91).

Perhaps it should not surprise us, then, that Løgstrup takes as the starting point for his discussion of British philosophy not Prichard but the Cambridge philosopher G. E. Moore. Moore's *Principia Ethica*, published in 1903, was understood by some of its readers, whether or not Moore himself intended this, as a rejection of the Victorian morality of rules and conventions that prevailed in nineteenth-century England. For example, it evoked an extraordinarily warm reception from the convention-flouting intelligentsia of the period, including the members of the literary and artistic circle known as the Bloomsbury group. The art critic Clive Bell called it a masterpiece, while the economist John Maynard Keynes, especially focusing on the final chapter, "The Ideal," wrote: "I know no equal to it in literature since Plato" (Keynes 1949, 94). In general, though, British moral philosophers, unlike their literary contemporaries, paid little attention to this chapter—a neglect that Løgstrup suggests led them astray. For they took as Moore's key contribution to ethical theory the brief passage in the preface to *Principia Ethica* which sets out the argument for the naturalistic fallacy—a choice which led them to focus from that point in time on the analysis of ethical predicates. This was, as Løgstrup says—and who could disagree with him?—an arid pursuit and a blind alley (see SGCN, 113–114).

Briefly, Moore argued in that short passage that equating "good" with any natural, i.e. empirical, property is a mistake. The mistake consists in not recognizing that such an equation can be challenged by a question that is not trivial but substantial. For example, if someone says "good" = "more evolved," it makes sense to ask, "But is what is more

evolved good?" However, if the identification were correct—if "good" and
"more evolved" were synonymous, the question would *lack* substance—
it would be an empty tautology. Moreover, the analysis of any concept,
according to Moore, must be offered in terms of concepts that are not
present in the original concept (the analysandum). This is only possible
in the case of complex properties whose constituents can be separately
identified. For example, "a bachelor is an unmarried man" correctly specifies the two features encompassed by "bachelor"—being male and
being unmarried. However, Moore believed he had demonstrated that
"good" was a *simple* notion, which could not be analyzed or broken down
further. The essence of Moore's intuitionism, then, could be said to be his
claim that "good" is a simple, unanalyzable concept. In contrast, other in-
tuitionists, in particular Prichard and W. D. Ross, took "ought" and "right"
as the fundamental terms—a significant difference in view of Løgstrup's
rejection of a morality which centers round these terms and his warmth
towards Moore's approach. Indeed, it is not impossible that Moore's suggestion that a situation of moral choice is to be resolved by a simple
and unmediated recognition of good, rather than by the application of
principles, might well have helped shape Løgstrup's own thinking on the
subject.

The same might be said of what Løgstrup identified as the next stage
of British philosophy, the emotivist position, although for the different
reason that it makes feeling or emotion central to moral judgment. However, while Løgstrup may be right in seeing a path from Moore's rejection of naturalism to emotivism, I doubt that it could be considered its
main source. As far as formal argument is concerned, emotivists were,
as a matter of fact, more interested in improving on a version of subjectivism according to which "x is good" = "I approve of x" than in responding to Moore's arguments. But the roots of emotivism lie more obviously in empiricism in general and logical positivism in particular, with
the acknowledged mediation of the philosophers of the Vienna Circle,
who had a strong pro-science bias. The explanation for this, put briefly,
is that in recognizing only two kinds of meaningful statements, namely,
analytic statements that were true in virtue of the meaning of the terms
involved (if true, they were truisms) and empirical statements (some sense-
experience must be relevant to determining their truth or falsity), the
positivist philosophers of this school placed the very meaningfulness of

94 ethical utterances in doubt. Indeed, such utterances could only be defended as useful communication if reinterpreted, not as statements, but as expressions or attempted evocations of emotions.

Hence, the focus within British philosophy, in its empiricist mode, on the way moral utterances were used and on their role in the language, and further, beyond the narrow claims of emotivism, on what Løgstrup identified as the later stages: the move to prescriptivism and thence to ordinary language philosophy. In accepting this chronology, however, it is worth remarking that the idea of a sequence of development in thinking about ethics should be treated with caution. British moral philosophy was more a matter of (politely) warring schools than a step-by-step progression to a consensus. For example, it is not unreasonable to say that Moore, notwithstanding the peculiarities of his views about analysis, did in fact originate the analytic approach in twentieth-century philosophy and was also, especially in connection with epistemology, a pioneer of ordinary language philosophy. This emerges, for example, in the way in which he appealed to the ordinary person's use of concepts of time or perception in writings such as "A Defence of Common Sense" (Moore 1925), taking their unreflective assumptions as trumping the complexity of philosophical reasoning.

It is also worth remarking that emotivism was not as detached from the idea of principle or pattern as is usually thought. So, for example, when A. J. Ayer wrote, "An action or a situation is morally evaluated always as an action or a situation of a certain kind. What is approved or disapproved is something repeatable. In saying that Brutus or Raskolnikov acted rightly, I am giving myself and others leave to imitate them should similar circumstances arise," he was tacitly creating a role for moral principles, whether or not he was willing to recognize the fact.[3] It is right, then, to treat with caution the appearance of diversity and the indisputable fact of rivalry between philosophical factions—a point that Anne Marie Pahuus stresses in her own interpretation of the writings of both Hans Lipps and Løgstrup. She sums it up in her essay in this volume with the paradoxical assertion that "[i]nterpreting our own situation is seeing it both as something unique and as something typical."

In Løgstrup's account of the sequence of British moral philosophy in the twentieth century, the two philosophers he sees as representing its next phases are R. M. Hare and P. H. Nowell-Smith. Nowell-Smith,

notwithstanding the widespread use and popular success of his *Ethics,*
would, I think, no longer be regarded as the representative of a distinctive phase in British moral philosophy, although it is true that in his
approach to ordinary language philosophy, which Løgstrup sees as a
more generalized form of emotivism and prescriptivism, he added diversity to its claims about the uses of moral language and gave greater
attention to context. But rather than focus on this, which Løgstrup
described as the end-stage, and which indeed provided something of a
foundation for his own view that language construes and interprets the
world (SGCN, 102), I will give attention here to Løgstrup's reflections
on Hare.

CONSTRUCTING A NEW MORAL LIBERALISM: LØGSTRUP AND HARE

Hare's philosophy, as Løgstrup recognized, marks a return to a Kantian
preoccupation with universalizability. But in so doing, it raises once again
the underlying problem of a duty ethic: how are conflicts of principles to
be resolved? It is clear that Hare shared with Løgstrup a desire to find
room for compromise when faced with the special demands of individual
situations. But Hare was prepared to give much more weight than Løgstrup to the need for simple, teachable moral principles for everyday living, as well as recognizing that they might be necessary for bringing up
children. We need principles, he said, that are "sufficiently general for the
ordinary man to build them into his character and those of his children in
such a way that they will not be in doubt as to what they should do in the
moral situations that they are likely to meet with, unless they are rather
unfortunate" (Hare 1972, 16).

The paper in which Hare made this statement did not appear, however, until the early 1970s, and it was not so clear in Hare's early writings
as it became in his later works—works which postdated publication of
Norm und Spontaneität—that he was willing to deal with this problem by
adding a utilitarian element to his prescriptivism. It would be a mistake,
then, to look for reaction to Hare's later theories in *Norm und Spontaneität*.
Nevertheless, it will be useful to say a little about those theories here, since
it is clear that in many ways Hare's solution was a solution to problems
that Løgstrup, too, had recognized.

In the essay mentioned above, "Principles" (1972), Hare outlined the early stages of an ethical theory which consisted in positing two kinds of people—shallow and deep thinkers. The first of these would be people, including children, who lack either the time or the ability to reflect on moral principles, while the second group would consist of people equipped to struggle with the fact that life sometimes seems to require a more situational approach. Later, in *Moral Thinking* (1981), he suggested the terms *proles* and *archangels*, making it clearer there, however, that he was regarding these as states of mind which we all experience at different points in life, rather than proposing an elitist distinction between philosophers and ordinary people. However, he still favored a systematic account of moral judgment, and for this he preferred to seek a solution in utilitarian calculation rather than, as Løgstrup does, in terms of feeling or emotion. The way in which Hare described his theory was that moral thought has two levels: an intuitive level, at which we operate with simple, general principles, and a critical and rational level, at which we construct complex principles. It is at the critical level, according to Hare, that we may be able to find broad justifications for some of the simple principles familiar at the intuitive level and also to settle some of the conflicts that can arise amongst those principles. Hare says that the critical level of moral thinking is a version of Kant's Categorical Imperative; but he believes that, because everyone's good counts equally, it is necessary in reaching a moral decision to take account of people's preferences. Thus, in Hare's account of moral judgment, the Kantian element is conjoined with a form of utilitarianism. This means that, according to Hare, a moral judgment is indeed reached, as the utilitarians hold, by balancing costs and benefits but also, as the Kantians maintain, is subject to the test of universalizability.

At this point it is worth asking, how does Hare's solution compare with that of other twentieth-century British philosophers? As mentioned above, W. D. Ross had also addressed the problem at the beginning of the 1930s. But he had specifically refused any hedonistic or utilitarian solutions—in morality, he insisted, you look to principles, not to consequences (e.g., "I made a promise," or "I incurred a debt," not "I could find a better use for the money"). Ross's solution, indicated in a brief but significant passage, was to distinguish between prima facie duties and absolute duties. While absolute duties hold in all circumstances, prima facie duties are essentially *conditional* duties. Ross writes: "When I am in a situation in which more than one of these *prima facie* duties is incumbent on me, what I have to do is to study the situation as fully as I can until I form the considered opinion (it is never more) that in the circumstances one of them is more incumbent than any other; then I am bound to think that to do this *prima facie* duty is my duty *sans phrase* in the situation" (Ross 1930, 19). Prima facie duties, then, have a shadow presence in a situation of moral choice, but they address only a part or aspect of a situation; what is actually a duty depends on looking at the whole situation—a point with which Løgstrup could have been expected to agree, even if he would not have expressed it in the same terms.

In contrast, Anscombe, in "Modern Moral Philosophy," insisted that there are "principles of absolute generality." This, she maintained, was the only possible stance consistent with the Judaeo-Christian tradition. Against what she saw as the prevailing utilitarian tendency of modern philosophy, she insisted that there are things that are forbidden within that tradition *whatever* the consequences, for instance, vicarious punishment, killing the innocent, adultery, and so on.

Neither of these solutions appealed to Hare. His solution, and his theory, were typically logico-analytic. His solution was to point to a common confusion between the ideals of generality and universality and to explain the difference between these concepts by pointing to their opposites: the opposite of "general," he said, is "specific" and that of "universal" is "singular." In this way Hare hoped to create a logical space for moral principles that could be at the same time both complex and specific. Indeed, he maintained, moral life consists in adding qualifications to brief simple principles in the light of experience. This is the theory to which he gives the name "specific rule-utilitarianism," and if it is correct it means that he does not have to defend what Løgstrup had denounced as moralism: that is, undeviating adherence to brief, simple, general principles such as "Do not lie" and "Do not kill."

But this may be to move too far ahead. The Hare known to Løgstrup had, like Stevenson, divided moral judgment into two elements: a descriptive element and a prescriptive element. And according to his analysis of the logic of moral language, Hare deemed that the prescriptive element could supply the universality and objectivity implicit in a moral judgment.

But as both Løgstrup and Hare saw very clearly, this approach generates a problem for someone whom I should like to call the moral liberal. By this, I mean someone who takes account of "hard cases"—who sympathizes, for example, with the plight of a person who has made a foolish promise, or for whom respect for property and ownership stands in the way of some good vital to another person's welfare. But if we accept this as one way of characterizing the moral liberal—as one who is ready to make concessions, to yield ground in the rigid application of principle—it opens up a more general debate about the nature of liberalism. Alasdair MacIntyre once described the attempt to combine Kantianism and utilitarianism as the central characteristic of contemporary liberalism, and I have always been intrigued by this comment, since for most commentators these two theories represent the ultimate ethical polarity. Its plausibility, however, seems to depend on a negative view of liberalism. It depends, that is to say, on failing to give due weight to the way in which liberalism can itself be characterized as a position of principle, involving a commitment to impartiality, truth, and respect for persons. But of course, these too are principles or can be expressed as such, and they can, in practical living, entail other more homely principles, including even fidelity and responsibility. But Løgstrup denies to the latter the name of principles, placing them instead within his system of ontological ethics. Insofar as Løgstrup can be seen as a moral liberal, then, it is in the negative rather than the positive sense. In this sense, a liberal approach to personal morality seems to entail shunning moralism—being nonjudgmental—and looking directly at the needs of the people involved in a situation of moral decision. It is worth noting that some of Løgstrup's brief remarks on welfare provision would suggest that, for him, this kind of moral liberalism could be carried over into politics and result in practical policies that, in the American context and increasingly in Europe, tend to be described as political or social liberalism.

CONCLUDING COMMENTS

In this chapter I have discussed Løgstrup's thoughts about British moral philosophy around the mid-twentieth century. As far as other areas of philosophy were concerned—logic, epistemology, and metaphysics—

ordinary readers in Britain at that time had little sympathy with the pre-occupations of professional philosophers, seeing in their focus on language a willful disregard of real life. As Moore pointed out, whatever metaphysicians had to say about the unreality of time or of physical objects, they actually had an unshakable confidence in the existence of tables, chairs, and their own bodies, and had no difficulty in getting to their appointments on time. Where moral philosophy was concerned, however, certain aspects, such as the analysis of value judgments as arbitrary emotive utterances, seeped rather *too* readily into public consciousness, generating a damaging skepticism and amoralism and an increasingly pervading moral relativism. This, combined with the determined secularity of British philosophy, prepared the ground for an even more morally and intellectually destructive philosophy—the hydra-headed theory known as postmodernism, the hallmark of which is to focus on the speaker or author of an opinion rather than on the content of the argument. It may be that the risk of this kind of intellectual and moral drift had begun to impinge on Løgstrup's thinking through his contact with students involved in the radical movements of the 1960s, for whom his objectivist and relatively unsophisticated approach would have had little appeal.

But, as was pointed out at the beginning of this chapter, Løgstrup would not have been willing to take refuge in either of the obvious refuges from philosophical isolation: the positivism common in the English-speaking world, or the existentialist theories favored in France and Germany. In the last paragraph of the appendix to *The Ethical Demand*, repudiating both, he writes: "I hope to have established against the positivist that there are essential things to say about reality, things that the exact sciences cannot say and that can be expressed only within an existential interpretation of natural language. And I hope to have established against the existential theologian that an ethical-religious relation very much contains an interpretation of human existence, nature, and the world" (Løgstrup 1997, 293).

Løgstrup, then, offers a challenge to both these approaches, aiming at a more generous vision—basically, the intuitionism of the situation. Perhaps we can better see a case for this perspective if we apply his reasoning to a phenomenon currently occupying the civilized world: terrorist bombing. To adapt Moore's argument to a different purpose, it is perhaps easier to see that the reasoning that may convince a bomber that it is right to explode a bomb in a crowded marketplace must be more unreliable than is the natural abhorrence generated by seeing or even simply imagining the situation that follows its explosion. Something has gone seriously wrong, ethically speaking, if the immediate reaction to the scene of carnage, of mutilated and detached limbs and the deaths of innocents, provokes, instead of horror and grief, applause and reference to extraneous goals. Of course, this example will itself generate an argument about moral consistency—an argument in which the voice of Løgstrup could have made a valuable contribution, for it is, in many ways, at the core of the issues with which he wrestled.

But while Løgstrup insisted on the rightness of following one's immediate inner response to a situation, it is undoubtedly necessary to recognize the risks involved in a deliberate limitation of perspective to the here and now, and necessary not to confuse this with a narrow situationism of the moment. But it would be wrong to suppose that Løgstrup himself was a shallow situationist in this sense. In his own lifetime he took the opportunity to show that he believed in standing for broader and more long-term commitments—something that can, in extreme cases, like those prevailing in Denmark during the Second World War, mean risking your own life for others' good. Nevertheless, he clearly wanted to avoid formalizing this conviction, and he quotes a remarkable passage from Bertrand Russell to justify this aversion to formalism: "When I am compelled, as happens very frequently in the modern world to contemplate acts of cruelty which make me shudder with horror, I feel myself constantly impelled towards an ethical outlook which I cannot justify intellectually. I find myself thinking: 'These men are wicked, and what they do is bad in some absolute sense for which my theory has not provided'" (Russell 1954, 285–286).

But Russell's intellectualism drove him to renounce dependency of this sort on feelings and to prefer a mature consideration of ethical theory. In contrast, Løgstrup regrets Russell's decision to let ethical theory win over his feelings and rejects his claim that the alternative is to build ethics on an illusory foundation. Løgstrup's own view of the matter is summed up in these terms: "an ethical demand takes its content from the unshakable fact that the existence of human beings is intertwined with each other in a way that demands of human beings that they protect the lives of others who have been placed in their trust" (Løgstrup 1997, 290).

Løgstrup offers us, then, an ethic of trust and responsiveness to dependency and community. It is a compelling vision and one with which it is tempting to sympathize. But, perhaps like Russell, and certainly like most of the authors mentioned here from the English-speaking tradition, we should be extremely cautious about foregoing the hard core of morality that is represented by concepts like rights, duties, and obligations. Situations are diverse and always new in the moral dilemmas that they create. Principles are the guiding torch that we cannot in the end manage without. Stripped of them, we are, morally speaking, left in a state of Heraclitean flux. The point can be illustrated with a trite example, the return of the borrowed book to its owner: Løgstrup suggests that one should consider whether its owner really needs to have it back at the agreed time or will otherwise suffer from the failure to return it. It is difficult to concur with this view, for, as Ross pointed out, these are not the appropriate considerations—the fact that that was the condition on which the book was lent is the salient moral consideration.

In conclusion, then, I would like to suggest that we do necessarily judge for others as well as for ourselves when we make a moral judgment and that we do not need to make these judgments as though we were the first to arrive on the scene—as if we were newborn, nonsocial entities. Instead, we can draw on the wealth of human experience to take our judgments out of the sphere of individual eccentricity and arbitrariness and into the realm of rational acceptability. In the end, and notwithstanding his attack on moralism, it is tempting to suppose that Løgstrup might have agreed with this and, to the extent that that is so, we can agree with him that our initial moral responses should indeed be responses to the facts of situations rather than the initiation of a chain of theoretical reflection.

NOTES

1. For discussion of this sequence, see SGCN, 96–100.

2. See A. Hägerström, "On the Truth of Moral Propositions," in Hägerström 1964.

3. See A. J. Ayer, "On the Analysis of Moral Judgements," in Ayer 1954, 237–238.

102   REFERENCES

Anscombe, G. E. M. 1958. "Modern Moral Philosophy." *Philosophy* 33: 1–19.
Ayer, A. J. 1936. *Language, Truth and Logic*. London: Gollancz.
———. 1954. *Philosophical Essays*. London: Macmillan.
Blegvad, Mogens. 1959. *Den Naturalistiske Fejlslutning*. Copenhagen: Gyldendal.
Fletcher, Joseph. 1997. *Situation Ethics*. Westminster: John Knox Press.
Gilligan, C. 1993. *In a Different Voice: Psychological Theory and Women's Development*. 2nd revised ed. Cambridge, Mass.: Harvard University Press.
Hägerström, A. 1964. *Philosophy and Religion*. London: Allen & Unwin.
Hare, R. M. 1952. *The Language of Morals*. Oxford: Oxford University Press.
———. 1963. *Freedom and Reason*. Oxford: Oxford University Press.
———. 1972. "Principles." *Proceedings of the Aristotelian Society* 73 (1972/73): 1–18.
———. 1981. *Moral Thinking*. Oxford: Oxford University Press.
Keynes, J. M. 1949. *Two Memoirs*. London: Rupert Hart-Davies.
Løgstrup, K. E. 1989. *Norm und Spontaneität: Ethik und Politik zwischen Technokratie und Dilettantokratie*. Translated by Rosemarie Løgstrup. Tübingen: Mohr. First published in Danish, 1972.
———. 1997. *The Ethical Demand*. Notre Dame: University of Notre Dame Press.
———. 2007. *Beyond the Ethical Demand*. Notre Dame: University of Notre Dame Press.
MacIntyre, A. 1957. "What Morality Is Not." *Philosophy* 32: 325–335.
Macmurray, J. 1996. *The Personal World: John Macmurray on Self and Society*, ed. P. Cornford, with an introduction by Tony Blair. Edinburgh: Floris Books.
Moore, G. E. 1903. *Principia Ethica*. Cambridge: Cambridge University Press.
———. 1925. "A Defence of Common Sense." In *Contemporary British Philosophy*, ed. J. H. Muirhead, 2nd ser. Reprinted in G. E. Moore, *Philosophical Papers*. London: Allen & Unwin, 1959.
Niekerk, Kees van Kooten. 1999. "Review Article" [on K. E. Løgstrup, *The Ethical Demand*]. *Ethical Theory and Moral Practice* 2: 415–426.
Nowell-Smith, P. H. 1954. *Ethics*. Harmondsworth: Penguin.
Ogden, C. K., and I. A. Richards. 1923. *The Meaning of Meaning*. London: Routledge and Kegan Paul.
Prichard, H. A. 1949. "Does Moral Philosophy Rest on a Mistake?" In *Moral Obligation*, 1–17. Oxford: Clarendon Press. First published in *Mind* 21, no. 81 (January 1912).
Ross, W. D. 1930. *The Right and the Good*. Oxford: Clarendon Press.
Russell, B. 1954. *Human Society and Ethics and Politics*. London: Allen & Unwin, 1954.
Stevenson, C. L. 1944. *Ethics and Language*. New Haven: Yale University Press.
Toulmin, S. 1950. *The Place of Reason in Ethics*. Cambridge: Cambridge University Press.

CHAPTER FIVE

The Use of Principles in Ethical Situations

A Response to Almond

Anne Marie Pahuus

Brenda Almond's essay in this volume is an important contribution to the understanding of K. E. Løgstrup's philosophical world. Løgstrup formulated some of his views in contrast to positions in British moral philosophy, and in doing so he challenged both a rationalist approach to ethics and an emotivist or expressivist position in ethics. Almond points out that Løgstrup wished to turn the focus away from principles and towards the situations people confront in their moral lives. Her conclusion is that Løgstrup's philosophy is an intuitionism of the situation insofar as he "insisted on the rightness of following one's immediate inner response to a situation," but she also maintains that what Løgstrup offers us is a generous vision of ethics focusing on trust and on responsiveness to dependency and community—which is no shallow situationism marked by decisionism or voluntarism, but a vision of ethics that embraces both reason and objectivity.

Almond throws light on Løgstrup's understanding of moral judgment through a clear and systematic account of the difference between philosophical positions that focus either on principles (as does R. M. Hare's) or on situations. Almond also convincingly demonstrates why philosophical factions should be treated with caution, and placing Løgstrup in a philosophical

104 faction is not the purpose of her discussion. With these cautions in mind, I would like to consider more closely the idea of an intuitionism of the situation. I focus on the question of how Løgstrup conceived of "the situation" and of the use of principles in situations, rather than on the question of whether Løgstrup's position is a form of intuitionism.

POLITICAL SITUATIONS VERSUS ETHICAL SITUATIONS

Among Løgstrup's analyses of the concept of situation, one is particularly relevant in this context. In his essay "Ethical Choice" (in *Kunst og etik* [Art and Ethics], Løgstrup 1961), Løgstrup points out the difference between ethical situations of an existential nature and ethical situations of a political nature, and further, the difference between the relevant use of principles as guidelines in political issues and the mistaken use of principles in situations of ethical-existential choice. Whereas the use of principles in the latter context removes their weight and their momentous character, according to Løgstrup, moral reasoning naturally and rightly leads to argument and justification by principles in situations of public deliberation. When moral agents are confronted with choices of a very complex nature—Løgstrup's examples are legislation on nuclear armament and on contraception—people choose on behalf of future generations, and in such choices principles should serve as guidelines. The political choice is a choice between real alternatives where compromise is often a necessary outcome. Even if the choice appears to be arational, the decision-making process is supposed to be rational and often implies the use of principles.

Contrary to ethical choice in political situations, ethical choice in existential situations ought not to be turned into an instance of principle (Løgstrup 1961, 148). What interests Løgstrup in existential situations is that moral agents choose between objective realities of good and evil, not between alternatives that can be weighted differently in compromises. Løgstrup here restates what he wrote in 1956 in *Den etiske fordring* (*The Ethical Demand*): the ethical choice is a limited choice. A person involved in ethical deliberation is the object of an appeal or a challenge implicit in the situation itself. The appeal itself—which is an appeal to our responsiveness—is what gives the situation its weight. The immedi-

ate discernment of this appeal is what ethical understanding is about.
Løgstrup points out here that we have to look at a certain ethical or
ontological structure in situations where doing good is not something
external to the action itself. Existential-ethical choices are choices in
situations that are strictly personal and demand a personal act.

One of the ethical structures Løgstrup mentions is a result of the
fact—as he puts it—that to speak is to speak openly. The self-surrender
in communication is not primarily a matter of what is said, but is an inherent ethical aspect of existential-ethical situations. All speech takes
place in an environment of such fundamental trust. To speak openly and
honestly is to act for the sake of a particular human being who has placed
his or her trust in us. Trust has an intrinsic claim on us. And it can only
be fulfilled by acting unselfishly.

Every choice made by a person involved in such direct, communica-
tive, and personal situations is of extreme importance here and now and
can be judged as morally relevant. Existential situations are the situations
in which attitude of mind and outcome of agency cannot be separated.

In parallel with the distinction between politics and ethics, Løgstrup
also points to the distinction between judging and choosing. In political
and public deliberation, attentive and reasonable understanding proceeds
as judging, whereas in existential situations, ethical choice is relevant.
According to Løgstrup, there has been a division of labor between two
different philosophical traditions: British moral philosophy focuses on
judgment, while German and French philosophy focus on ethical choice.

Mary Warnock comes to a similar conclusion in her 1960 work *Ethics
since 1900*:

> There is one respect, however, in which subsequent philosophers
> did follow Moore. Whereas Bradley, following Hegelian, and ulti-
> mately Kantian models of ethical theory, regarded human choice as
> the only proper subject matter of morals, and further, thought of
> choice as something which must essentially be viewed from inside,
> from behind the eyes of the agent, Moore and moral philosophers
> after him were concerned only secondarily with choices. Their main
> interest was in judging things to be good or bad, right or wrong.
> The central question became "What is moral judgement?" (Warnock
> 1960, 199)

106 THE COMPLEXITY OF SITUATIONS

Løgstrup argues for the importance of dividing up situations according to the distinction between ethics and politics without embracing the existentialist identification of morality and choice. Choice, in Løgstrup's understanding, is not self-determination in any heroic or voluntaristic sense, as it is understood by existentialists.

By making situations of an existential nature and not situations of public deliberation the focus of morality, Løgstrup is in complete agreement with other thinkers in the phenomenological tradition, such as Martin Heidegger, Hans Lipps, and Karl Jaspers. Existential phenomenology, or *Lebensweltphänomenologie*, was Løgstrup's primary philosophical world. The concept of situation is fundamental in phenomenology's paradigmatic shift from the epistemological subject to the constantly changing interrelations of the human being with the world.

One of the most basic ideas of phenomenology is that an object is an identity in manifold appearances. In the words of Lipps, our conceptual understanding of the phenomenon is marked by dissemination: "*Gestreutheit* gehört zum Begriff der Dinge als Phainomena" (Lipps 1938, 59, emphasis in original). Situations cannot be defined without going through the manifold appearances and perspectives determined by the standpoints of the persons involved in interpreting and conceptualizing what is going on. In keeping with Heidegger's interpretation of concern pervading all human activity, both Lipps and Løgstrup claim that all thinking reflects our situation and ourselves, and that every situation is part of an act of interpretation to which we bring assumptions both intellectual and emotional. Interpretation assumes that something identical manifests itself in the manifold appearances—which, however, by no means simply reduces those appearances to cases of something universal. Interpreting our own situation is seeing it both as something unique and as something typical (in that something identical pervades different situations in our lives). Even so, nothing practical can be derived from principles without taking into consideration the complexity of the situation.

In *Ophav og omgivelse* (Source and Surroundings), Løgstrup describes the complexity of historicity as twofold (Løgstrup 1984, 243): the complexity of contexts, and the complexity of planes of familiarity (in Danish, *fortrolighedsplaner*). The first is politically relevant, because any course of events is politically complex when it is intertwined with other courses of events. Many different kinds of scientific studies, for example, are valuable to our understanding of the complexity of political situations. Any political decision has consequences in many different contexts—economic, sociological, psychological, and environmental—and, as different courses of events affect each other and intertwine, the complexity of these connections poses a challenge to our political understanding.

The second kind of complexity is particularly relevant to understanding existential-ethical situations. Every phenomenon contains manifold alternatives in itself, and whereas the complexity of political situations is the complexity of a collision of courses of events, the complexity of ethical phenomena must be analyzed through linguistic studies, since their complexity is due to the fact that individual people are constantly interpreting their own situations. In *The Ethical Demand*, Løgstrup explains this by saying that "it is characteristic of human existence that we always give our needs a definite form. . . . It is therefore in the nature of human conduct and demeanor that one takes a position with respect to it" (Løgstrup 1997, 64–65). In "forming" or interpreting one's own life, many different aspects of the situation are molded into one's unified understanding of it. In *Ophav og omgivelse* Løgstrup gives as an example the fact that in communication, speech is both appeal and reference. Neither of the two can exist without the other, and every speaker unconsciously knows it. Another example is objectivity in attitude (*saglighed*), which he terms "a concrete unity," meaning a combination of different aspects of human conduct. The concrete unity (which I have called "a unity in the multitude") in the case of objectivity in attitude is a supple relationship between contrasting phenomena, such as compliance, or openness to objections, and confidence, or the ability to stick to one's own opinion. Compliance without confidence becomes vacillation, and confidence without compliance and tolerance changes into obstinacy. In human life, however, objectivity in attitude is fulfilled in a direct and simple way. The philosophical analysis might try to explain the phenomenon by disassembling the concrete unity into its manifold parts. But in doing this, Løgstrup says, the philosopher must be aware of the unity of the phenomenon in question and its simpleness when fulfilled in concrete situations.

The simpleness of an attitude is the simpleness of its appearance, but its simpleness is not equal to the simpleness of, say, a color. Løgstrup

108   does not share Moore's notion of simpleness as the unanalyzable and in-
tuitively available phenomenon. Løgstrup's own conception of simpleness
means the simpleness of a phenomenon in its fulfillment in concrete situations. The simpleness of objectivity in attitude is the fulfillment of it as
it appears in its subtle difference from both vacillation and obstinacy. Both
the attitude itself and our description of it are an act of interpretation.

     In his 1976 work *Vidde og prægnans* (Breadth and Concision), Løg-
strup compares his own understanding of such phenomena as objectivity
in attitude with Derrida's deconstructive understanding of signs as "difference." Whereas Derrida considers the complexity of situational understanding in terms of a postponement of meaning, Lipps, and Løgstrup
with him, considers it in terms of the evanescence of meaning. Løgstrup
believes that every word has an indeterminacy or a multiplicity of significatory content that forms a kind of halo around the word as it appears
in the sentence. The significatory content of "objectivity in attitude" can
even be seen as a guideline for our understanding of situations in which
tolerance, compliance, and confidence converge.

     The significatory content of a word, or the meaning of the word, is
thereby sought through distinctions in ordinary language between the
word and its semantic cognates. In *Ophav og omgivelse*, Løgstrup in-
vestigates the distinctions between "situation" and its close semantic cognates, such as position, perspective, circumstance, context, and episode.
The difference between expressions like "being put in a position" and
"being in a difficult situation" makes us aware of the difference between
our positions' complexity as the constellation of certain objective traits
and the complexity of our situation as it appears in its indeterminacy.

     As a result, we might say that every situation—political or ethical—
is historically unique and complex, but only the ethical situation is equally
personal. Being ethical or existential, the situation is mine: it is open to
an act of interpretation presented by me. The situation is "up to me" and
must be dealt with by me.

ETHICAL SITUATIONS RECONSIDERED

In given situations, people act in a certain way and thereby intervene in
a network of human relationships. Any intervention—even the most

immediate and ethically salient intervention—is based on individual **109** discernment on the actor's part. Løgstrup describes this in *The Ethical Demand* in the following way:

> A person's relation to the radical demand is and remains invisible. . . .
> The radical demand gives no detailed directions concerning the ac-
> tions and conduct through which the other person is to be served. A
> person must use his or her own experience and insight, his or her
> own judgment of the other person's situation and of their mutual re-
> lationship. And, not least of all, he or she must use his or her imagi-
> nation to determine whether the other person is best served through
> certain words he or she may speak or through his or her remaining
> silent, through certain actions he or she may take or through his or
> her not acting at all. (Løgstrup 1997, 105)

In some passages Løgstrup expresses himself as if he is univocally critical vis-à-vis the reflection inherent in the discernment of the ethical appeal. As he points out, bringing in the other's perspective in ethical situations of an existential nature can be motivated by one's own need to be taken care of, by one's feeling of having certain rights that should be taken care of by others. If that is the case, reflection has nothing to do with moral imagination; it is selfishness. From this kind of selfishness it is only a small step to real egoism and self-righteousness, where the other person exists only for the purpose of assuring me that I get my return. In existential situations the alternative, as we have seen, is absolute be-tween good and evil, between responsiveness to others and selfishness. This is also the point on which one might criticize Løgstrup's thinking. In my view, part of letting our moral capacities of thinking do their work consists in mobilizing all our mental skills in understanding a situation and integrating both intellect and emotion in our response to others. Here one could move in the direction suggested by Jørgen K. Bukdahl, which Løgstrup mentions but rejects in *Opgør med Kierkegaard* (Contro-verting Kierkegaard) (SEL, 79–80). Bukdahl suggests that there is a way in which the individual person is integral to the sovereign expression of life because the individual must vouch for, or commit himself to, the sovereign expressions of life. I believe Bukdahl is right in implying that Løgstrup considered the relationship between the ontologically given

110   appeal and the person's own contribution in terms that were overly anti-
thetical.

Yet even in *The Ethical Demand*, Løgstrup may be said to welcome the
use of principles and the process of reflection, if using principles means
bringing into focus the universality of the Golden Rule as a rule governing the use of imagination. The Golden Rule, he states later in *Norm
og spontaneitet* (Norm and Spontaneity), is "anything but a tepid rule of
reciprocity. . . . On the contrary, it is a rule governing the use of the
imagination. It requires of us that we seek to imagine how we would wish
to be treated were we in the other's stead—and then that we actually go
on to act towards the other in that way" (SGCN, 85–86). In the earlier
The Ethical Demand, the use of imagination also plays an important part
in discernment:

> The radical demand says that we are to care for the other person in
> a way that best serves his or her interest. It says that but nothing
> more. What this means in a given situation a person must discover
> for him or herself in terms of his or her own unselfishness and in
> the light of his or her own understanding of life. This is why in the
> very nature of things it is impossible to obey the radical demand on
> the basis of motives which are foreign to the demand. (Løgstrup
> 1997, 55)

The appeal is inherent in the ethical situation and demands an unselfish
answer, but the response to this appeal is mediated by and determined by
attentive people with suitably informed powers of judgment—people
who judge rightly and answer for what they do: "To be an individuality,
a self, implies that something is claimed of me. And this in turn means
that the moment something is claimed of me, it is I who must answer for
what I do or do not do" (Løgstrup 1997, 66).

Løgstrup's aversion to the use of principles is an aversion to the belief that reflection on moral rules is what makes the moral rules rational
and justifiable. Justification is thought of as something positive by Løgstrup when it means an exercise of mind in order to determine whether
I am making an exception of myself. This role-reversal exercise depends
on the imagination of the individual, and it is an effort of both reason
and feeling.

I think that Prichard's way of talking about moral thinking in *Moral Obligation,* referred to by Almond, is close to Løgstrup's. The activity of moral thinking is described by Prichard as the opposite of a process of general thinking. Moral thinking is a thinking that brings us back to the knowledge we once had in our "unreflective consciousness" and "unquestioning confidence." This kind of moral thinking, I suggest, cannot be solely a question of immediate discernment; it must be understood as imaginative understanding evolved through practice. Thinking and acting are inherent parts of living the communal life, through involvement in the communal life. I think Løgstrup recognized this very clearly when he pointed to the fact that sovereign expressions of life and character traits often converge (SGCN, 90–95). What Løgstrup says here seems identical to the Aristotelian concept of virtuous action (*eu prattein*) as the choices that reveal character.

Løgstrup's own reason for distinguishing between sovereign expressions of life and character traits is that, in his view, the first cannot be produced by practice. Sovereign expressions of life transform the situation, but they are not produced by practice. They must be there already as possibilities of life. What he means by this is that the self or the individuality is not part of the ontological structure of ethics. As he sees it, reflection on the freedom to act is never an impetus to action. I would argue, however, against Løgstrup, that reflection on the self can be an element in the integration of all our personal powers, especially in very demanding situations. Løgstrup says in *The Ethical Demand* that it is "*with a view to* and *out of consideration for* the position which the others take with respect to my conduct and demeanor that I give my behavior the form of conduct and demeanor" (Løgstrup 1997, 65–66, emphasis in original). In such a "view," I believe that even the insufficiency of my own responsiveness is made available to me by a kind of self-reflection. A rational reaction to the situation sometimes demands that we stop and think. This is of some importance, especially in situations where our negative responses issue spontaneously. To take an example, antipathy and repugnance are natural responses to people's self-pity or their defeatist reactions to their own misfortunes. Our spontaneous and immediate understanding of self-pity includes aversion. Being merciful, even towards self-pitying people, and forgetting our aversion to or distaste for self-pitying person, is not brought about by an unselfish response to

112   him or her. It is by means of a self-reflective process, by using all our personal powers, that we might move beyond our antipathy. It is as a result of our personal effort, through the use of emotional as well as reasoning capabilities, that we can forget the repugnance and even, perhaps, become absorbed in the task of helping the unfortunate person. The self-reflective understanding of the inadequacy and immorality of our first spontaneous reaction leads to the imaginative use of reason. Løgstrup's idea of the unselfish fulfillment of the ethical demand and the absolute choice between mercy and selfishness is not very useful in this context.

To conclude, the main point of Løgstrup's aversion against principles is his insistence upon the importance of our immediate response to the ethically given content of situations in which we interact with others. But the actuality of his philosophical analyses of the situations people confront in moral life is not a result of the fact that he insists on the unselfishness and immediacy of our reaction. It is a result of the fact that his ethics contain important insights concerning the imaginative use of reason and the cognitive powers of emotions such as fear, joy, grief, love, and compassion.

REFERENCES

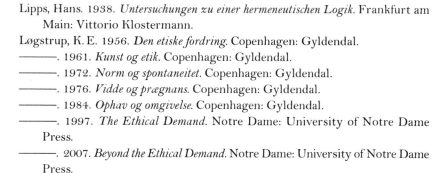

Lipps, Hans. 1938. *Untersuchungen zu einer hermeneutischen Logik.* Frankfurt am Main: Vittorio Klostermann.

Løgstrup, K. E. 1956. *Den etiske fordring.* Copenhagen: Gyldendal.

———. 1961. *Kunst og etik.* Copenhagen: Gyldendal.

———. 1972. *Norm og spontaneitet.* Copenhagen: Gyldendal.

———. 1976. *Vidde og prægnans.* Copenhagen: Gyldendal.

———. 1984. *Ophav og omgivelse.* Copenhagen: Gyldendal.

———. 1997. *The Ethical Demand.* Notre Dame: University of Notre Dame Press.

———. 2007. *Beyond the Ethical Demand.* Notre Dame: University of Notre Dame Press.

Warnock, Mary. 1960. *Ethics since 1900.* Oxford: Oxford University Press.

CHAPTER SIX

The Liquid Modern Adventures of the "Sovereign Expression of Life"

Zygmunt Bauman

I came across the first English edition of Knud Ejler Løgstrup's *The Ethical Demand* by chance, during a sabbatical term in the Newfoundland Memorial University. While collecting ideas and sources for my *Postmodern Ethics*, I browsed through the library shelves in search of a version of contemporary ethical thought betraying, however weakly, an affinity for and resonance with, or at least a sharing of the ground with, Emanuel Levinas's ethical teachings, focused on *Fürsein* and the idea of "unconditional responsibility." I believed then, as I believe now, that the Levinasian unique location of ethics "before ontology" was crucial for a sober critical assessment of modern ethical practice and for facing the challenge presented by its current transformations.

Before I opened the Newfoundland copy of *The Ethical Demand* (I was perhaps the first reader to do this), my hunt, having brought thus far not a single worthwhile trophy, had been an utterly frustrating experience; indeed, I remember being a day or two away from abandoning further efforts. But the wasted time was suddenly, in a flash, compensated for me many times over once I had read on the first page of the great Aarhusian's book his declaration of intent: "If a proclamation is to have any relevance for us it must answer to something in our own existence: a perplexity in which we find ourselves, an inescapable contradiction, a fate we refuse to accept, expectations we entertain, or difficulties that loom before us" (Løgstrup 1997, 1).

113

114   THE RISE AND FALL OF LEGISLATIVE ETHICS

Mainstream ethical philosophy, which is abominably slow to incorporate and assimilate Levinas's and Løgstrup's inspiration, has sound reasons to worry these days. Having invested its hopes of ethical progress in the moral self's conformity to a rule and in the ultimate noncontradictoriness of moral attitudes and moral actions, that philosophy is bound to view the current ongoing transformations of life-politics[1] and its social setting with apprehension, as retrograde developments, auguring a profound moral crisis of contemporary society. The vision of crisis is, however, as always whenever a crisis is announced, a by-product of a preconceived ideal pattern: a projection of the assumptions that overtly or tacitly underpin mainstream ethical philosophy onto social realities that no longer seem to validate them (that is, if they ever did).

Ethical philosophy of the modern era could not but reflect the legislative and order-building ambition, the defining trait of modernity. It also had to be animated by the foremost characteristics of modern spirit—the unshakeable trust in the ultimate and irrevocable triumph of reason over other human faculties. That confidence re-presented the ambition as the forecast of imminent future. The pronouncements of ethical philosophers could not but bear an indelible mark of that ambition and that trust. Like the statesmen and social reformers bent on legislating harmony, peace, and conflict-free order into social reality with the help of a legal code meticulously cleansed of blank spots and all traces of ambiguity, the philosophers vested their hopes in a code of ethical rules purified of all ambivalence and contradiction and bound to be designed, sooner or later, with the reliable assistance of reason. The confidence of philosophers was regularly endorsed, reinforced, and replenished by the legislative energy and determination showed by the political rulers in their pursuit of the order-building ambitions. That confidence and the imposing ethical/philosophical edifice founded on it, however, suffered a tremendous blow and were shaken beyond repair once the ambitions began to fade and the attention and concerns of the statesmen drifted to other targets.

With ever growing numbers of life-servicing tasks shifting away from the legislating powers of the state to impersonal forces of the financial and consumer markets and to the personal but much less powerful resources of individual life-politics, a progressive diversification rather than the hoped-for universality is fast becoming the dominant trend. The prospects of divergence now seem considerably more credible than the cultural convergence and leveling of differences of traditions, customs, *Weltanschauungen,* life strategies, and lifestyles anticipated by the philosophers and worked and fought for by the statesmen. This in itself would be a good enough reason to proclaim the advent of a moral crisis. Decisive for the perception of moral crisis, however, is the ever more conspicuous absence of the tools and vehicles of effective action available to a would-be ethical legislator—were there still statesmen left willing to adopt that mission. Authoritative public institutions amenable to the promotion of ethical causes are increasingly unwilling to instill moral standards and to force ethically inspired or ethically approved solutions onto the grassroots negotiations of the patterns of human cohabitation. On the other hand, forces that are able to exercise compelling influence on individual conduct are unlikely to be concerned with the promotion of moral principles and would rather stay programmatically indifferent to the ethical aspects of human choices. Integrative functions performed, attempted to be performed, and hoped to be performed through the normative regulation orchestrated by the public organs of enforcement and persuasion tend to be replaced these days by the seductive powers of the consumer market, while the ubiquitous yet diffuse and uncoordinated influences of public relations agencies, commercials, and the media take over a good deal of the behavioral regulation once expected to be performed mainly by the centralized, ubiquitous, panoptic policing helped by uniform school curricula.

The now all but discredited vision of morality winning the battle with the weapons of logically impeccable, no-reasonable-doubt-left arguments rested its credibility on the tacit assumption of the presence of conformity-commanding powers waiting and willing to carry the torch of ethical enlightenment in order to make the world hospitable to morality and intolerant to whatever the universally binding ethical principles would condemn or declare out of court. The gap between that assumption and sociopolitical realities of the day is now widening, apparently unstoppably, and so the vision that assumption supported seems ever more nebulous. The business of promoting morality through philosophical argument risks becoming an esoteric pastime conducted at an

116   enormous and nonnegotiable distance from the business of daily life, where moral issues are conceived, born, confronted, and resolved. It is this collapse of the modern ambitions, hopes, and intentions regarding the ways in which the "problem of human morality" can be handled and ultimately "resolved" that has been articulated by the mainstream ethical philosophy as the moral crisis of contemporary (postmodern, late modern, hypermodern—liquid modern) society.

A society in which morality is no longer identified with (or, more to the point, no longer reduced to) the obedient observance of a set of law-like ethical prescriptions and proscriptions is indeed reminiscent of a killing field of the moral homunculi conceived in the philosophers' test tubes. It is in such a society, however, that K. E. Løgstrup's moral self, moved by the "sovereign expressions of life" and prompted (though not exactly guided, let alone goaded) by the "ethical demand," comes into its own. From the point of view of such a moral self, moralism of the kind propagated by Steven Toulmin or R. M. Hare "is morality's way of being immoral" (SGCN, 103). Toulmin's moral person who returns a borrowed book to John because everyone who borrows must return the borrowed, and not because John needs the book, is in Løgstrup's view a "dreadful fellow": he cares not a bit about John "but is merely concerned with his own fidelity to his promises so that the social order may be preserved" (SGCN, 104).

FROM ETHICAL CONFORMITY TO MORAL RESPONSIBILITY

Of the ethical demand (the demand to be concerned with and to take care of another person just because I and the other person share the same world and so our fate and welfare are intertwined and interdependent— we are *delivered* to each other's care), Løgstrup says that it "gives no directions whatever about how the life of the person thus delivered is to be taken care of. . . . To be sure, the other person is to be served through word and action, but precisely which word and which action we must ourselves decide in each situation" (Løgstrup 1997, 56). The ethical demand is *silent*. It does not *command* what action is to be taken—it *demands* that an action is to be taken. The demand "does not refer us to some kind of divine instruction with respect to what is to be said and done, thereby helping us *skip over the matter of our own responsibility*, our own reflection and effort together with all the attendant possibilities of failing and defaulting" (ibid., 109, emphasis added).

I suppose that Levinas and Løgstrup never met face to face, or exchanged letters; and I have found no evidence that they ever read each other's works. But the affinity between them is truly striking. For both thinkers the *conditio sine qua non* of moral stance is the assumption of responsibility. For both, that responsibility is intrinsically under-defined and needs to be given content by the moral actor. For both, the act of filling the responsibility "which is always there" yet always unspecific is a risky decision, involving the possibility of "failing and defaulting." For both, the essential demerit of acting-by-the-rules or by behest, the flaw of any form of *conformist* behavior, consists in glossing over that primary circumstance that the act cannot be moral unless it is taken on the actor's own responsibility and risk. This is the message contained in Løgstrup's adamant verdict on moralism and on all other ways to free (or expropriate) moral actors from the agony (and dignity) of responsible choice.

Indeed, if the ethical demand "could be spelled out in detail, . . . [it] would in that event be purely an external matter . . . without any responsibility on our part, without any investment of our own humanity, imagination, or insight." That would not stop, though, the attempts to do just that — to "pretend to possess a divinely attested knowledge of what is to be said and done in the given situation and of what our mutual relationships ought to be." In case such attempts are taken, we break the silence of ethical demand "often in a very noisy and self-opinionated manner and with an unbearable and loquacious sense of superiority" (ibid., 110). We dream of "absolute certainty"—but absolute certainty "is the same as absolute irresponsibility. The wisdom, insight, and love with which we are to act are then no longer our own; they belong to the message itself. We ourselves are then not really involved" (ibid., 112).

To cut a long story short: what we learn from Løgstrup is that the state of certainty—be it genuine or putative, factual or contrived, gained or imposed—is not the hoped-for haven of morality. In the realm of certainty the conjecture of responsibility wilts and the push of responsibility grinds to a halt. Expeditions to the dreamland of certainty are guided by Thanatos. The spiritual balance promised by the strict and unambiguous ethical code that contains a recipe for any circumstance of life and declares out of court all situations without a recipe attached is the tranquility of a graveyard. On this side of the life-and-death boundary, such a tranquility is, and is bound to remain, an illusion. Though a potent illusion it is: a mirage, deceitful yet seductive, glittering and tempting. Its temptation is as impossible to escape as death itself.

The Paradise inside which the torments and the agony of choice between good and evil were unknown appears within the *Lebenswelten* of people daily confronted with the stern choice between good and evil only as a "Paradise lost." But the truth that the Paradise has been lost *forever*, that the apple from the Tree of Knowledge of good and evil cannot be un-eaten, made whole again, and returned to where it belongs—to the paradisiac Forbidden Tree—is, it seems, difficult to digest, perhaps unbearable; and the deeper are the torments and the more excruciating the agony, the stronger is the compulsion to deny it. And there is never a shortage of false prophets eager to oblige. Modern history, which threw open breath-taking expanses of choice, has been strewn with the promises of certainty—of return to Paradise, that serene state of no choice.

Løgstrup charges another great Danish philosopher, Kierkegaard, with the error of ignoring a large part of human life. He focuses his anger on Kierkegaard—but among the philosophers guilty of a similar error his target was neither the only nor a particularly insidious case. The incapacitating tendency of all philosophers defiant and contemptuous of the banality and meaninglessness of most human lives was to view their own, philosophical life-formula as the only alternative to thoughtless conformity that marks the nonphilosophizing "mass" (that is, the rest of human kind). Critical of Kierkegaard's haughty suggestion that without "living in relation to the infinite idea," living a life of conformity would inevitably follow, Løgstrup seems to resort to the ancient, yet by no means outdated or falsified, observation: *primum vivere, deinde philosophari.* For most of us, most of the time, serving eternal values (un-aging, death-proof, or at least death-insured values, ones bound to survive or ones we hope will survive the pitiably brief corporeal life and its ephemeral pleasures) is an option neither available nor easy to take up. This does not mean that we are doomed to sink in conformity. (Let us note that it does not mean, either, that dedicating life to eternity is a guaranteed cure or effective preventive medicine against conformity. Calls to sacrifice individual life to an "eternal cause" of one kind or another are known to be frequently and keenly resorted to as principal weapons in all sorts of *Gleichschaltung* crusades, whenever a depersonalized conformity is being installed or promoted.)

LIFE'S ONGOING WAR OF INDEPENDENCE

The "sovereign expression of life" is another brute fact—just like Levinas's "responsibility" or indeed Løgstrup's own "ethical demand." Unlike the ethical demand, perpetually *noch nicht geworden*—always unfulfilled and perhaps forever, in principle, unfulfillable—the sovereign expression of life is always-already fulfilled and complete, though not by choice, but "spontaneously, without being demanded" (SEL, 69). It is, we may assume, the "non-choice" status of life expressions that justifies the ascription of sovereignty. The "sovereign expression of life" may be seen as another name for Martin Heidegger's *Befindlichkeit* (being situated—an essentially ontological notion) combined with *Stimmung* (being tuned—the epistemological reflex of being situated) (Heidegger 1926). As Heidegger intimated, before any choosing may start, we are already immersed in the world and tuned to that immersion—armed with *Vorurteil, Vorhabe, Vorsicht, Vorgriff,* all those capacities with the "vor" prefix, that precede all knowledge and constitute its very possibility. But Heideggerian *Stimmung* is intimately related to *das Man*—that "nobody, to whom all our existence . . . has already surrendered." "At the beginning, I am not 'me' in the sense of my own self; to start with, being is *Man* and tends to remain so" (Heidegger 1967, 128, 129). Such a state of "Being as *das Man*" is in its essence the state of conformity *an sich,* conformity unaware of itself as conformity (and thus not to be confused with the sovereign choice of solidarity). As long as it appears in the guise of *das Man, Mitsein* is a fate, not the destiny, let alone a vocation. And so is the conformity of the surrender to *das Man:* it needs first to be unmasked as conformity before it can be either rejected and fought back in the critical act of self-assertion, or wholeheartedly embraced as life-strategy and life-purpose.

On the one hand, by insisting on its spontaneity, Løgstrup suggests the "an sich" status of life-expressions, reminiscent of that of *Befindlichkeit* and *Stimmung.* On the other hand, however, he seems to identify the

120   sovereign expression of life with the rejection of the primeval, "naturally given" conformity (he strongly objects that the "sovereign expressions of life are engulfed by conformity, are drowned in a life where the one individual imitates the other" [SEL, 54]), though he would not identify them with the original act of the self's emancipation, of breaking through the protective shield of the *an sich* status. He insists that "there is no foregone conclusion that the sovereign expression of life will prevail" (SEL, 53). Sovereign expression has a powerful adversary—the "obsessive" expressions, expressions externally induced, and so heteronomous instead of autonomous; or, rather (it seems to be an interpretation of "obsessive expressions" more in tune with Løgstrup's intention), expressions whose motives (re-presented in the process, or rather misrepresented, as causes) are projected upon the outside agents.

As examples of the obsessive expressions, offence, jealousy, and envy are named. In each case, the striking feature of conduct is the self-deception aimed at disguising the genuine springs of action. For instance, the individual "has too high an opinion of himself to be able to bear the thought of having acted wrongly, and so offence serves to deflect attention from his own misdemeanor, and this it achieves by making him the wronged party. . . . Taking satisfaction in the conception of oneself as the wronged party, one has to invent wrongs with which to feed it" (SEL, 51–52). The autonomous nature of action is thereby concealed; it is the other party, charged with the original misbehavior, with the starting-it-all felony, that is cast as the true actor of the drama. The self stays thereby wholly on the receiving side; the self is a sufferer of the other's action rather than an actor in his own right. Once embraced, such vision seems to be self-propelling and self-reinforcing. The outrage imputed to the other side must be ever more awesome and above all ever less curable or redeemable, and the resulting sufferings of the victim must be declared ever more abominable and painful, to justify ever harsher measures undertaken by the self-declared victim "in just response" to the committed offence or "in defense" against offences yet to be committed. Obsessive actions need to deny their autonomy; for that reason they constitute the most radical obstacle to the admission of the self's sovereignty and to the self's acting in a fashion resonant with such an admission.

The overcoming of self-imposed constraints, by unmasking and discrediting the self-deception they rest on, emerges therefore as the preliminary, indispensable condition of giving free rein to the sovereign life's expression; the expression that manifests itself, first and foremost, in trust, compassion, and mercy.

THE WORLD INHOSPITABLE TO TRUST

Løgstrup held a more optimistic view of the natural inclination of humans in *Den etiske fordring* (*The Ethical Demand*), published twelve years before his work on Kierkegaard (*Opgør med Kierkegaard*) and probably conceived in the eight years following his marriage to Rosalie Maria Pauly, which were spent in the small and peaceful parish of Funen Island. "It is a characteristic of human life that we normally encounter one another with natural trust," he wrote then. "Only because of some special circumstance do we ever distrust a stranger in advance. . . . Under normal circumstances, however, we accept the stranger's word and do not mistrust him until we have some particular reason to do so. We never suspect a person of falsehood until after we have caught him in a lie" (Løgstrup 1997, 8). With due respect to the friendly and sociable residents of Aarhus, I doubt whether such ideas could gestate in Løgstrup's mind once he settled at that town's university and faced point-blank the realities of the world at war and under occupation, as an active member of the Danish resistance.

People tend to weave their images of the world out of the threads of their experience. The present generation might have found the sunny and buoyant image of a trusting and trustworthy world far-fetched— sharply at odds with what they themselves learn daily and what the common narratives of human experience and recommended life strategies that they daily hear insinuate. They would rather recognize themselves in the acts and confessions of the characters of the recent wave of avidly watched, hugely popular television shows of the *Big Brother, Survivor*, and *The Weakest Link* type. These TV spectacles that took millions of viewers by storm and immediately captured their imagination were public rehearsals of the *disposability* of humans. They carried an indulgence and a warning rolled into one story, their message being that no one is indispensable, no one has the right to his or her share in the fruits of join effort just because she or he has added at some point to their growth, let alone because of being, simply, a member of the team. Life is a hard game for hard people, so the message goes. Each game starts from scratch, past merits do not count, and you are worth only as much as the results of your last duel. Each player in every moment is for herself (or himself), and to progress, not to mention to reach the top, one must first cooperate in excluding those many others eager to survive and succeed who block the way, but only to outwit in the end, one by one, all those with whom one used to cooperate. The others are, first and foremost, competitors. The assets that help one to emerge victorious from the cutthroat battle, to outlive the competition, may be of all sorts, ranging from blatant self-assertiveness to meek self-effacement. And yet whatever are the assets of the survivors and liabilities of the defeated, the story of survival is bound to develop in the same monotonous way: the successive installments of the *Survivor* series bear the telling-it-all subtitle: TRUST NO ONE. In the game of survival, trust, compassion, and mercy (the paramount attributes of Løgstrup's sovereign expression of life) are suicidal. If you are not tougher and less scrupulous than all the others, you will be done in by them, with or without remorse. We are back to the somber truth of the Darwinian world: It is always the fittest who survive.

Were the young people of our times readers of books, and particularly of old books not currently on the bestseller list, they would in all probability agree with the bitter, not at all sunny picture of the world painted by the Russian exile and philosopher of the Sorbonne, Leon Shestov: "*Homo homini lupus* is one of the most steadfast maxims of eternal morality. In each of our neighbors we fear a wolf. . . . We are so poor, so weak, so easily ruined and destroyed! How can we help being afraid! . . . We see danger, danger only" (Shestov 1970, 70). They would insist, as Shestov did and as the *Big Brother* shows promoted to the rank of common sense, that this is a tough world, meant for tough people. It is a world of individuals left to rely solely on their own cunning, trying to outwit and outdo each other. On meeting a stranger, you need first vigilance, and then vigilance second and third. Coming together, standing shoulder to shoulder and working in team, makes a lot of sense as long as it helps you get your way; there is no reason why it should last once it brings no more benefit or brings less benefit than shedding the commitments and canceling the obligations would.

Young people born and growing at the turn of century would also find familiar, perhaps even self-evident, Anthony Giddens's description of "pure relationship" (1992, 58 and 137), which today tends to be the prevailing form of human togetherness and which one enters (always "until further notice") "for what can be derived by each person" and "which is continued only in so far as it is thought by both parties to deliver enough satisfactions for each individual to stay within it" (ibid., 58). The present-day pure relationship is, in Giddens's description, "not, as marriage once was, a 'natural condition' whose durability can be taken for granted short of certain extreme circumstances. It is a feature of the pure relationship that it can be terminated, more or less at will, by either partner at any particular point. For a relationship to stand a chance of lasting, commitment is necessary; yet anyone who commits herself without reservations risks great hurt in the future, should the relationship become dissolved" (ibid., 137).

Commitment to another person or persons, particularly an unconditional commitment and most certainly a "till death do us part," for better and worse and richer and poorer kind of commitment, looks ever more like a trap that needs to be avoided at all costs. Of something they approve, young people say it is cool. Whatever other features human acts and interactions might bear, they should not be allowed to warm up; they are OK as long as they stay cool, and being cool means being OK. If you know that your partner may opt out at any moment, with or without your agreement, just because her or his sources of enjoyment have dried up or the grass appears greener on the other side of fence, then investing your feelings in the current relationship is a risky step. Investing strong feelings in your partnership and taking an oath of allegiance makes you *dependent* on your partner (and let us note that dependency, now fast becoming a derogatory term, is what the responsibility for the Other is all about—for Løgstrup as much as for Levinas). And to rub salt into the wound, your dependency—due to the "purity" of your relationship—may not and need not to be reciprocated. Therefore you are bound, but your partner is free to go, and no kind of bond that may keep you in place is enough to make sure that she or he won't. The widely shared, indeed commonplace awareness that all relationships are pure, that is, frail, temporary, and always "until further notice," is hardly a soil on which trust may take root and blossom.

I have dwelled on partnerships that replaced the model of a "till death do us part" personal union that, for better or worse, still held (even if showing a growing number of off-putting cracks) at the time Løgstrup

124 recorded his belief in the naturalness and the normality of trust and his judgment that it was the suspension or cancellation of trust, rather than its unconditional and spontaneous gift, that was an exception prompted by extraordinary circumstances and therefore requiring explanation. The present state of partnerships is not, however, the only feature of today's life that saps the credibility of Løgstrup suppositions. An unprecedented fluidity, frailty, and built-in transience (the famed flexibility) mark all sorts of social bonds which, but a few dozens of years ago, combined into a durable, reliable framework within which the network of human interactions could be safely plotted. They affect in particular, perhaps most seminally, employment and professional relations. With skills falling out of demand in less time than it takes to acquire and master them, with educational credentials losing their purchase value long before their allegedly lifelong "sell-by" date, with places of work disappearing with little or no warning, and with the course of life sliced into a series of ever shorter "one-off" projects, life prospects look increasingly like meanderings of smart rockets that follow ephemeral, restless, and elusive targets, rather than like the predesigned and predetermined, predictable trajectory of a ballistic missile.

   If you feel ill at ease in that fluid world and are lost among the profusion of contradictory road signs that seem to be on wheels—visit one or several expert counselors, for whose services there has been at no time a greater demand and of whom there has never been a richer supply. Unlike the astrologers of past ages, who told their clients, ignorant of what to expect, what their already decided future would be alike regardless of what they did, the experts of our fluid-modern era would most certainly return the buck to their confused and perplexed clients. They would trace the trouble back to the client's doings and undoings and find errors in the clients' ways: not enough self-assertion, not enough self-care and self-drill, but above all, not enough flexibility, an obstinate clinging to old habits, places, or people, and lack of enthusiasm for change and of readiness to embrace it once it comes. The counselors would advice more self-appreciation and more self-concern, more attention to one's own inner ability for pleasure and satisfaction—and less dependence on others and less attention to their demands of attention and care. A client who diligently learned his or her lessons and followed the advice faithfully should more often ask himself or herself the question "What is there for me?" and inform the partners that he or she "needs more space"— that is, that the others should keep their distance and not expect, foolishly, that commitments are bound to be held forever.

Trust may remain, as Løgstrup suggests, a natural outpouring of the sovereign expression of life—but once emitted it now seeks in vain a place to anchor. Trust is doomed to a life full of frustration. People (singly, severally, or conjointly), companies, parties, communities, causes, or life-patterns invested with authority to guide one's life fail time and again to repay the devotion or else lead one astray. At the least, they are seldom paragons of consistency and long-term continuity. There is hardly a single reference point on which the attention of the guidance-seeker could be securely fixed, so that she can be absolved from the vexing need for constant vigilance and incessant revision. Nothing in the world seems to have a longer life-expectation than the guidance seekers, however abominably short their own corporeal lives may be. Individual experience stubbornly points to the self as the most likely home for the duration and continuity so avidly sought and craved.

To sum up: the world today seems to be conspiring against trust. Certainly, trust is not assisted by reflection. Sober scrutiny of the data supplied by life's evidence points to the opposite direction—repeatedly revealing the perpetual fickleness of rules and frailty of bonds.

THE AGE OF UNCERTAINTY, OR LØGSTRUP VINDICATED

Has Løgstrup's decision to invest hopes of morality in the spontaneous, endemic tendency to trust been invalidated by the endemic uncertainty saturating the world of our times?

One would be entitled to say so, if not for the fact that it was never Løgstrup's view that moral impulses arise out of reflection. On the contrary: in his view, the hope of morality was vested precisely in its pre-reflective spontaneity: "Mercy is spontaneous because the least interruption, the least calculation, the least dilution of it in the service of something else destroys it entirely, indeed turns it into the opposite of what it is—namely, mercilessness" (SGCN, 85). Levinas is known to insist that the question "Why should I be moral?" (that is, asking for arguments of the kind "What is there in it for me?" "What did he do for me to justify my care?" "Why should I care if so many others do not?" or "Could not someone else do it instead of me?") is not the starting point of moral conduct but signals its demise—just as all amorality began with the Cain's question "Am I my brother's keeper?" Løgstrup seems to agree. The *need* of morality (an expression that is already an oxymoron) or merely the advisability of morality cannot be discursively established, let alone proved. Morality is nothing but an innately prompted manifestation of humanity—it does not serve any purpose and surely is not guided by the expectation of profit or self-enhancement. It is true that good, merciful deeds are time and again performed out of the actor's calculation of gain, be it the earning of divine grace, purchase of public esteem, or purchase of absolution from mercilessness shown on other occasions; these, however, cannot be classified as moral acts precisely because of having been *motivated*.

In moral acts, "the least ulterior motive is excluded" (SGCN, 85), Løgstrup insists. The spontaneous expression of life is *radical* precisely because of the absence of ulterior motives—both immoral and *moral*. This is one more reason why the ethical demand, that "objective" pressure to be moral emanating from the very fact of being alive and sharing the world with others, is and must remain silent. Since obedience to the ethical demand can easily turn (or be deformed and distorted) into a motive for conduct, the ethical demand is at its best when it is forgotten and not thought of: its radicalness "consists in demanding its own superfluity" (SGCN, 87). "[I]mmediacy of human interaction is sustained by the immediate expressions of life" (SGCN, 84–85) and it needs, or indeed tolerates, no other supports.

In practical terms, it means that however a human may resent being left alone with (ultimately) his or her own counsel and own responsibility, it is precisely that loneliness that contains a hope of a morally impregnated togetherness. Hope—not certainty, nor a guarantee. Spontaneity and sovereignty of life expressions do not ensure that the resulting conduct will be the ethically laudable choice between good and evil. The point is, though, that blunders *and* right choices arise from the same condition, as do the cravenly impulse to run for the cover of authoritative command or self-deception *and* the boldness of accepted responsibility; and that without accepting the possibility of wrong choices, little could be done to persevere in the search for the right choice—and above all the right *moral* choice. What I have learned from Løgstrup is that far from being a major threat to morality (and so an abomination to moral philosophers), uncertainty is the home-ground of the moral person and the only soil on which morality can sprout and flourish.

ETHICAL DEMAND IN A WORLD OF GLOBALIZED DEPENDENCY

As Løgstrup rightly points out, it is the "immediacy of human interaction" that is "sustained by the immediate expressions of life." I presume that this connection and mutual conditioning acts both ways. "Immediacy" in Løgstrup's thinking about moral impulse seems to play a role similar to "proximity" in Levinas's writings. "Immediate expression of life" is triggered by the proximity or immediate presence of the other human being—weak and vulnerable, suffering and needing help. We are challenged by what we see; and we are challenged to act—to help, to defend, to bring solace, to cure or save. For most of human history (also, I suppose, in Funen or Aarhus of Løgstrup's times), "immediacy of the presence" overlapped with the potential and feasible "immediacy of action." Our ancestors had few if any tools that would enable them to act effectively at a large distance—but they were rarely exposed to human suffering too distant to be reached by the tools they had. The totality of moral choices our ancestors confronted could be almost completely enclosed within the narrow space of immediacy, of face-to-face meetings and interaction. The choice between good and evil, whenever faced, could be therefore inspired, influenced, and in principle even controlled by the sovereign expressions of life.

Today, though, the silence of ethical command is deafening as never before. That command prompts and covertly directs the sovereign expressions of life; but those expressions have retained their immediacy, while the objects that trigger and attract them have sailed away from the space of proximity. In addition to what we may see in our immediate vicinity with the naked (unassisted) eye, we are now daily exposed to the mediated knowledge of distant misery. We all have television; but most of us have no means of tele-action. If human misery we can not only see but also mitigate or heal casts us in a situation of moral choice that the sovereign expressions of life may find excruciatingly difficult but

128   nevertheless possible to handle—then the gap between what we are (indirectly) made aware of and what we can (directly) influence raises the uncertainty that accompanies all moral choices to the unprecedented heights, at which our ethical endowment is unused, and perhaps even unable, to operate.

Keith Tester (1997, 5–6) elaborates on Karl Jaspers's inventory of the types of guilt, in which moral guilt (of which culprits with a moral conscience, such as are "given to repentance," are aware) is set apart from metaphysical guilt. The latter, in Jaspers's view, stretches "beyond morally meaningful duty." Metaphysical guilt occurs whenever human solidarity has stopped short of its absolute, indeed infinite, limits. Unlike moral guilt, metaphysical guilt does not require proof or even a suspicion of the causal link between the action (or inaction) of the supposed culprit and the case of human suffering. In a metaphysical sense, I am guilty whether or not I have contributed, deliberately or inadvertently, to the pain suffered by another human being.

Knud Løgstrup, as well as Emmanuel Levinas, would perhaps incorporate Jaspers's metaphysical guilt into the category of moral guilt as such. For Jaspers the absence of causal connection between the culprit's conduct and the sufferer's pain was not sufficient to efface guilt, and this because the postulate of absolute human solidarity was the foundation stone of all morality and not detachable from a moral stance. For Levinas, what made the presence or the absence of causal connection irrelevant was the postulated un-conditionality of human responsibility for the Other; for Løgstrup, it was the unspokenness of the ethical demand.

Løgstrup, Levinas, and Jaspers may cut their categories differently, but the resulting disagreement is mostly terminological. In all cases, their terms are meant to convey the essential distinction between the realm inhabited by legal subjects and the universe of moral self. The cause-and-effect link, the principal *differentia specifica* of Jaspers's categorization, is devoid of potency and assigned only a secondary significance in Løgstrup and in Levinas.

Dethronement of causality and the endowment of interhuman solidarity and responsibility with the power to dismiss all ontological argument might have been the constitutive feature of the moral self—indeed, its transcendental prerequisite—at all times. In the era of globalization, however, the long-standing dispute between ethics and ontology loses much of its past sharpness, together with its subject matter. In our world of universal interdependency the realm of the causes and effects of human action, and the scope of humanity, overlap. Virtually no human action, however locally confined and compressed, can be certain to have no consequence for the lot of the rest of mankind. Nor can the lot of any segment of humanity be self-contained and depend in its entirety on the actions of its members alone.

Commenting on the memorable 1979 work by Edward Lorenz whose title that has become one of the best-known phrases coined in the past century ("Does the Flap of a Butterfly's Wings in Brazil Set Off a Tornado in Texas?"), Roberto Toscano (2001, 73) suggests that "today the fact of global interconnectedness demands, in international relations, ethical standards that go beyond a strict, legalistic concept of responsibility. The butterfly does not know about the consequences of the flapping of wings; but the butterfly cannot rule out that consequence. We move from responsibility to a related but more restrictive concept: that of precaution."

While retaining its eternal function of giving birth and life-sustaining nourishment to the moral self, "responsibility for the Other," a fully and truly unconditional responsibility that now includes as well the duty of prevision and precaution, becomes in our times the brute fact of the human condition. Whether or not we recognize and willingly assume responsibility for each other, we already bear it, and there is little or nothing at all we can do to shake it off our shoulders. Five percent of the planet's population may emit 40 percent of the planet's pollutants and use or waste half or more of the planet's resources, and they may resort to military and financial blackmail to defend tooth and nail their right to go on doing so. They may, for the foreseeable future, use their superior force to make the victims pay the costs of their victimization (were not the Jews under Nazis obliged to pay the train fares on the way to Auschwitz?). And yet responsibility is theirs—not just in any abstract philosophical, metaphysical or ethical sense, but in the down-to-earth, mundane, straightforward, causal (ontological, if you wish) meaning of the word.

Our responsibility extends now to humanity as a whole. The question of coexistence (of mutually assured survival) has stretched far beyond the problem of neighborly relations and peaceful cohabitation with people on the other side of the state border, to which it was confined for most

130   of human history. It now involves the human population of the earth—those already alive and those yet to be born. The factual, if not the recognized and the assumed, responsibility has already reached the limits of humanity—but the odds are that it won't stop even there for long. The full, wholehearted acceptance of the humanity of so-called savages, aborigines, tribesmen, travelers, and other varieties of half-humans, not-fully humans, or not-really humans, may still remain an unfinished project, but the roll call of the beings yet to be admitted into humanity (that is, as objects of ethical concerns and moral responsibilities) expands as quickly, perhaps faster yet, than the list of those already given the residence permit. The growing popularity of the declarations of rights of animals as living beings—like the widely read studies of Frans de Waal, Francis Kaplan, or Jared Diamond (cf. Vandegiste 2001, 22–23)—signal a radical shift in the perception of the ultimate limits of human responsibility.

Keith Tester (1997, 17) puts in the nutshell the quandary that is fast becoming the crucial and most vexing in our globalized world: "[T]he world is, amongst other things, a producer of horror and atrocity yet seemingly there are no resources which might be the basis of the generation of moral response to many of these instances of suffering." In other words, Tester asks why there are so many bystanders in this world of ours; how come our world has turned into a huge, uncharacteristically efficient branch of modern production, an admirably efficient factory of bystanders?

And so we are all bystanders now: we know that something needs to be done, but also know that we have done less than needs be and not necessarily what needed doing most; and that we are not especially eager to do more or better, and even less keen to abstain from doing what should not be done at all. To make the bystander's plight, distressing as it always is, more harrowing yet—the gap between things done and things to be done seems to be swelling instead of shrinking. There are more and more goings-on in the world which we sense to be crying for vengeance or remedy, but our capacity to act, and particularly the aptitude to act effectively, seems to go into reverse, dwarfed ever more by the enormity of the task. The number of events and situations that we hear of and that cast us in the awkward and reprehensible position of a bystander grows by the day.

Watching terrifying pictures of famine, homelessness, massive death, and utter desperation has turned by now, says Tester, into a new "tradition" of our age of mediocracy. Like all things traditional, they have lost the power to shock: they have been made "unproblematic through the practices of mundane and habitual everyday routine" (Tester 1997, 30). This is, as Tester points out, another (to be expected) case of Georg Simmel's "blasé attitude": "just like the city, television offers so much that our powers of discrimination actually cease to be able to work effectively" (ibid., 32). Henning Bech, a most insightful analyst of contemporary urban-living experience, coined the concept of the "telecity" to make salient the intimate kinship between the detached responses or nonresponsiveness of the flaneur (always in, but never of the urban crowd) and the TV addict's experience. Established charities and the animators of one-off "carnivals of pity" complain about "compassion fatigue." Yet this is exactly the kind of reaction they should have expected from the residents of the telecity. The telecity residents find tiring (boring) anything that lasts beyond a fleeting moment, thereby threatening to outlive the excitement its novelty has triggered. Why should some images of misery be exempt?

The most obvious answers are not necessarily the best, however. At least two other factors deserve a close look whenever one ponders the riddle (and abomination) of the notoriously short-lived and flickering, seldom more than lukewarm, responses to the televised horrors of distant suffering.

One of these factors has been spotted and recorded by Ryszard Kapuscinski (1999, 8–9), a most indefatigable explorer of the paradoxes, antinomies, and inanities of our shared global home: the gap between seeing and knowing. Depending on what is presented to view, the absorption of images may thwart rather than prompt and facilitate the assimilation of knowledge. It may also bar the understanding, let alone the ability to penetrate the causes, of what has been noted and retained.

The suffering as seen on TV is in most cases conveyed through the images of the emaciated bodies of the hungry and the pain-twisted faces of the ill. Hunger calls for the supply of food; disease cries for drugs and medical know-how. Both promptly arrive: lorries loaded with surplus food that, to keep prices high and the stockholders' income rising, clutters the

132 warehouses of affluent countries; and the earnest, devoted, and noble volunteers of Médicins sans frontières carrying surplus drugs that clutter, for much the same reason, the warehouses of the pharmaceutical multinationals. Nothing is shown, and no word is spoken, of the causes of the famine and chronic illness. There is no inkling of the steady destruction of livelihood by the trade sans frontières, of the tearing apart of the social safety nets under the pressure of finances sans frontières, or of the devastation of soils and communities by monocultures promoted by the merchandisers of genetically engineered seeds in close cooperation with the missionaries of economic reason from the World Bank or International Monetary Fund. Instead, we hear a persuasive and pervasive suggestion that what we see on TV was a self-inflicted disaster visited upon distant, exotic tribes "very unlike us" who had blundered themselves out of decent human living. And that—thanks to God (or our prudence)—some fortunate folks with good hearts like us, fortunate because sensible and industrious, are around, ready to salvage the hapless from the blood-curdling consequences of their bad luck and ill-considered conduct brought about by ignorance or sloth. Come the day of Band Aid or Cosmic Relief and the celebrities meant to prompt us to switch on—surrounded by seasoned entertainers meant to keep us switched on and computers meant to keep us proud of having switched on—anchor the spectacle of our benevolence and choke on our behalf with emotions while keeping us abreast of the vertiginous progress of our charity. As if by a magic wand, we are transported from the dark and mean hiding places of the wrong-doers' accomplices to the all-singing, all-dancing holiday camps of the selfless and magnanimous chevaliers sans reproche. Our joint responsibility for the human disasters we are invited to help repair is not implied and does not spoil the festival of mutual absolution. Conscience is pricked and placated in one go—in one charitable gesture.

Kapuscinski lays bare the gap between seeing and knowing. Yet a wider and truly abysmal gap yawns between knowing and acting. Were we to become, despite the adverse odds, aware of the real roots of human misery on display, what (if anything) could we do to eradicate them, let alone prevent them from taking root? Luc Boltanski asks the most pertinent of questions that can and ought to be asked: "What form can commitment take when those called to act are thousands of miles away from the persons suffering, comfortably installed in front of the television set in the shelter of their homes?" (Boltanski 1999, xv).

Tester (1997, 22) recalls Alfred Weber's anxiety caused by the emergence of a global network of radio broadcasting: "the world has become a much smaller place—it is scarcely possible honestly to maintain any kind of pretence of ignorance of what is going on"—anywhere, in however remote the corner of the globe. But things have moved much further still since Weber's expression of anxiety.

It is not just the volume of available (indeed, ubiquitously obtrusive) knowledge that has grown beyond all expectations: the quality of the information has radically changed as well. What we know and know of is not just a version of the events we have not seen—a hearsay that we are free to believe or not, a third-person story that we may trust or doubt, accept as true or dispute and with a modicum of effort argue out of conscience. Once images replace the words (photo- or videographic images, those frozen and preserved pieces of "reality," its ever more faithful replicas, not just "analogue" but digital—read "undistorted" copies), the processed, mediated nature of information is concealed from view and no longer can be held against the veracity of the message or authorize a truth-contest. Virtually or not, we are now witnesses to what is going on in those faraway places. We not only hear about the pain people suffer, we see it with our own eyes. As Stanley Milgram's famed experiments had shown, eyes are incomparably more morally sensitive than ears. Even if comfortably installed in the shelter of our living rooms, we watch, at close quarters, people dying of famine and of other people's cruelty. Our moral selves are daily accosted and molested, prodded, challenged, pressed to respond.

The snag, though, is that as the circulation of knowledge about ours and other people's plight becomes more effective, the same cannot be said of our capacity for ethically inspired acts. The network of our mutual dependence gets tighter with every advance of globalization—but the gap between the reach of the unanticipated (or simply ignored or unreckoned with) consequences of our actions and the scope of whatever we can do consciously and deliberately to mitigate such consequences grows wider. The outcomes of our action and inaction reach far beyond the limits of our moral imagination and our readiness to assume responsibility for weal and woe of the people whose lives have been directly or indirectly affected. This is why, paradoxically, our shared capacity to do harm seems infinitely greater than our shared capacity to do good. It is as if the tools and technologies of causing (collectively,

134   though unintentionally) misery surge forward, while leaving behind the tools and technologies of causing (collectively and deliberately) bliss. The tools of happiness, unlike the vehicles of misery, all seem small-scale, for individual use only, fit solely for servicing private life and individual action. What we can do to alleviate the plight of those affected seems much less potent than what we do, intentionally or by default, to contribute to its misery.

A GLIMPSE INTO THE FUTURE

There is no reason to suppose that we have become, or are becoming, less sensitive to human suffering than our ancestors used to be. If anything, the opposite seems to be the case. We are increasingly less tolerant of pain—also of the sight of pain. This is not to say that globalization promotes callousness and moral indifference to the suffering of others, humans or animals (if we are assured, that is, that the pain is real). Many varieties of human misery once meekly accepted as unavoidable, ordinary, and indeed indispensable accompaniments of human life, have been recast as superfluous and gratuitous, unjustified or downright offensive, and above all calling for remedy, revenge, or—short of these—(pecuniary) compensation.

The problem is that, unlike in the past, the volume of our awareness of the fate of others and the scope of our ability to influence that fate (whether to damage it or to repair it) do not overlap. Our ancestors were direct witnesses to most consequences of their actions because these consequences seldom, if ever, reached further than their unarmed eye (and armed hands) could reach. With the new, global network of dependencies and with the technology potent enough to allow for equally global effects of actions, that morally comfortable situation is gone. Knowledge and action no longer overlap, and the realm of their encounter shrinks steadily by comparison to the rapidly expanding area of their discordance. They are out of joint more often than they merge.

No wonder that it is easy to refuse commitment without much moral torment and easy to find arguments legitimating the denial of guilt. Admonished to seek (as Ulrich Beck memorably phrased it) biographical solutions of systemic contradictions and to rely solely on our own, individually owned and individually managed resources, and told or shown daily that everyone else follows or tries hard to follow that admonition, we grow used to the idea that our individual life-itinerary is the sole realistic concern and the sole ground on which to focus any action one wishes to be effective instead of time-wasteful. It hardly occurs to us that there may be some reason (and hope) in trying to reform the wider conditions under which our biographies (and the biographies of our fellow humans) are shaped and biographical solutions are desperately sought. If it were suggested to us to try such reform we would treat the advice with disbelief and we would mistrust the advisers. Refusal of commitment, on the ground of the assumed idleness and ultimately the impotence of collective action, seems to be a rational step to take, a legitimate conclusion from the sober, rational evaluation of the possible and the feasible.

And yet . . . however rational the refusal of commitment appeared to be, its logical elegance would not always lay the pangs of conscience to rest. Conscience is known to stubbornly disregard the reasons of Reason and to have reasons of which Reason knows not. We do not always switch off the pictures of horror. Time and again we do wish to help the victims, though we seldom go beyond mailing a check or phoning the credit card number to the address of a charity agency displayed on the screen. Sometimes we add our voices to the chorus of condemnation of the invidious perpetrators of atrocity (when named) and to the chorus of praise for the victims' helpers (if picked up by the reporters from their self-chosen anonymity). The commitment rarely goes far enough to strike at the roots of wrongdoing. If we wished to take up such a commitment, we would be hard put to find out where to start and how to proceed from there.

Commitment is not inconceivable; neither is the long-term commitment, or the fruitful, effective, changing-the-world commitment. But powerful forces conspire to bar its entry. The absence of a proper insight into the tightly sealed cocoon of interdependence, in which the horrors already seen have gestated and those yet unknown and still to be hatched incubate, is one hurdle most difficult to leap over or kick out of the way. The chain of causal connections is too ramified, twisted, and convoluted to be followed by people untrained and in a hurry; but in addition, many of its links tend to sink in secret compartments plastered all over with "entry forbidden" warnings and impenetrable without security screening

136   and stingily issued passes. The fragments of the chain accessible to view seldom form a cohesive system with clearly marked points of entry and "install" and "uninstall" buttons.

Admittedly, the obstacles to effective long-term commitment are numerous and many of them are intractable. It can be argued, though, that the barrier most difficult to negotiate is the one-sidedness of the globalizing process. The progressive interlocking of global dependencies is not paralleled, let alone checked and balanced, by similarly global, and potent, instruments of political action. Diffuse and sporadic anti-globalization protests, however brave and dedicated, are a poor match for the concentrated might of the multinationals, which are cosseted, shielded, and kept out of trouble day in and day out by governments vying for the Michelin stars of hospitality and by the heavily armed forces they command. To remove that hurdle, a better insight would not suffice. But at least it will be (to use Churchill's memorable phrase) "the end of the beginning."

And rereading Løgstrup in the light of the new planet-wide interdependence of humankind would be an excellent point to start the effort to end that beginning.

NOTE

1. "Life politics" is a household concept in current sociology, coined by Anthony Giddens and referring to the shift from "state politics" to "individual politics": things once debated and resolved (?) in the public arena by the state organs are now relegated to the reflection, decision making, and undertakings of individual men and women.

REFERENCES

Boltanski, Luc. 1999. *Distant Suffering: Morality, Media and Politics*. Translated by Graham Burchell. Cambridge: Cambridge University Press. First published as *La souffrance à distance*.

Giddens, Anthony. 1992. *The Transformation of Intimacy: Sexuality, Love and Eroticism in Modern Societies*. Cambridge: Polity Press.

Heidegger, Martin. 1967 [1926]. *Sein und Zeit*. 11th ed. Tübingen: Max Niemeyer Verlag.

Kapuscinski, Ryszard. 1999. "Les médias reflètent-ils la réalité du monde?" *Le Monde diplomatique.* August 8–9.

Løgstrup, K. E. 1997. *The Ethical Demand.* Notre Dame: University of Notre Dame Press.

———. 2007. *Beyond the Ethical Demand.* Notre Dame: University of Notre Dame Press.

Shestov, Leon. 1970. "All things are perishable." In *A Shestov Anthology.* Edited by Bernard Martin. Athens: Ohio University Press.

Tester, Keith. 1997. *Moral Culture.* London: Sage.

Toscano, Roberto. 2001. "The Ethics of Modern Diplomacy". In *Ethics and International Affairs: Extents and Limits,* ed. Jean-Marc Coicaud and Daniel Werner. Tokyo: United Nations University Press.

Vandegiste, Pierre. 2001. "Le proper de l'homme et la culture chimpanzée." *Le Monde de debats.* June 22–23.

The Ethical Demand in a Global Perspective

A Response to Bauman

Øjvind Larsen

Zygmunt Bauman has written an engaging and thought-provoking essay on the ethics of K. E. Løgstrup in which he raises the important question of how Løgstrup's ethics could be understood in a modern global society. Bauman's questions are all the more stimulating to me in light of my work *Den Samfundsetiske Udfordring* (2005), which deals with the same topic but reaches different conclusions.

Bauman's most significant hypothesis is that Løgstrup's ethics has gained new meaning because it is no longer possible to maintain shared legislative forms of ethics in a postmodern global society. Bauman believes that Løgstrup outlines a kind of spontaneous ethical responsibility that could form the basis of morally oriented political behavior in the global society. I, on the other hand, propose that Løgstrup's ethics cannot endure the transformation into the global sort of ethics for which Bauman makes his case. The following discussion of Bauman's essay is set against the backdrop of these two contradictory hypotheses.

Bauman's enthusiasm for Løgstrup's *The Ethical Demand* has to do with his perception that it can provide an alternative to the legislative forms of ethics that, according to Bauman, have been dominant in modern society. Regrettably, Bauman

140 offers no precise explanation in his essay of the particular theories he has in mind. Instead he presents a general polemic against "mainstream ethical philosophy." In using the phrase "legislative forms of ethics," Bauman means forms of ethics that have been used by politicians and social engineers to establish substantial moral norms for how we should all behave in society and thus to lay down a kind of social morality. In this way the personal and free dimension so crucial to ethics wanes.

The legislative forms of ethics, Bauman says, have increasingly lost their significance, since centralized control is no longer sustainable in a modern society. Our society has entered the postmodern age. One characteristic of a postmodern society is that even though it is dominated by impersonal market forces, it is also typified by individuals' own personal life strategies, which do not allow themselves to be subordinated to fit a common moral code. Postmodern society no longer has firmly established authorities that can prescribe moral norms for the individual. In Bauman's view, this has triggered a kind of moral crisis, and it is against this background that Løgstrup's ethics take on a new meaning.

The important point for Bauman is that Løgstrup's ethics is able to uphold a sense of moral responsibility and commitment in a historical situation where the norms in the legislative forms of ethics have become conformist and thereby casual and noncommitted, insofar as the authoritative nature of conformity has also been watered down in postmodern society. Social relations between people have become associated with an uncertainty and a randomness for which no fixed norms can be prescribed. This is where Løgstrup's view of ethics can be brought in, since it, by its thesis that the ethical demand is a *silent* demand, does *not* operate on the basis of predefined norms. In this context, Bauman emphasizes that the ethical demand is always present as a silent demand.

Upon closer investigation, however, Bauman also finds that Løgstrup's ethics is not quite as disconnected from social aspects as it might seem at first glance. According to Løgstrup, we always meet one another with trust, and Bauman sees that this claim is indeed socially rooted in a delineated world in which people meet each other as acquaintances, and hence they also know a good deal about one another and experientially know they can meet the other with trust. According to Bauman, however, this precondition has also broken down in postmodern society, where all individuals must fight for their own particular life strategies. The world has become, as Bauman says, "inhospitable to trust." In this connection Bauman quotes Leon Shestov's dictum that *homo homini lupus* has become the predominant moral stance in postmodern society. Anthony Giddens's descriptions of the provisional, temporary, and coincidental nature of the postmodern society's love relationships point in the same direction. Modernity has now become a "liquid modernity." The conclusion is that although our social relations are fundamentally characterized by trust, our trust lacks a place where it can drop anchor. The world has become a place full of uncertainty.

This analysis would seem to invalidate Løgstrup's theory. Even so, faced with this apparent contradiction, Bauman maintains that it is precisely the spontaneousness and the silence of Løgstrup's ethics that comes into its own here. The sovereign expressions of life spontaneously assert themselves, and this is the circumstance on which we can rely. Bauman concludes that the lesson he has learned from Løgstrup is the following: "uncertainty is the home-ground of the moral person and the only soil on which morality can sprout and flourish."

Bauman does not believe that this assertion applies only to immediate, close relations between people, as in Løgstrup's own presentation. Bauman also applies it to distant, that is, global, relations. But when he goes on to analyze the distant, global relations that we encounter only through the media, the assertion turns out to be greatly weakened, if not untenable, even for Bauman himself. Certainly a sense of unlimited responsibility can be awakened via the media, not least through the images we see on television, but the reality of the matter is that we also come to feel powerless when faced with such images. We therefore have a strong tendency to become bystanders, impotent observers of the pictures on the screen. In this connection Bauman derives support from Ryszard Kapuscinski's analysis of the gap between what we *see* and what we *know*, and then between what we *know* and what we can *do*. As a consequence, it is difficult for Bauman to uphold his position that it is possible to establish a link between the ethical demand and the taking of political action in the global society. What remains, according to Bauman, is that we have a responsibility that we cannot sidestep, since the demand made to us rises up as a silent demand for us to assume our responsibility, and it must be this demand that gets us started thinking about how we should behave in the global society.

Summing up, one could say that through his interpretation of Løgstrup's ethics, Bauman attempts to advocate a form of unconditional responsibility in the postmodern global society, which otherwise seems to
be characterized by cynical and irresponsible bystanders, each of whom
is solely preoccupied with his or her own strategic optimization of personal advantages, not only on an individual level but on a social level as
well. However, his interpretation of Løgstrup's ethics raises a number of
problems that I will discuss in the following.

It is true that in *The Ethical Demand* Løgstrup places a pronounced
emphasis on the silence and unconditionality of the ethical demand. In
addition, Løgstrup, in *Opgør med Kierkegaard* (Controverting Kierkegaard), introduces the elemental concept of what he calls the sovereign
expressions of life. Their significance is that the ethical demand can be
spontaneously fulfilled through the sovereign expressions of life (SEL,
69). According to Løgstrup, the sovereign expressions of life are "premoral" (SEL, 77). As an extension of this idea, morality becomes a sort
of substitute motivation for a substitute action, which is then meant to
replace the spontaneous good action that is generated by the sovereign
expressions of life.

Løgstrup's ethics can be understood as an ethical theory in its own
right, and indeed, this is what many of those interpreting his ethics in recent years have done. Here it would seem appropriate to observe that
Løgstrup himself offers *The Ethical Demand*, from cover to cover, as a
contribution to a theological discussion of how Christianity ought to
be understood. On its first page he outlines his project as an attempt, in
purely human terms, to determine the attitude towards the other that is
contained in the religious proclamation of Jesus of Nazareth. He ends his
book with a lengthy polemical critique of the Kierkegaardian theological interpretation of Christianity, which is precisely the opposite of Løgstrup's interpretation in rejecting the priority of purely human existence
and maintaining that the unconditional nature of our relationship to God
is the decisive determining factor for human existence. I do not believe it
does Løgstrup justice to disregard the theological and metaphysical context within which his phenomenological analysis of human relations was
meant to rest. One could counter this by asserting that a modern non-
Christian and indeed nonreligious reader is not necessarily prepared or
able to read Løgstrup's exposition on its own terms. In all fairness, we do

not read the rest of the philosophical tradition on its own terms, either. We always come to the text with our own questions, which can be completely detached from the tradition of the text itself. Basically, I accept an objection of this nature as valid. There is, however, one crucial point on which it is untenable to disregard the entire theological and metaphysical context in which Løgstrup was originally intended to be understood. This point is the definition of the ethical demand: in other words, the most pivotal point in Løgstrup's whole undertaking.

What is important here is that Løgstrup, in his phenomenological analysis, seems to say that the ethical demand is silent and unconditional, and that as such it is not dependent on anything else. It is sovereign. But if one removes the demand completely from its theological and metaphysical context, it not only becomes nondefinite in the concrete situation, as Bauman emphasizes. It is also nondefinite in theological and metaphysical terms. However, this renders it bland and meaningless.

Løgstrup's essential claim is that the demand has been uttered aloud *once*, namely, by Jesus of Nazareth, and through being uttered has also been given a name: charity, or love. This means that the demand can be contemplated theologically and metaphysically in a discussion with other perceptions of love, and this is precisely what Løgstrup does throughout his work. Løgstrup's undertaking is not simply to describe and define love in general and purely human terms. His theological hypothesis is that it is in one's relation to the other that one's relationship to God is determined. And it is this hypothesis that stands in opposition to the Kierkegaardian hypothesis Løgstrup wishes to refute, which states that it is in our relationship to God that our relationship to the other is determined. This is the pivotal issue in Løgstrup's work, and this is the issue on which the postsecular and postmodern reader should also take a stand if Løgstrup's undertaking is to be relevant to our time.

This leads us to another interesting discussion. While Løgstrup certainly claims that the demand is silent, this is not to be understood in the sense that its content cannot be discursively determined. It can, in fact, be discursively determined through reflection on the ethical demand itself. If, in this connection, one sets aside the Christian theology along with the accompanying metaphysics as a reference for such reflection, then surely one must be able to present a different context for understanding in which the significance of the ethical demand can be contemplated.

144   In one passage, Bauman deals with the metaphysical significance of the demand, and hence of guilt. In this connection he emphasizes Karl Jaspers's discussion of the problem of guilt, which Jaspers presented in the light of Auschwitz after the end of World War II (Jaspers 2000). Jaspers distinguished between moral guilt and metaphysical guilt. Moral guilt relates to a limited and specific situation between the parties involved. Metaphysical guilt, on the other hand, is typified by the absence of any connection between the action of the individual and his or her guilt in relation to a specific situation. So in the metaphysical sense, I can be guilty even though I have not contributed to the suffering of the other. There is no connection between cause and effect associated with metaphysical guilt. Jaspers introduced this distinction in order to allow himself to address the moral problems raised in connection with Auschwitz, including the question of the German people's guilt. Jaspers believed that one could argue the case for a metaphysical guilt of the German people in connection with Auschwitz, even though each German as an individual had not been factually involved in its atrocities.

Bauman suggests that perhaps Løgstrup would have incorporated metaphysical guilt as a part of moral guilt. In my view, however, this is not the case. The guilt that Løgstrup is concerned with in *The Ethical Demand* is always defined in relation to one or more persons or to a social relationship in a particular situation. The nature of metaphysical guilt, Løgstrup would say, is different, and would have to be contemplated theologically and metaphysically in a different way. But this is not Løgstrup's concern in *The Ethical Demand*.

Bauman waters down Jaspers's material distinction between the two forms of guilt to the point where it is a distinction between moral guilt, which relates to the legal subject, and metaphysical guilt, which relates to the moral self. Bauman concludes: "The cause-and-effect link, the principal *differentia specifica* of Jaspers's categorization, is devoid of potency and assigned only a secondary significance in Løgstrup." Thus, for Bauman the ethical demand is linked with Jaspers's metaphysical concept of guilt. According to Bauman, we can be guilty even though we have not caused a particular problem.

This, I think, is where things go wrong for Bauman's argument. The ethical demand of Løgstrup, which in my interpretation always has to do with the relationship to one particular individual, or to several, or to a body of people in a particular situation, is transformed in Bauman's reasoning to a metaphysical relationship in which a responsibility can be placed on each individual, thereby imposing a guilt that is limitless in a global world. Løgstrup would have rejected this, arguing that the demand and the guilt are always bound by the relationship to particular people in a particular situation. But if, in spite of this objection, Bauman wishes to maintain the account of guilt that he has presented here, I believe that it gives rise to an obligation to contemplate in greater depth how individual human beings are supposed to be equipped to deal with such guilt, and to prevent the misery of the world from becoming a deadly millstone round their neck. I do not believe that a philosophical metaphysics would be sufficient in this case. What we are dealing with is a kind of guilt that is far more radical than the metaphysical guilt conceived by Jaspers. Despite its horrendous enormity, Auschwitz was still a definable historical and social occurrence. A guilt that relates to the misery of the world is solely definable in religious terms.

It is understandable that Bauman attempts to incorporate Løgstrup's idea of the ethical demand into a new and larger context, as an unlimited demand and guilt. But if one does not take along Løgstrup's theology and metaphysics as part of the deal, one creates an obligation to contemplate the theological and metaphysical issues in a new and different way. Otherwise the consequence would be that each individual is regarded as being to blame for the world's misery—a burden of guilt that no person would be able to bear, since no one would ever be capable of remedying that misery. This problem is abundantly discussed in Christian theology, and I will refrain from introducing this discussion here. Stated very briefly, however, only God can assume such a burden of guilt and bear it. If one does not choose to pursue this theological path, and there are many excellent reasons not to pursue it, then to avoid that unbearable burden one becomes obliged to contemplate the ethical demand and the issue of guilt in some other metaphysical and theological context.

In contrast, in Løgstrup's undertaking he is concerned with discussing the ethical demand and the issue of guilt in the definite sense that the ethical demand is always a demand related to particular people, or related to a particular historical situation. The discussion as such raises various theological and metaphysical problems that Løgstrup also discusses in *The Ethical Demand*. Ultimately, the ethical demand cannot stand alone. It calls for a theological and metaphysical determination.

146 REFERENCES

Jaspers, Karl. 2000. *The Question of German Guilt.* New York: Fordham University Press.

Larsen, Øjvind. 2005. *Den Samfundsetiske Udfordring.* Copenhagen: Hans Reitzels Forlag.

Løgstrup, K. E. 1968. *Opgør med Kierkegaard.* Copenhagen: Gyldendal.

———. 1997. *The Ethical Demand.* Notre Dame: University of Notre Dame Press.

———. 2007. *Beyond the Ethical Demand.* Notre Dame: University of Notre Dame Press.

Human Nature and Human Dependence

What Might a Thomist Learn from Reading Løgstrup?

Alasdair MacIntyre

Thomism does not confront its philosophical rivals as a completed system of thought, and not primarily even as a set of propositions, but rather in the first place as a set of questions, questions that do indeed presuppose the truth of certain assertions and the soundness of certain arguments, but that nonetheless are important as questions. They are questions with a history, the questions successively of Socrates, of Plato, of Aristotle, and of medieval Islamic and Jewish Aristotelians, before they ever became Aquinas's questions; and at each stage they were refined and reformulated, so as to take account of a wider and wider range of relevant considerations. This process did not come to an end with Aquinas's articulation of that theological and philosophical whole to which these questions turned out to be contributory parts. In the last hundred years, for example, Thomists have learned a great deal to their profit from the development of logic since Boole and Frege, from Wittgenstein, and, perhaps most importantly from the phenomenology of Husserl and Ingarden. And it is, I am going to suggest, from Løgstrup as a phenomenologist that we now have much to learn.

148   It is important to emphasize that I speak only as "a" Thomist. There are numerous issues on which Thomists are divided, both on the interpretation of Aquinas's texts and on substantive philosophical questions, some of which are relevant to the dialogues between Thomists and protagonists of other standpoints. Thomists have, for example, differed widely among themselves in their attitudes to phenomenology. So that in writing about Løgstrup and in thinking about the phenomenological aspects of his work—although not only about these—I unavoidably enter disputed territory, bringing with me much that is shared with other Thomists, but also a good deal less widely shared, including my view of how the kind of psychoanalytic understanding that we owe to D. W. Winnicott is to be integrated into a Thomistic understanding of human nature.

In phenomenological claims it is important to distinguish between what is reported as given in experience of the object of phenomenological attention and what derives instead from the theoretical framework in terms of which particular phenomenologists present their reports and interpret the experience. The point that I am making here is similar to that made by Løgstrup, when he warned moral philosophers of the dangers involved in not distinguishing adequately between what belongs to the phenomenological description of the moral act and what is a matter of the logical entailments involved in statements of general principles and moral arguments (SGCN, 104). This danger has two dimensions. Sometimes, when we share the phenomenologist's theoretical presuppositions, we may too easily accept as an account of the object itself what is in fact an account of the object as interpreted from that theoretical standpoint. And sometimes, when our theoretical standpoint is at odds with that of the phenomenologist, we may be insufficiently receptive to what does in fact belong to the account of the object as it presented itself, as it disclosed itself to phenomenological attention, and therefore to the account of the object as it is.

An important precaution therefore is to begin by identifying possible obstacles to genuine receptivity, both obstacles that may rise from shared agreements and those that may be the result of difference and disagreement. For a Thomistic reader of Løgstrup these are not difficult to catalogue.

The agreements are of at least three kinds. First, Løgstrup as a Lutheran theologian shared an Augustinian inheritance with Aquinas. And it was one of Augustine's central theses that our lives are given to us by God and that we only perceive and understand ourselves rightly insofar as we perceive and understand our lives as gifts. It is of course possible to experience one's life as a gift without recognizing that it is God's gift. Katherine Mansfield described in one of her letters a surge of gratitude for her existence without being able to say to whom she was grateful. But insofar as one finds oneself unable not to acknowledge that one's life is a gift, the questions of who it is to whom gratitude is owed and of how that gratitude is to be expressed become inescapable.

Secondly, the need for trust is recognized by Aquinas just as it is by Løgstrup, although he speaks about it in a different context. Løgstrup rightly emphasized the priority of trust over distrust for human beings: "It is a characteristic of human life that we normally encounter one another with natural trust" (Løgstrup 1997, 8). We may and do learn by hard experience to distrust certain others. But we do not have to learn to trust. We have indeed initially no alternative to trusting others and by doing so laying ourselves open to them. "In its basic sense trust is essential to every conversation" (ibid., 14). And this is because "the definitive feature of speech is its openness" (SEL, 55).

Aristotle and Aquinas too recognize the importance of trust, something presupposed in a good deal that they say about friendship and made explicit by Aristotle in his remarks in Book VIII of the *Nicomachean Ethics* (1157a20−25), where he lists trust as among the prerequisites of true friendship, remarks endorsed by Aquinas in his *Commentary* (at 1592). They come even closer to Løgstrup when they speak of the natural friendship that all human beings have for one another. Here Aquinas as a commentator adds to what Aristotle asserts (1155a20−22) with an example that anticipates Løgstrup: "This is evident when a human being loses his or her way; for everyone stops even an unknown stranger from taking the wrong road, as if every human being is by nature a familiar friend of every other human being" (1541). That is, we invite and expect the trust of others, even when we are unknown to them.

It is important to note that any fuller statement of Løgstrup's views and of the views of Aristotle and Aquinas would reveal certain disagreements, but for the moment I put these aside in order to identify a third area of agreement. About the characterization of some features of the ethical demand Løgstrup and Aquinas disagree, but that there is such a thing as the ethical demand they agree. Some of the relevant passages in Aquinas occur in his discussion of the virtue of *misericordia.* The extreme and urgent need of another, whoever she or he is, makes a claim upon me that is stronger than any other human claim, stronger than claims that arise from the closest ties of kinship and family (*Summa Theologiae* IIa-IIae 31, 3). Aquinas's discussion enables us to understand what it would be to fail or to succeed when confronted by the ethical demand. What he does not supply is any account of what it is from a first-person standpoint to be confronted by the ethical demand and consequently of what is involved in recognizing the demand as and for what it is rather than failing to recognize it. It is here that the work of the phenomenologist is indispensable and that a Thomist needs to supplement and to enrich Aquinas's account by drawing upon phenomenological resources. Yet doing so is not straightforward.

The best phenomenological reports of the ethical demand that we have—and here I think of Levinas as well as of Løgstrup, and indeed not only of them—are generally presented in texts that tie them to theses and presuppositions notably at odds with those of Aquinas. So that it is not just a question of adding a set of phenomenological reports to Aquinas's account, but also one of inquiring about the relationship between the phenomenological reports and the theoretical presuppositions of these particular phenomenologists, and whether or not Aquinas's account needs to be revised, if it is to accommodate what is undeniably so in the light of the phenomenological reports. Before we can profitably attempt to do this, however, it is necessary to consider three aspects of Aquinas's positions that generate disagreements with Løgstrup.

SOME IMPORTANT DISAGREEMENTS

The first is his teleology. Løgstrup opened his discussion of teleology in his 1980 article "Ethics and Ontology" (translated as an appendix to *The*

Ethical Demand [1997, 265–293]) by saying that he intended to "discuss exclusively a teleological conception for which it is characteristic that it rejects a ranking of the goods and that it can be placed in a schema of a psychology of desires" (Løgstrup 1997, 265). By so doing he excludes from consideration Aquinas's teleology and obscures from view some of its central characteristics. Perhaps most importantly, Aquinas's teleology requires a rank-ordering of goods, both of goods as such and of goods in respect of the part that they should play in the life of this or that particular agent here and now. There is indeed an ultimate good for human beings towards the achievement of which they are directed by their specific nature, and other goods are rank-ordered in respect of their contribution to the kind of life through which that ultimate good can be achieved.

Moreover, on Aquinas's view, the psychology of desire has to be elucidated with reference to that teleology and not vice versa. How the different appetites and passions need to be criticized, disciplined, and redirected depends upon the nature of the goods to be pursued by this or that particular agent. What those goods are and how they are to be achieved depends in turn not only upon the circumstances of the particular agent, but also and primarily upon the teleologically directed character of human life. Our desires, that is to say, are never to be taken as given. They need to be transformed. And of themselves they never provide us with a sufficient reason for action. We have to become the kind of agents whose desires are disciplined and ordered, so that we are directed towards our good and take pleasure in performing those types of action that have as their end that good.

Løgstrup's use of "teleology" to name a set of very different views was designed to contrast teleology with deontology. Yet teleology, conceived as Aquinas conceived it, is not only not incompatible with deontology of a certain kind, but requires it. What kind of deontology? It has as its background a view of human beings as able to achieve their ultimate end only in and through social relationships that are law-governed. To speak of law, as Aquinas understands it, is to speak of precepts of reason directed towards our common good, precepts that bind just because to flout them is to violate one's nature as a rational being. For to be rational is to be directed towards one's good, and there is no way to achieve one's individual good except in the company of a variety of others with whom

152   one shares a common good. Hence one cannot aim at the achievements of one's individual good without also aiming at the achievement of the common good. But initial human awareness of the precepts of the natural laws and of their binding character does not derive from reasoning about the common good and the human good. Such awareness does not require the prior exercise of our reasoning powers, but is exhibited in the standards presupposed by the accountability that is commonly taken for granted in the transactions of our everyday life.

For it is not that we are able first and independently of any awareness of the precepts of the natural law to frame an adequate conception of our good and only then and secondly to ask and answer the question of what rules we must follow if we are to achieve that good. It is rather that the goods of human beings as agents whose relationships are informed by the precepts of their shared reason are goods achievable only in and through a law-governed life. How the precepts of the natural law are formulated and understood does of course vary from culture to culture, and in some societies those precepts are more adequately formulated and understood than they are in others. But the norms and rules of all cultures are to be understood as variously imperfect apprehensions of the natural law and not relativistically. And this of course puts Aquinas and those who follow him at odds with Løgstrup in another way.

Løgstrup believed that the differences between cultures in respect of norms and the history of moral change warranted a relativistic view of moral rules and their authority. And he decried any attempt to differentiate "between *lex naturae* and *lex positiva*" and so "to tie in with the metaphysical tradition in western European culture" (Løgstrup 1997, 100). He also believed that a relativistic view of the history of moral change could not issue in a relativistic attitude to the norms and rules of one's own culture, and asserted that our dispositions will have been so shaped by whatever moral culture we inhabit that it is not in our power to set its norms aside (ibid., 101). This latter claim, although I take it to be false, I shall not discuss. I note only Løgstrup's rejection of the Thomistic conception of the natural law.

Finally, in this catalogue of disagreements something should be said about character traits. "In the old days, traits of character acquired through practice were called virtues" (SGCN, 91), wrote Løgstrup. To which it must be replied that even in those old days to which Løgstrup relegates us Thomists, only some character traits were classified as virtues, while others were not. I am not making the point that some character traits were classified as vices and justifiably so, but rather that of the items on Løgstrup's list of character traits only some can be justifiably accounted virtues. His list includes perseverance, trustworthiness, reliability, loyalty, self-criticism, and fortitude (SGCN, 91). But perseverance as such, reliability as such, and loyalty as such are not virtues but rather traits whose moral significance depends entirely upon whether they are put to the service of virtues or of vices. To persevere in bad ways, to be reliably vicious, and to be loyal to those who are vicious is to be a worse human being than one who is too lazy to persevere in bad projects or only intermittently vicious or disloyal to the protagonists of injustice.

What then is the mark of a virtue? A virtue is a disposition to act in accordance with the judgments of reason, that is, to act so as to achieve that immediate end or good which in this or that situation is ordered to our ultimate good. Virtues differ both from skills and from character traits, such as reliability and perseverance, precisely in that they are habits directed towards goods. They are not neutral powers, equally available for the pursuit of either goods or bads. Particular virtues have to do with particular aspects of our nature, as temperance has to do with the appetites and courage to do with the passions of fear and confidence. To act virtuously is to act as a human being with practical intelligence would act, not only so as to achieve what is required by the virtues in this or that particular situation, but also so as to perfect oneself in their exercise, to make oneself into the kind of human being who is able to achieve both the common good and her or his own individual good.

The relevance of this to Løgstrup's thought is not just a matter of his—from a Thomistic point of view—misconception of the virtues, but also of the part played by the virtues in those actions that exemplify trust and spontaneity.

TRUST AND TRUSTWORTHINESS

Whatever our positive or negative assessment of this or that particular thesis of Løgstrup's concerning trust, spontaneity, mercy, human life as a gift, the ethical demand, and their interrelationships, we are all indebted

154   to him for his insistence on the centrality of these features of the moral
life and for his searching questions about those interrelationships.

About trust I have already noticed the common ground shared by
Løgstrup and Aquinas. But when in the *Summa Theologiae* (IIa-IIae 129,
6) Aquinas discusses the confidence that we repose in others, he says that
on occasion we have confidence in those others because we have observed
in them something that gives us reason to hope for good from them. And
since no one, not even the most self-sufficient of human beings, can dis-
pense with the assistance of others, we need at hand just those others
in whom we can have such confidence. This is, at least at first sight, at
odds with Løgstrup, according to whom we can and do have reasons
for distrust, but not for trust. "Only because of some special circumstance do we ever distrust a stranger in advance. . . . Under normal circumstances . . . we accept the stranger's word and do not mistrust him
until we have some particular reason to do so" (Løgstrup 1997, 8). Yet
perhaps Løgstrup and Aquinas are not as far apart as might appear. To
explain why let me construct a fuller account of trust and distrust than
either of them provide.

Initially as small children we trust others, exhibiting what Løgstrup
calls "natural trust" and Aquinas the "natural friendship" of human beings
for each other. But even at this early stage the capacity for trust can be
either enlarged or damaged by the actions of parents and especially of
mothers, as D. W. Winnicott has emphasized (Winnicott 1971, 108–110).
Children at a later stage are often warned by their elders not to be too
trusting and they are commonly taught to be suspicious of strangers,
often of course with justification. Or they may learn to be less trusting in
another more harmful way, by having their confidence in others abused.
So children may come to have good reason to distrust certain others and
perhaps certain types of others. But this must at a certain point raise the
question: In whom then should I have confidence? We confront two op-
posing dangers, that of being over-suspicious and that of being insufficiently on our guard. The extreme version of the former is paranoia, of
the latter a kind of naiveté and credulity that makes us ideal victims for
the unscrupulous. Løgstrup seems to have underestimated the need for
cultivating discriminating suspicion in the modern world when he wrote,
"Only because of some special circumstance do we ever distrust a stranger
in advance." Here he presumably had in mind such special circumstances

as those of the German occupation of Denmark in World War II. Løgstrup added, "We never suspect a person of falsehood until we have caught
them in a lie" (Løgstrup 1997, 8). But when we have caught just too many
people either in lies or in misleadingly selective truth-telling—and the
advertising and public relations industries make this a common experience in the consumer societies of advanced modernity—then the question "Whom may I reasonably trust?" becomes inescapable for adults as
well as for children.

As adolescents and even as adults we therefore have to learn to
trust all over again. It is to the point that the context in which Aquinas
discusses confidence in others and security of mind in ourselves is that
of an inquiry into the parts and aspects of courage. Magnanimity is
characterized as a part of courage and confidence in others and security
of mind are characterized as aspects of magnanimity (*Summa Theologiae*
IIa-IIae 129, 6 and 7). So, to trust others with reason is to exhibit the
virtue of courage. Why is it courage that is required? It is, I suggest, because although we may have sufficient reason to distrust some particular individuals, we never have *sufficient* reason to trust anyone, although
there are those whom we have some good reason to trust or at least no
reason to distrust. Reasoning, that is to say, is far from irrelevant to
our placing trust in someone, as Aquinas pointed out. But all trust, even
with the strongest possible reason to support it, involves a measure of
genuine risk-taking, and the risks are as considerable as they are because
of that uncalculating opening up of ourselves to others that, as Løgstrup rightly and so often emphasized, is involved in all trust. But the
virtue concerned with risk-taking is courage. To be too little and too seldom prepared to take risks is to be both over-suspicious and cowardly.
To be too much or too often prepared to take risks is to be not only
credulous but also rash. And the mean between the vices of cowardice
and rashness is of course the virtue of courage, exhibited in reasonable
risk-taking.

What emerges then is a contrast between the initial trust of children, some element of which is preserved throughout our lives in the
trust that we continue on occasion to repose in perfect strangers, and a
mature trust in particular individuals for which we can sometimes give
reasons that are good, although not sufficient, to justify that trust. We
have, however, sufficient reasons for taking it to be rational to go beyond

our reasons in this way. An insightful psychoanalyst has narrated how he responded to the irrational suspicions of a paranoid subject, who believed that those who should have been aiding him—his lawyer, for example— were leagued in a conspiracy against him, not by trying to allay his suspicions, but by suggesting that he had at least the same grounds for imputing hostile motives to a much wider range of persons, including the analyst himself. The paranoid subject's response was one of indignant protest: "But, doctor, you have to trust someone!" Indeed—and it is therefore against reason not to trust, although there are better reasons for trusting some individuals rather than others, even if there are no conclusive reasons for trusting any particular individual.

How, then, in the perspective afforded by this larger account of trust are we to view the relationship of Løgstrup's views to those of Aquinas? It is clear that Løgstrup's thesis that trust and openness are primary, distrust and suspicion secondary, is indispensable to our understanding of trust and that any view that is unable to accommodate this thesis ought to be rejected. But the developmental account that I have sketched enables us to integrate Løgstrup's central thesis and Aqinas's arguments into a single account, one which preserves Løgstrup's insight that there is such a thing as "natural trust" and that it is an essential feature of human nature.

To this it will be retorted that this purported acceptance of Løgstrup's thesis has involved a distortion of Løgstrup's view. For trust, as I have described it, can change its character in the course of an individual's development and is something for which, in its mature form, reasons can be given. But this is quite incompatible with Løgstrup's account. For trust and openness are "expressions of life" and these always "remain the same" throughout history, let alone through the development of a single individual. Furthermore, although they are not irrational, "they have a primordiality which precedes any distinction between rationality and irrationality" (LI, 151). But, if this is so, then any conception of trust as reasonable or unreasonable seems to have been ruled out by Løgstrup. So we may have learned something from our reading of Løgstrup, but what we have learned is not what he intended to teach. To respond to this objection it will be necessary to examine Løgstrup's views further, focusing on what he has to say about spontaneity and about reflection.

What did Løgstrup mean by "spontaneity"? "Admittedly, 'spontaneous' is not the most felicitous term," he wrote, "especially if it is associated with a bubbling, welling gush of life. Etymologically, however, the word is appropriate because it means that what persons do, they do in accordance with the nature of things and of their own accord. . . . what persons do spontaneously they do unconstrainedly and without ulterior motives" (SGCN, 85). And he then says of spontaneous acts, such as acts of mercy, that they "are elicited solely by the condition or situation in which the other finds himself" (SGCN, 85).

Spontaneity is an all-or-nothing concept. "Spontaneity is not something of which there can be more or less" (SGCN, 85). For any action to be a "sovereign expression of life," then spontaneity must inform it in such a way as to exclude other determinants of action. Indeed Løgstrup partially defines spontaneity by a series of contrasts with other features of human action which, when present, exclude spontaneity. Four of these contrasts are of particular interest to Thomists.

The first is that between spontaneous actions and actions performed for the sake of something further. Løgstrup speaks of spontaneity as ruling out "ulterior motives" and also of the spontaneous agent—the example of spontaneity that he is discussing is mercy—as not "deriving any benefit from his deeds, not for himself nor for any third party or institution" (SGCN, 85). But this invites questioning by Thomists. Aquinas takes it that there are many types of action that are to be performed for their own sake, that are worthwhile in and for themselves. But insofar as they are thus worthwhile, they contribute to the goodness of a life through which the ultimate good can be achieved, and we perform them both for their own sake and for the sake of achieving that ultimate good. If this is so, if they are indeed performed for the sake of something further, then they must, it seems, on Løgstrup's view, lack spontaneity. Yet, for Aquinas, as for Løgstrup, among such worthwhile types of action are just such spontaneous acts of mercy as those of the good Samaritan.

A second contrast is between the decisiveness of a spontaneous action and that of actions that result from a decision to do one's duty. So Løgstrup asks, "But what is meant by a spontaneous decision?" and answers by making a comparison with "decisiveness in relation to duty" (SEL, 79). Duty, for Løgstrup, is a concept that finds application only when the sovereign expressions of life with their spontaneity have failed to elicit from us the kind of responsiveness that is necessary for their expression in action. But for a Thomist, when we act because it is our duty, that is, because of what we owe to another, we act for the sake of that other and, at our best, spontaneously. To act from duty and to act spontaneously are not, on a Thomistic view, in the least incompatible. Is this perhaps because what Løgstrup means by "duty" is different from what the Thomist means by it? To answer "Yes" to this question is only to gesture at the task of showing how different Løgstrup's moral vocabulary is from Aquinas's.

This difference in idiom is also relevant to a third contrast by reference to which Løgstrup partially defines spontaneity. Løgstrup says of the sovereign expressions of life that "[e]ither the will, allowing itself to be overmastered, surrenders to the expression of life, or it relies on its own efforts" (SEL, 68). That is, the will has only two alternatives: to let the spontaneity of the sovereign expressions of life have its own way or to substitute itself for that spontaneity. Spontaneity itself cannot be willed. At first sight what Løgstrup asserts seems obviously true. I cannot by making a deliberate effort to do so act spontaneously. But what this suggests is that Løgstrup equates willing to act with making a deliberate effort to act. And this is not what Aquinas means when he speaks of willing and of the will. What he does mean can best be brought out by first considering a fourth contrast.

Spontaneity is, in Løgstrup's view, incompatible with reflection. The moment that reflection or calculation come between the agent and her or his action, spontaneity becomes impossible. Løgstrup gives us two examples, that of the individual who, prior to acting, reflects on his freedom to act (SEL, 80), and that of the woman visited by the secret police (SGCN, 83–84). He writes of the first that "even as he begins to reflect, a paralysis sets in." In the second the woman must deliberately inhibit her impulse to speak in a way that would be a sovereign expression of life, frankly and openly, that is, spontaneously. And not to speak openly seems to her "to be contrary to nature."

To act spontaneously, and therefore without allowing reflection to intervene, is, as Løgstrup sees it, to act naturally. Yet on Aquinas's view it is our nature to be reasoners. Our goods are the specific goods of rational animals, and right action is action that not only accords with reason but issues from deliberative reasoning. What Aquinas asserts about deliberation therefore seems irreconcilable with what Løgstrup says about reflection, and it would be wrong to underestimate what divides them. The root of their difference is perhaps, however, other than it seems to be.

Consider the difference, on Aquinas's account, between the virtuous agent and the merely continent agent (*Summa Theologiae* IIa-IIae 155, 156). The continent agent knows by the exercise of her or his reason what it is right to do, but desires, even strongly desires, to do otherwise, perhaps because of anger, perhaps because of erotic desire. The continent agent, who also desires to do what reason prescribes, is able to resist and does successfully resist these nonrational and antirational impulses, while the incontinent agent fails to do so, although able to do so. The latter acts impulsively, on occasion even spontaneously; the former acts after reflection. So here we seem to be at the furthest from Løgstrup, since what in this type of case issues from spontaneity is wrong action. And indeed not only incontinent but also vicious people do seem to be sometimes spontaneously bad and not only reflectively bad.

Løgstrup's account apparently leaves no room for this possibility. When he gives examples of human badness, they are examples of what he calls "obsessive" thoughts and actions: taking offence without having good reason to do so, indulging in jealousy or envy. These are states in which individuals are, as he says, fixated. Their "paltry emotionality consists in the self's forcing them to revolve around him" (SEL, 52). But these are only one kind of badness, and they contrast with, for example, the joyful malice of *Schadenfreude* or the witty and hurtful sneer that is voiced spontaneously and issues equally spontaneously in unreflective and unconstrained words and deeds. In them there need be no trace of fixation or obsession.

So much for the incontinent and the vicious: what we now need to consider is how virtuous agents differ from merely continent agents. Fully virtuous agents have through habituation and reflection so reordered their desires and so developed their capacity for judgment in accordance with right reason that they are undivided in their inclination to act rightly. They know how to act on many types of occasions without immediately prior deliberation. Confronted by such situations they

160   respond wholeheartedly and spontaneously. Notice now that continence is a stage that we reach and pass through on the way to becoming fully virtuous. We have to learn to overcome and to put behind us the dividedness of the desires that characterizes a continent agent and the consequent need for reflection in order to deal with that division, so that we can become wholehearted and spontaneous in the right way. The spontaneity that issues in right action has to be learned. To say this is not to deny that such spontaneity is natural. For it is our nature to learn, and part of what we have to learn is when and where to be spontaneous.

There is empirical evidence that spontaneity has to be learned and that the way in which children are brought up in their early years can help or hinder such learning. Such evidence also discloses that there is an original spontaneity from which such learning begins. But that spontaneity can be destroyed by bad parenting. Winnicott has described how one effect of the imposition of harsh and strict standards of cleanliness on an infant can be to deprive that child of any hope of "retaining his valuable spontaneity and valuable impulsiveness" (Winnicott 1987, 123). But how and when to exhibit that spontaneity in later life has to be learned and "a great deal of the joy of spontaneity has to be given up" (ibid., 128). Why so? In part because the spontaneity that is creative in later life, in, for example, acts of teaching, often encounters frustrations, and being able to tolerate such frustrations is a necessary condition for continuing to be, on appropriate occasions, spontaneous (ibid., 202–203). Løgstrup did of course recognize the relevance to his accounts of trust and spontaneity of psychological and psychiatric discoveries about the effects of early childhood upbringing (Løgstrup 1997, 15 and 47–48). But he seems to leave no place in his account for the fact that spontaneity has the kind of history that I have suggested, while Aquinas with his Aristotelian view of development does provide us with at least a framework within which there is a place for just such a history.

So with regard to spontaneity there are two fundamental differences between Aquinas and Løgstrup. Where Løgstrup seems to identify spontaneity as itself a good, Aquinas requires us to distinguish between the spontaneity of the good and the spontaneity of the bad. And where Løgstrup treats spontaneity as something that presents itself spontaneously, Aquinas suggests to us that the spontaneity of the good has to be acquired through learning. To understand this allows us to view the contrasts through which Løgstrup defines spontaneity in a new light.

On Aquinas's view I can only achieve my ultimate good as a human being by, on occasion, devoting myself wholly to the needs of some other, by taking it to be worthwhile in itself to do so, and by having in mind for the moment nothing but the needs of that other and directing my actions wholly to the needs of that other. So I exclude from my mind for that moment any thought of that ultimate good for the sake of which I have become the kind of person who on occasion acts without thought of that ultimate good. And, in *this* sense, I have, just as Løgstrup requires, no ulterior motive.

When I so act, I do what duty requires. And part of what duty to another may require is that I devote myself for a given period of time wholly to the good of that other. So to act from duty and in accordance with duty is not incompatible with acting for the sake of the other. And, finally, what I do intentionally, whether reflectively or spontaneously, is always an expression of my will, that is, my actions have that voluntary directedness that distinguishes actions from nonvoluntary bodily movements. Willing is not a matter of making some special effort, as Løgstrup seems to have thought, and, on those occasions when I do make a special effort, that involves my will no more and no less than does any other action of mine.

THE ETHICAL DEMAND

When I suggested earlier that Aquinas, like Løgstrup, understood the significance of the ethical demand, I cited a passage (*Summa Theologiae* IIa-IIae 31, 3) in which Aquinas speaks of what is required when we are confronted with the urgent need of another. But it may seem that Aquinas cannot be speaking of the ethical demand, as understood by Løgstrup, since it is only on some particular occasions that we are confronted by others in great need, whereas the ethical demand is present, on Løgstrup's account, whenever trust is present and trust is taken to be a universal or near universal phenomenon. So Løgstrup writes that "our existence demands of us that we protect the life of the person who has placed his or her trust in us" (Løgstrup 1997, 17).

However he adds that "How much or how little is at stake for a person who has thus placed his or her trust in another person obviously varies greatly." And it is therefore worth thinking about those situations, apparently ignored by Aquinas, in which nothing very much is at stake and yet, according to Løgstrup, the ethical demand is nonetheless present. So in a casual encounter with a stranger who asks me if he is standing in the right line at the bus station, where we are both waiting to buy tickets, in what way am I confronted by the ethical demand? Certainly I am required to give the stranger a truthful answer, but, even if I did not, he would soon discover the truth. So not too much seems to be at stake. But now consider possibilities that might be, even if they are not in fact, realized.

The stranger might suddenly faint. Or he might put his hand in his pocket, searching for his wallet, so as to pay for his bus ticket, only to discover that his wallet has been stolen. Or he may be hassled or attacked by an aggressive drunk. It is true of all of us all the time that we may without warning fall into some predicament from which we can only be rescued by the mercy of strangers. Løgstrup did not believe that it is only if such contingencies in fact occur that we are confronted by the ethical demand. When someone has put their lives in our hands by trusting us, even momentarily, all that may be at stake may be that individual's "passing mood." But it may also be "his or her entire destiny" (ibid., 26). Surely the ethical demand has the significance it has because, even in those situations in which nothing much seems to be at stake, things might always change, so that "his or her entire destiny" is at stake. I conclude that in focusing upon situations of urgent or great need, Aquinas is not mistaken. Were it not the case that every situation is potentially one of someone's urgent or great need, the ethical demand would not be the universal phenomenon that it is.

That Løgstrup might not have disagreed with this is suggested by his own further characterization of the demand. For he says of the situation in which the demand is presented that "either we take care of the other person's life or we ruin it" and that "there is no third alternative" (ibid., 18 n. 6). And evidently this is not true of situations in which little is and continues to be at stake. The ethical demand then presents itself in situations of varying importance. And what the demand is does not in the least depend upon the individual whose life is given over into our hands. Its content does not depend upon what that individual asks of us. For the demand is necessarily silent. It is the "individual to whom the demand is directed" who must "decide what the content of the demand is" (ibid., 22).

What that individual has to decide is what is best for the other, but in acting for the good of the other he has to let the other "remain sovereign" and not intrude upon "his or her individuality and will" (ibid., 27). Why? Løgstrup offers us assertion rather than argument here, but Aquinas is able to supply a reason. If the good that I seek for the other is genuinely that other's good, it is one that she or he will be able to make his or her own and it will be for the good of the other that he or she should make it her or his own. But this can only be achieved through the other's sovereign exercise of reason and will. Hence that sovereignty must be treated as inviolable.

I have here used Thomistic concepts to explain, expand, and perhaps modify one of Løgstrup's central theses. But this should not be allowed to obscure how much Løgstrup is putting Thomists in his debt by his phenomenological account of the ethical demand, an account that is generally consistent with a Thomistic understanding of the moral life. And, as Løgstrup's characterization of the demand continues, it provides even more that can and should be integrated into a Thomistic account. So it is, for example, with Løgstrup's insistence on the radical character of the demand and his accompanying reminder that the responsibility imposed by the demand is not without limits (Løgstrup 1997, chapter 3, sections 1 and 2). Yet there is a point at which Løgstrup's characterization becomes—as he himself perhaps to some extent recognizes—deeply problematic.

For Løgstrup insists *both* that we are to be measured by our success or failure in responding to the demand *and* that the demand is by its very nature unfulfillable. Why is the demand taken to be unfulfillable? What makes it so is that, on Løgstrup's account of it, every attempt to obey the demand inevitably frustrates obedience to the demand. This is because "what is demanded is that the demand should not have been necessary" (Løgstrup 1997, 146) or, as he put it later "the demand demands that it be itself superfluous" (SEL, 69).

Løgstrup asserts—he does not argue—not only that the ethical demand is a demand that such and such should be done for the good of this or that individual, but also that it includes the requirement that what is done be a spontaneous fulfillment of a sovereign experience of life. Since, however, the demand presents itself only on occasions when the sovereign experience of life has already failed, the demand is a demand for the impossible. Agents confronted with the demand must therefore have recourse to substitute motives and dispositions. To act from duty or because the required action is virtuous is to have just such a substitute motive or disposition. What do substitute motives and dispositions substitute for? "When the intended outcome of the act constitutes its motivation, that motivation consists in spontaneous expressions of life" (SEL, 78). Løgstrup's thesis is then that to act from duty or to act as virtue requires is necessarily to act without spontaneity, to substitute something else for spontaneity.

Løgstrup's account is flawed. The notion that we can be required to respond to a demand that is always and inevitably unfulfillable is incoherent. If I say to you "This cannot be done; do it," you will necessarily be baffled. And I suggested earlier that Løgstrup himself betrays some awareness of this difficulty. I was referring to the passage in which he wrote that "[t]heoretically, these two claims cannot be reconciled—life's claim that its demand . . . can be fulfilled, and our own claim . . . that it cannot be fulfilled" (Løgstrup 1997, 167). But Løgstrup then goes on to say that "if our life is, ethically speaking, a contradiction, it is important not to remove the contradiction theoretically." To this it must be said, parodying Gertrude Stein, that "a contradiction is a contradiction is a contradiction. . . ." A contradiction is a sentence in which nothing is asserted. It has no substantive content, whether in theoretical or practical contexts. Yet it is of course possible for Løgstrup's position to be restated in a less self-destructive way. And it is illuminating that in *Norm og spontaneitet* he no longer treats the demand as unfulfilled, although he insists—and we may be reminded of Kant here—that "it becomes impossible to see whether the act is performed from mercy or for the sake of the moral ulterior motive or for the sake of some other gain" (SGCN, 87).

Yet we should not treat Løgstrup's earlier insistence on the unfulfillability of the demand as a mere mistake. For it is perhaps bound up with fundamental aspects of his position. Certainly it relies on just those contrasts between *acting because it is one's duty so to act* and *acting because virtue requires one so to act* on the one hand, and *acting spontaneously* on the other, that I criticized in the preceding section of this paper. And my suggestion there was that these contrasts presuppose misleading conceptions of duty, virtue, and spontaneity. But to this I now want to add a further criticism, one that may be even more revealing of what is at stake in the disagreements between Thomists and Løgstrup. For Løgstrup is mistaken on a matter of fact. The condition of those who cannot fulfill the demand—and there certainly are such—is not in fact the condition of every agent, but only that of those not yet so advanced in virtue that they are able to respond spontaneously to the demand presented to them in this or that concrete situation. Such agents may have reached various points in their progress towards perfected virtue. But they are still at a stage when the demand is less than completely fulfillable for them, because of that factor in their insufficiently reordered desires that still holds them back. Yet there are also lives that have progressed beyond that stage, the lives of those in whom openness to the grace of charity has allowed them to become spontaneously responsive to whatever is demanded of them.

What lives are these? They are the lives of the saints. But to say this is to have reached a point at which the issues that divide Thomists from Løgstrup in moral philosophy turn out to reflect theological issues that have always divided Catholics from Lutherans. And the unfulfillability of the ethical demand is perhaps best construed as a reinstatement in secular terms of one aspect of Luther's theology of grace. Kees van Kooten Niekerk has drawn our attention to the importance of Luther's influence on Løgstrup in this regard (see his essay in this volume). But I cannot pursue this issue further here.

WHAT NEXT?

To carry this inquiry further then, we would need to move beyond ethics to metaphysics and to theology. For the disagreements that I have so far catalogued, disagreements about how central questions of ethics are to be answered, are rooted in disagreements about human nature and about the place of human beings in the order of things. As I have just suggested, some aspects of these disagreements reflect Løgstrup's Lutheran inheritance and the differences between Catholic and Lutheran theology. Others have to do with Løgstrup's metaphysics of life and others again with his complex relationship to the work of Hans Lipps. But the investigation of these are tasks for another time and place.

166 REFERENCES

Aquinas, Thomas. 1963 –. *Summa Theologiae.* Latin and English texts. 60 vols. Oxford: Blackfriars; London: Eyre & Spottiswoode; New York: McGraw-Hill.

———. 1993. *Commentary on Aristotle's Nicomachean Ethics.* Translated by C. I. Litzinger, O.P. Notre Dame: Dumb Ox Books.

Aristotle. 1980. *The Nicomachean Ethics.* Translated by David Ross, revised by J. L. Ackrill and J. O. Urmson. Oxford: Oxford University Press.

Løgstrup, Knud Ejler. 1997. *The Ethical Demand.* Notre Dame: University of Notre Dame Press.

———. 2007. *Beyond the Ethical Demand.* Notre Dame: University of Notre Dame Press.

Winnicott, D. W. 1971. *Playing and Reality.* London: Tavistock Publications.

———. 1987. *The Child, the Family and the Outside World.* Reading, Mass.: Addison-Wesley.

CHAPTER NINE

Sovereign Expressions of Life, Virtues, and Actions

A Response to MacIntyre

Svein Aage Christoffersen

Thomism is not a closed system of thoughts and propositions, or even a system at all, according to Alasdair MacIntyre, but a kind of inquiry, an open-ended quest with reference to a particular kind of question evolving through history. This way of describing the historicity of Thomistic thinking holds true, I think, for theology and ethics in general—Løgstrup's way of thinking included—and makes it appropriate to respond to MacIntyre's contribution to this volume by looking more closely into his objections and questions to Løgstrup. In turning my attention to MacIntyre's criticism of Løgstrup, however, I am not forgetting the important agreements MacIntyre finds between Løgstrup and Aquinas. Nor am I forgetting his assurance that a Thomist has much to learn from Løgstrup. But I think an important road, even to these points of agreement, goes via the crucial questions MacIntyre is asking.

A main issue in MacIntyre's critique is the relationship between spontaneity and virtue. According to MacIntyre, Løgstrup holds that spontaneity and virtue are irreconcilable, and for several reasons MacIntyre refutes Løgstrup on this point. Do these objections to Løgstrup from a Thomistic point of view ultimately signify two incompatible ways of thinking, or is it possible to reformulate the disagreements in such a way

168 that some points of connection may appear? MacIntyre's article is inconclusive and open to further consideration, so let us look more closely at some of his objections.

MacIntyre draws attention to the blurred distinction between character traits and virtues in Løgstrup's writings. Many of Løgstrup's writings are unavailable in English, so MacIntyre has had to restrict his arguments to a limited number of texts. Other parts of Løgstrup's oeuvre may contribute to a more complex picture of his thinking. I still think, however, that MacIntyre has drawn our attention to an important objection, leading the way to some of Løgstrup's fundamental concerns.

Let us take loyalty as an example. Loyalty is treated as a virtue by Løgstrup, but is not a virtue, as MacIntyre convincingly argues. Loyalty is a character trait. Løgstrup seems to handle the concept of virtue carelessly by mixing virtues together with character traits

But Løgstrup was not careless. If we look more closely into his arguments in *System og symbol* (of which an extract is now available in English in *Beyond the Ethical Demand* but was not available to MacIntyre when he wrote his essay), we have to admit that Løgstrup was well aware of problems associated with the treatment of character traits as virtues. Løgstrup seizes upon the crucial point when he says that thoroughness is just as necessary for a philosopher reading Kant as for a burglar committing a successful break-in (NEL, 125). So thoroughness as such is neither good nor bad. The goodness or the badness stems from the goals at which we are aiming. In spite of the fact that a thorough burglar is a better burglar than a careless one, burgling is still a bad thing. From an ethical point of view, the reasons for doing this or that cannot be derived from the character traits themselves. The reasons must be derived from the goals we are aiming at and the tasks we are to carry out. This is Løgstrup's point of view, and I think it is very much in accordance with MacIntyre when he underlines the teleological nature of virtues.

In other words, Løgstrup could very well have made the distinction between character traits and virtues. He had the necessary presuppositions at hand. So why did he not do it? Was it just because he was not challenged by a revitalized virtue ethics? This, I think, would be too simplistic an answer. Løgstrup was always very careful in making necessary distinctions when they were of importance to his train of thought. It is thus more reasonable to assume that he did not make the distinction between virtues and character traits in *Norm og spontaneitet* (Norm and Spontaneity) because he did not need the distinction with regard to the points at which he was aiming there. He wanted to consider a specific aspect of the sovereign expressions of life compared to which the distinction between virtues and character traits was of minor importance or of no importance at all. When MacIntyre elaborates this distinction as an argument against Løgstrup, it becomes apparent that Løgstrup's own concern lay elsewhere. He did not merely misunderstand or disregard the virtues of virtue ethics; he had something else in mind.

Let us now take a closer look at trust and trustworthiness. With reference to Winnicot, MacIntyre describes trust in the perspective of personal growth and development. He refers to the "natural trust" in very small children, describes the transformation of this basic trust through their interaction with other people, and ends up by pointing to the difference between the initial trust of children and a mature trust in particular individuals. According to MacIntyre, this understanding of how trust is and has to be transformed is lacking in Løgstrup. Løgstrup ignores the fact that our basic trust sooner or later comes to an end and we must learn to trust all over again. Løgstrup also seems to have underestimated the need for cultivating discriminating suspicion in the modern world.

I believe that this critique is both right and wrong. Many passages in Løgstrup's writings demonstrate that he was well aware of the need to be suspicious and not to put one's trust and confidence in everyone (for instance, see SGCN, 115). But MacIntyre is right in assuming that Løgstrup lacked interest in the cultivation of this discriminating suspicion. This lack of interest, however, did not derive from the idea that trust is, after all, more important than suspicion. Had this been the case, Løgstrup would have emphasized the importance of cultivating trust, but he did not do that either, as MacIntyre rightly notices. Løgstrup's lack of interest has to be understood in the light of his distinction between psychology and phenomenology. What he aimed at was not the psychological relationship between trust and suspicion, but what he called "the foundational relationship between trust and distrust." Trust is the basic phenomenon; distrust is the negation of trust. This goes for small children, and for mature adults as well. Cultivation makes no difference from a phenomenological point of view, but in my understanding this does not contradict what MacIntyre says. MacIntyre explicitly subscribes to

170   this phenomenological point of view when he holds as indispensable to our understanding of trust Løgstrup's thesis that trust and openness are primary, distrust and suspicion secondary.

At first glance, MacIntyre's objections seem familiar. Objections to the phenomenological analysis of trust from academic or everyday psychology followed in the wake of *The Ethical Demand*, and Løgstrup dealt with them in a collection of essays entitled *Kunst og etik* (Art and Ethics), as well as other writings (see R, 2–8). However, in looking more closely at MacIntyre's criticism, it becomes apparent that he is heading in another direction than the usual criticism. MacIntyre is using psychology not to challenge the foundational relationship between trust and distrust, but to challenge Løgstrup's assertion that reasons cannot be given for trust. For some reason or another, Løgstrup has dismissed reasonableness and teleology from his description of the sovereign expressions of life. This is the problem. MacIntyre has seized upon an issue that is crucial, not only from his own point of view, but from Løgstrup's point of view as well. So the question is, why did Løgstrup persistently oppose every attempt to mix sovereign expressions of life and teleology?

A puzzling, but nevertheless important, distinction in Løgstrup is between sovereign expressions of life and actions. Sovereign expressions of life express themselves in actions, but they are not the same as actions. Let us consider the following example taken from one of Woody Allen's many fascinating movies, *Manhattan*. In the opening scene we are introduced to four of the principal characters dining at a crowded restaurant. The meal is just coming to an end, and the friends are chatting, none too seriously, in an amicable, comfortable atmosphere. Then Allen suddenly says: "The important thing in life is courage. . . ." And he continues, "Listen to this example. If the four of us were walking home over the bridge and there was a person drowning in the water, would we have the nerve, would one of us have the nerve to dive into the icy water to save the person that is drowning?" Then he quickly adds, "I can't swim so I never have to face it."

Let us imagine that I am walking with Woody Allen over the bridge. Suddenly we realize someone is drowning in the river. We both have to choose what to do. Allen will not jump into the water because he cannot swim, so merely jumping into the water would be a very silly thing to do. But I am a good swimmer, so I jump into the water while Allen—I hope—runs for a lifeline. Both actions are reasonable, and if asked, both of us would be able to give good reasons for acting as we did. We might even have to state our case and defend our actions if someone later asked the question, Why did you do that? I jumped because I am a good swimmer. Allen ran for a lifeline because he actually noticed a lifeline mounted on the railing a little further on.

In this imaginary example, Allen and I acted spontaneously, but this does not prevent us from giving very good reasons for doing precisely what we did, and Løgstrup would not have dreamed of denying us the right to give reasons for our actions. However, there are two things he persistently would have denied us the right to do. First, he would not have accepted a reference to the sovereign expressions of life as the reason for our actions. If I were challenged to defend or explain my action, I could not say that I jumped into the water because I was merciful. Why would that be unacceptable? Partly because referring to mercy as a sovereign expression of life is no answer. Allen was merciful too, yet he did not jump, so mercy does not explain my action. More importantly, however, Løgstrup would have opposed a reference to mercy as a reason simply because mercy itself points to the person needing help as the reason for action (SEL, 77–78; SGCN, 85). The paradox is that if jumping into the water was a merciful action, mercy was not a reason for jumping. I jumped because the person was drowning and I am a good swimmer. If I explained or defended my action by referring to myself as being so merciful, then the person asking would rightly suspect me of being more self-absorbed than merciful.

But suppose the person asking is puzzled by the merciful nature of my action and follows up his first question by asking, Why be merciful? I could, of course, explain the necessity of mercy in human relationships and even quote Løgstrup by saying that if mercy disappears from our lives, life collapses. But I cannot state the reason for merciful actions by referring to something other than the person in need of mercy. This is the second thing Løgstrup would have refused to let me do. If I explain that I wanted to act in mercy because mercy sustains society, or because next time I myself may be the one in need of mercy, then mercy is turned into something else. Mercy may be very useful to society and to me personally, but if I turn this usefulness into a reason for performing merciful acts, then mercy as a sovereign expression of life is destroyed. Incidentally, turned the other way around, this is the reason why I am able to act in accordance with mercy without being merciful. But that is another story.

What is the difference between sovereign expressions of life and actions in the light of this example? The difference lies in the shape and the form. The sovereign expressions of life have to be shaped. They are unconditioned, but their shape is conditioned by the situation. The sovereign expressions of life do not belong to me, but shaping them is up to me (Løgstrup 1995, 90). I have to answer for their shape; I have to answer for the things I do or fail to do. Acting in a particular situation, I have to choose between different possibilities, and I must be prepared to defend my choice if necessary. And my choice depends, albeit not entirely, on how virtuous I am. I agree with MacIntyre on this point. If I jump into the icy water to save someone from drowning, some kind of courage is required, although I would add that my spontaneous choice in this situation also depends on conventional morality. My spontaneous act is prefigured by the society I live in. The easiest way to recognize this is to look at Allen. He ran for a lifeline, and this was possible and reasonable because someone had prefigured this act and mounted a lifeline on the railing. I, for my part, was able to jump only because someone had taught me how to swim, and how to save a person from drowning. We both acted spontaneously without much deliberation, because we acted according to a prefigured morality, established by convention.

This distinction between sovereign expressions of life and actions is a crucial point in Løgstrup's thinking. In examining Løgstrup's sovereign expressions of life, MacIntyre concludes that several distinctive features of the virtues are missing, such as reason-giving, teleology, and even development. And he is right: these traits are actually missing, but that is because they belong to the shape that we give the sovereign expressions of life. They are distinctive features of actions, not of sovereign expressions of life—which means, however, that when we act there is no such thing as "pure" sovereign expressions of life. This, I think, is a consequence that we tend to ignore in our reading of Løgstrup, and I admit that Løgstrup was not always crystal-clear on this point himself. It is not difficult to find passages where he gives the impression that acts of mercy or of trust and confidence are "pure" sovereign expressions of life. I nevertheless think this is a misreading, or a misunderstanding. Sovereign expressions of life can be recognized only when they are executed and shaped in actions, and then they are shaped and conditioned by the situation. If we wish to "see" them stripped of the different shapes we give them, then we have to carry out a phenomenological analysis.

But is acting spontaneously not *the* ideal from Løgstrup's point of view, and is a spontaneous action not a kind of "pure" sovereign expression of life, so to speak? I do not believe it is. Actions are always shaped, conditioned by the situation, or to put it more precisely, conditioned by the doer. There is no exception. On the other hand, this does not prevent me from acting spontaneously in the sense that I am acting without any mental reservations or ulterior motives. Jumping into the water to save someone's life is spontaneous in this sense of the word, but it is not a "pure" sovereign expression of life.

We tend to stress spontaneity too much. Spontaneity is not the main point here. MacIntyre argues against Løgstrup by saying that some of us, or all of us, are occasionally able to do bad things spontaneously, and I think he is right. Moreover, I think Løgstrup would have agreed. Yet that does not make bad things into sovereign expressions of life. *Sovereign* is the important word, which is why Løgstrup often used the word "sovereign" instead of "spontaneous," and why I consider *sovereign* expressions of life to be a much better rendering of Løgstrup's idea than *spontaneous* expressions of life.

Although there is no such thing as a "pure" sovereign expression of life, this does not mean that we cannot act in accordance with the sovereign expressions of life and thus accomplish or fulfil a sovereign expression of life. Of course we can. Of course we can act out of mercy and do a merciful act, which makes it is easy to mistake such an action for a "pure" sovereign expression of life—but precisely for this reason we must bear the difference in mind if we are to understand our own actions.

But if actions are never "pure" sovereign expressions of life, then why speak of sovereign expressions of life at all? Is this not an unnecessary doubling? Are sovereign expressions of life not just a figment of the imagination, or a ghost in the machine? This would be the positivist point of view, but Løgstrup did not accept positivism. He insisted on the

174   importance of ontology as a presupposition for the understanding of ethics, and sovereign expressions of life primarily have to do with ontology in a Heideggerian sense of the word. They belong to a fundamental and constitutive definition of being, to use Løgstrup's own definition of ontology (Løgstrup 1997, 171 n. 2).

One way of putting this is to say that sovereign expressions of life are present in, with, and under the kind of actions we are dealing with here. And it is not by accident that this way of phrasing the relation leans heavily on Luther's wordings when he explains how Christ can be present in the elements of the sacrament.

As an ethicist Løgstrup did not deny the importance of reason-giving or personal growth and development, but he found it of greater importance to draw attention to realities beneath our reason-giving and personal development. Ontology occupied his mind even when he was doing ethics. He searched for the basic conditions of life prior to cultivation. His provocative assertion or idea was that sovereign expressions of life are prior to both our actions and our virtues. Our entire activity and our responsibility as moral beings are rooted in ontological presuppositions that we are unable to change by our actions. Because he was so preoccupied with this idea, Løgstrup neglected the virtues of virtue ethics, and that is why he did not draw a sharp distinction between virtues and character traits. This distinction is less important when the ontological basis for our actions is at stake. And because of Løgstrup's ontological concern, contrary to MacIntyre, the concept of natural law may fit very well into the thinking of Løgstrup, albeit in a different way than that of Aquinas.

Sovereign expressions of life are unconditional, unchangeable, and impossible to rationalize, whereas actions are by necessity conditioned, changeable, and open to rationalization. Sometimes we must suppress the sovereign expressions of life, and sometimes we must fulfil them through action. It all depends on the situation. Sovereign expressions of life are not virtues, either, but when shaping sovereign expressions of life into actions, virtues are of great importance. Since Løgstrup paid little attention to virtues from this point of view, it would be a significant step in the right direction to pursue and develop Løgstrup's thoughts by attempting to incorporate some key perspectives presented in the virtue ethics of Alasdair MacIntyre.

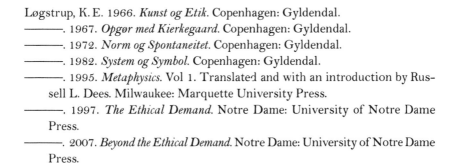

REFERENCES 175

Løgstrup, K. E. 1966. *Kunst og Etik.* Copenhagen: Gyldendal.

———. 1967. *Opgør med Kierkegaard.* Copenhagen: Gyldendal.

———. 1972. *Norm og Spontaneitet.* Copenhagen: Gyldendal.

———. 1982. *System og Symbol.* Copenhagen: Gyldendal.

———. 1995. *Metaphysics.* Vol 1. Translated and with an introduction by Russell L. Dees. Milwaukee: Marquette University Press.

———. 1997. *The Ethical Demand.* Notre Dame: University of Notre Dame Press.

———. 2007. *Beyond the Ethical Demand.* Notre Dame: University of Notre Dame Press.

CHAPTER TEN

Donum or Datum?

K. E. Løgstrup's Religious Account of the Gift of Life

Hans S. Reinders

Man's relationship with the other is *better* as difference than as unity: sociality is better than fusion. The very value of love is the impossibility of reducing the other to myself, of coinciding into sameness. From an ethical perspective, two have a better time than one (*on s'amuse mieux a deux!*).

—Emmanuel Lévinas

K. E. Løgstrup's reflections on ethics proceed from what he regarded as "the foundational relation," which is that human beings live together on the basis of trust rather than distrust.[1] There is, in Løgstrup, a strong protest against philosophical attempts to ground morality in a conception of ourselves as sovereign beings who exist prior to their relationships with others. With his "foundational relation," Løgstrup opposes the tradition of ethical naturalism as it appears, for example, in the work of Hobbes and Hume. These philosophers regard morality as a social institution created to overcome problems of social cohesion. In their philosophies, people are rationally compelled to accept moral obligations in order to counteract the condition of mutual fear (Hobbes) or of limited sympathy (Hume).

Løgstrup opposes such views and the moral culture they have produced. Again and again he points out that we can only maintain the illusion of being sovereign individuals by forgetting that not mistrust but trust is the condition from which morality proceeds.[2] We have received our lives as a gift, and that is the reason we accept moral responsibility for others who put their lives in our hands.

This reasoning explains why the notion of life as a gift lies at the heart of Løgstrup's reflections. He develops this notion in *The Ethical Demand*, where he takes as his point of departure what he calls "the proclamation of Jesus of Nazareth" as it is found in the New Testament (Løgstrup 1997, 1). But his using this point of departure does not mean that he intends to offer an account of Christian ethics. Instead, Løgstrup presents the book as a philosophical reading of the ethical content of that proclamation. From the very first page Løgstrup makes it quite clear that he wants to interpret its message "in strictly human terms." This holds true for the notion of "the gift of life" as well. Even though the message of the gospel was historically proclaimed by Jesus of Nazareth, its content is universal. We do not need the gospel to understand why the fact that we have received our lives as a gift constitutes the foundational relation of morality.

However, this notion of the gift of life turns out to be questionable for precisely those authors who did a great deal to reintroduce Løgstrup's work in Anglo-Saxon moral philosophy, namely, Alasdair MacIntyre and, especially, Zygmunt Bauman. Bauman develops his own views on postmodern ethics on the basis of what he learned from both Løgstrup and Lévinas, which is that moral responsibility for the other is unconditional. In Bauman's view, gift language in Løgstrup's account is to be rejected because it is a residue of what Løgstrup was trying to get away from, which is the idea that moral responsibility is grounded in reciprocity (Bauman 1993, 57; 1995, 61–62). Gift-giving presupposes a social system of mutual expectations that is regulated by social rules of appropriate giving as well as receiving. Appropriate gifts, such as giving each his due, require appropriate responses. Consequently, gift-giving reinforces relationships of reciprocal exchange. To take the notion of the gift of life as fundamental, one therefore necessarily ties moral responsibility to the framework of conventional morality. This cannot be the source of the ethical demand, in Bauman's view, because as such it would undermine the primordial character of the demand as one-sided and unconditional. Since, for Løgstrup, reciprocity was the key to the conception of conventional morality that he wanted to leave behind, his clinging to the notion of the gift of life indicated a limited understanding of his own project. In Bauman's view, Løgstrup is unclear about what he himself thought he was doing.

Another objection to the use of gift language in Løgstrup's writing is signaled by Fink and MacIntyre in their introduction to the second English edition of *The Ethical Demand*. With regard to his use of gift language, some commentators have accused Løgstrup "of *covertly* presuppos[ing] theological commitments derived from his faith" (Løgstrup 1997, xxxv, emphasis added). The objection is that gift language betrays a religious perspective, in spite of the fact that Løgstrup claims to offer a philosophical account of the primordial source of moral responsibility. At first sight Fink and MacIntyre only seem to flag a *possible* objection, which leaves undecided the issue of whether they themselves regard it as pertinent. However, they then indicate what, in their view, a defense of Løgstrup at this point would have to show, and it is this suggestion that effectively denies the possibility of gift language in the sense that Løgstrup uses it. When he maintains that no one can deny his or her life is a gift, Fink and MacIntyre say, it would have to be demonstrated "that his argument does not rely on what he says about life being a *gift* but merely on life being something *given* in the ordinary philosophical sense of being prior to and a precondition of all we may think and do" (Fink and MacIntyre, 1997, xxxv). The language of life as a gift, as distinct from the language of the given, must be abandoned, according to these authors, if Løgstrup's account of the ethical demand as non-theological is to be sustained. Several other critics of Løgstrup, whose ranks I intend to join in this contribution, have raised a similar objection (see R, section 6). They maintain that Løgstrup was much more of a Christian thinker in his ethics than he himself was prepared to acknowledge.

Both objections, as stated by Bauman and by Fink and MacIntyre, imply that Løgstrup had a limited understanding of his own project. In reverse order, these authors argue that in making gift language pivotal to that project, he was "covertly" building on theological commitment, even while that same language tied him to the framework of conventional morality that he rejected. By discussing a theological reading of his work, this essay is intended to shed more light on both of these objections.

In order to be clear about the nature of the discussion presented here, let me try to clarify my intentions as follows. There are at least three ways of commenting upon the relation of an author to his or her own work. The first is to present an account of what the author claimed to be doing, and why. Comments of this kind are, in effect, contributions to the history of philosophy. My comments, however, will not be of this kind, because my main interest is not in the question of what Løgstrup claimed he was doing. The second way is that of the "schoolmen." Their goal is to elaborate the thought of the original author into a "position" and then try to interpret his work such that it provides the strongest possible defense of that position. My comments on these pages will not be of this kind, either, for I do not belong to the Løgstrupian school, if there is such a thing. The typical question guiding academic debates of this sort is what the author would have said or should have said in order to avoid this or that misinterpretation, or to correct this or that mistake in his arguments. Instead, my comments will be of the third kind, which is to present a critical rereading of the author's work in order to see whether his philosophical account of the gift of life "in strictly human terms" is sustainable in any relevant sense. I believe the answer to this question to be negative. Løgstrup's account of the ethical demand is rooted in Christian belief, and this can be shown by looking at how he uses the notion of the gift of life. Therefore his account of the ethical demand "in strictly human terms" is implausible as a purely philosophical account.

To arrive at this conclusion I will discuss both of the objections to gift language set out above, beginning with that mentioned by Fink and MacIntyre, namely, that Løgstrup's use of gift language betrays a religious perspective. I think this objection is valid, but I fail to see that one can defend Løgstrup's view — *pace* Fink and MacIntyre — by switching from speaking of "a gift" to speaking of "the given" without seriously undermining that view. Second, I address Bauman's objection to gift language. In that connection I will argue not only that the notion of "the gift" is crucial to Løgstrup's ethical position, but also that this position can be adequately defended on theological grounds. In short, what I will argue is that Løgstrup's view of the ethical demand was committed to a religious perspective, regardless of whether he himself accepted this, and that it is highly implausible not to read Løgstrup as an author committed to Christian belief.

In his introduction to *The Ethical Demand*, Løgstrup defines what he takes his task to be: "to give a definition in strictly human terms of the relationship to the other person which is contained within the religious proclamation of Jesus of Nazareth" (Løgstrup 1997, 1). In reading what he says about this task, however, one notices a striking lack of clarity as to what the "proclamation" entails. Apparently, at this stage Løgstrup is interested only in making a formal point. He wants to establish the possibility of taking the moral content of Jesus' message as a starting point for his ethical reflections, without being dependent on the gospel for its justification.

To see how his argument works, let me focus my attention on two distinctions that he builds upon, although he does not make them explicit. My aim here is to see what, exactly, Løgstrup has in mind when he speaks of "the proclamation." Careful reading suggests that the answer to this question is more complex than it might seem at first glance. The first distinction is the one between the content of Jesus' proclamation, on the one hand, and the attitude towards the neighbor implicit in it, on the other (ibid., 3). Although that attitude is included in the religious content of the proclamation, it "should be susceptible of formulation in strictly human terms" (ibid.). The second distinction is the one between understanding and accepting the proclamation. It is one thing, Løgstrup tells us, to understand the proclamation's content as addressing "decisive features" of our existence; it is quite another thing to accept it. The one does not entail the other: "A proclamation may conceivably arouse us to an opposition so intense that we constantly seek to evade it, but this does not negate the fact of its understandability in this personal and objective sense" (ibid., 2).

With regard to the first distinction, Løgstrup is attempting to say that the particularly Christian content of the proclamation concerns Jesus' message of God's forgiveness for our sins. This message is something that "no human being could have foreseen." Therefore it can have "no relation to philosophy" (R, 13). The human mind could not have discovered it, being guided only by the light of its own powers. However, this does not include the issue that the message is concerned with, namely, our attitude towards our neighbor. Its "object," so to speak, is a

182   concern of human existence that we can speak of independently of the message itself. Whereas the content of the message is Christian and therefore particular, its object is human and therefore universal. Consequently, the relation to the neighbor is a concern that we can understand without being dependent on the message itself. Thus, we can ask: "What attitude to the neighbor is implicit in it? What does it conceive to be the essential thing in our life with and against each other and how can that be stated in strictly human terms?" (Løgstrup 1997, 3).

The image emerging from this distinction is that of a theatre stage on which a certain dramatic scene is put in a spotlight. The spotlight is the religious message of the gospel, which is about forgiveness. The scene that it highlights is our attitude towards our neighbor. Plausible though it may seem, however, the situation is more complicated than it initially looks at first sight. Why should our attitude towards our neighbor be the scene highlighted by the message of God's *forgiveness?*

The point to which I want to draw attention in view of this question is how Løgstrup introduces the proclamation in *The Ethical Demand*. If it is to have any relevance for us, he says, it must answer to something in our existence, but it must also address something not yet understood. Otherwise the notion of a "proclamation" would not make sense. So what it addresses—the author suggests—is a problem: "a perplexity in which we find ourselves, an inescapable contradiction, a fate we refuse to accept" (ibid., 1). Løgstrup speaks as if he is introducing the concept of a proclamation in a general way, but I do not think it is accidental that he explains it as revealing a serious problem in human existence. What strikes me in his account is that the proclamation does not straightforwardly give us the moral law enveloped in a religious message. The proclamation is repeatedly said to "answer to" the feature of our existence that it reveals. Apparently, there is a question to be addressed.

What, then, is this feature of our existence? What, exactly, does Løgstrup have in mind when speaking about the proclamation that confronts us with perplexity and contradiction in our lives? To be sure, it is implausible that he should have in mind the message of God's forgiveness per se. With regard to this message Løgstrup would never have said that once we have understood it, we can do without it (ibid., 1). But it is also implausible that he would have in mind the moral law per se, for as a moral teaching the law itself does not confront us with a perplexity.

Moreover, we did not need the proclamation to instruct us morally about our relation to our neighbor. Jesus never claimed to bring a new law, nor was the demand to love the neighbor a new law. Quite the contrary—a fact of which Løgstrup is well aware when he states that Jesus' proclamation regards the intimate connection between the "two great commandments in the law" (ibid., 5).[3]

It is curious to notice, then, that in his introduction Løgstrup does not make explicit what he has in mind when speaking of the proclamation, and so we are obliged to make an assumption. My assumption is derived from the fact that in his "Rejoinder," Løgstrup explains the proclamation's religious content as the message of God's forgiveness in relation to the moral law. What he has in mind, I assume, is the fact that the proclamation puts the finger on the problem of our ambiguous response to the moral law. As humans we revolt against the demand that we take responsibility for our neighbor.[4] We do so even when we know that the demand is grounded in a fundamental feature of human existence, which Løgstrup explains by reference to Luther's expression that we are "daily bread" in the life of one another (Løgstrup 1997, 5). The "religious" message of Jesus that we could not possibly have foreseen is concerned with God's forgiveness for our failure to respond to this fundamental feature of our existence. The feature that the proclamation "answers to," then, is the "perplexity" that the moral law confronts us with, namely, that we do not do what we know we should do. Løgstrup has in mind the classical Lutheran distinction between two different functions of the law: the first is to teach us of our failure to obey God's command, the second is the moral content of that command. The particularly Christian aspect relates to the first meaning, but with regard to the second—what our relation to our neighbor ought to be—Løgstrup wants to maintain that this can be explained "in strictly human terms." In other words, in speaking of the proclamation that can be discarded once it is understood, Løgstrup has in mind the fundamental experience that the moral law teaches us not only how we should live with our neighbor, but also of our failure to do so. Løgstrup was, after all, a Lutheran theologian.[5]

The second distinction to which I want to draw attention is the one between understanding and accepting the proclamation. This distinction also reveals an ambiguity. Løgstrup indicates several times that understanding the proclamation "as answering to decisive features of our

184   existence" does not exclude the possibility of rejecting it. We may, in fact,
oppose it intensely. However, this does not "negate" the fact of its understandability. Here, again, the question is what the author has in mind. The
simple answer would be to say that people may reject the gospel of God's
forgiveness and still accept the truth about our attitude towards the neighbor that it entails. People often make this kind of distinction: "they reject
Christianity out of hand because it is a religion" while at the same time
approving "the attitude to the neighbor which is set forth in and through
the religious proclamation" (ibid., 3). When people reject the message
of God's forgiveness, it is, presumably, because they reject that there is a
problem with our attitude towards our neighbor, which is rightly seen as
"sin." What they reject is "sin" and "grace," but what they understand and
recognize is human nature. That is to say, they recognize our ambiguous
attitude towards our neighbor and towards what the moral law demands.
The more complex answer is, then, that people may understand and accept the perplexity that the moral law confronts us with, but they reject
the Christian interpretation of it in terms of their sinfulness.

What these considerations help to show is that the proclamation
of Jesus that Løgstrup wants to bring to his ethical reflections is not
simply a secular version of the moral law that states that we should love
our neighbor. If that is what he had in mind, he could have done without the notion of a proclamation. The actual content of the proclamation
is more complex than that. It not only regards the ethical demand as responding to a fundamental feature of our existence, but also regards it
as a fundamental problem.

THE ETHICAL DEMAND

The ethical demand that we should love our neighbor is a problem because of our ambiguous response to it. In the introduction to *The Ethical
Demand*, Løgstrup touches upon this ambiguity only indirectly, as when
he asks, for example, what the proclamation regards as essential in our
life "with and *against* each other" (Løgstrup 1997, 3, emphasis added).
The ambiguity also appears, as indicated, in the way he introduces the
proclamation as revealing a perplexity. It is only later in *The Ethical
Demand*, when Løgstrup has explained the ethical demand as "radical,"
"one-sided," and "unfulfillable," that the problem it confronts us with as

human beings bears down with its full weight. Therefore, in this section I follow the various stages of his argument, and then come back to what I take to be the implications for his argument of the ambiguous response to the ethical demand.

The primordial fact out of which the ethical demand arises is the fact of basic trust. Explaining this is the first stage of Løgstrup's argument. Human beings would not be able to exist in the world without trusting one another. When approaching another person, we present ourselves to be accepted by the other for something we want or need. "In expecting something of the other person we undertake an action which amounts to a delivering of ourselves over into his hand" (ibid., 17). To address others is to give them some degree of control over me. They have to make up their mind about what I ask or say. How they will respond is beyond my control. In my encounter with other people, I am therefore giving myself partly over into their power, which requires a basic trust. Yet there is no decision on my part to do so. The reality of basic trust is not something we can profess or deny, because it speaks from everything we do as human beings. In this sense trust is the main characteristic of the foundational relation with the other person from which the ethical demand arises.

As already indicated, the phenomenon of trust as Løgstrup describes it is intended as a critique of moral atomism, a philosophy that explains morality as a system of rules intended to regulate accidental collisions between independent and sovereign subjects:

> We have the curious idea that a person constitutes his own world, and that the rest of us have no part in it but only touch upon it now and then. If the encounter between persons therefore means, as it normally does, nothing more than that respective worlds touch upon each other and then continue unaffected on their separate courses, the encounter can hardly be very important. According to this reasoning, it is only when a person accidentally breaks into another person's world with good or bad intentions that anything important is at stake.
>
> This is really a curious idea, an idea no less curious because we take it for granted. The fact is, however, that it is completely wrong because we do indeed constitute one another's world and destiny. (Ibid., 16)

186   According to Løgstrup, mutual dependency constitutes the very fabric of our moral world. However, to reject the ontology of moral atomism and to assert the primacy of trust is not to deny that power is part of human exchanges and relationships. Being in the hands of another person is a precarious situation, which explains why human encounters are couched in moral language (ibid., 11). In view of the risk of being rejected or denied, we seek "insurance" through moral claims. However, this is not the moral life that the proclamation of Jesus of Nazareth envisions. The ethical demand, as Løgstrup describes it, is radical and one-sided: it addresses me in the approach of the other person who delivers himself or herself into my hands. In the very act of that person in which he or she approaches me with a question or a need, the demand manifests itself:

> Through the trust which a person either shows or asks of another person he or she surrenders something of his or her life to that person. *Therefore*, our existence demands of us that we protect the life of the person who has placed his or her trust in us. (Ibid., 17, emphasis added)

As it happens, some of Løgstrup's critics have objected to this "therefore" because it links the fact of basic trust with a moral "ought" that is supposed to follow immediately. Løgstrup himself responded to this objection by saying that phenomenologically the fact-value distinction is not a very relevant one (R, section 2).[6] It presupposes a scientific reduction of "fact" to "data," meaning things we describe and theorize about. But the ethical demand corresponds to a fact of the "world in which we live enterprisingly and emotionally" (R, 9). He writes, "It is therefore impossible in a given situation to recognize that the other person's life has been surrendered to one without taking a position in respect of that circumstance" (R, 8). As it turns out, however, Løgstrup is careful not to imply that with the recognition of the demand, the response, too, is given:

> The demand arises directly out of the fact. Whether we wish to or not, we heed or disregard the demand of taking care of the other person's life, simply because both he and I live through enterprise and

emotion, and not just through cognition. Therefore there is no problem in finding out how a demand arises out of a fact. It happens of
its own accord and is, simply, unavoidable. (R, 8)

The "ought" following from the fact that the other person delivers himself
or herself into my hands is phenomenologically given, but my recognition
of this "ought" does not determine my response. I may heed it or discard
it. I may accept my responsibility for the other, or I may turn away.

> When the demand is despised, the fact on which it rests comes to
> mean that the other person is subjected to my self-assertion and to
> my desire to promote myself. The radical demand gives no protec-
> tion against this sort of thing, since through our disobedience to it
> we render it impotent. (Løgstrup 1997, 54)

The demand does not simply reflect our inclinations. Responding to it
does not come naturally.[7] So, even when the demand arises immediately
from an undeniable fact, that does not in itself assure a positive response.

At a later stage of his argument in *The Ethical Demand*, however,
Løgstrup gives a more complicated account of the demand. Important
for the present argument is the fact that he declares the demand to consist of two elements rather than one, namely, the fact of basic trust *and*
the belief that life is a gift (ibid., 123). I am particularly interested in this
second element, the element of belief. Both elements, Løgstrup tells us,
are necessary in order to account for the one-sidedness of the demand.
Before turning to this subsequent stage of his argument, let us first try
and discern why Løgstrup needs both these elements in his account.

As has been indicated already, we often act so as to protect ourselves
against the other person. Løgstrup regards this resentful attitude towards
the demand as resulting from the Kantian influence on our moral culture (ibid., 23). In our culture we are not primarily supposed to take responsibility for the other person, but we are supposed to respect his or
her autonomy. Apparently, we often regard ourselves in relation to the
other in quite a different way than that which the fact of basic trust suggests. Awareness of the fact that we "constitute one another's world and
destiny" is a "highly disquieting" phenomenon (ibid., 16). It is better for
our peace of mind not to be too much aware of the extent to which our

188   actions actually determine "other people's joy or pain in living" (ibid.). The radicality of the ethical demand is disturbing.

This radicality, Løgstrup goes on to say, implies that the demand can only be fulfilled unselfishly (ibid., 44). It requires that I act for the sake of the other person rather than for my own sake. It asks that I take care of the other person's life, not only when this is expedient, "but also when it is very unpleasant, because it intrudes disturbingly into my own existence" (ibid., 45). Responding to the demand cannot be a matter of prudence. The demand is not grounded in a mutual agreement within which one good turn deserves another. The demand is "one-sided" and "unconditional" (ibid., 46), which rules out that how we respond is measured by what we get in return from the other person.

At this point Løgstrup anticipates resistance. The one-sidedness of the demand will evoke protest.

> In his own way each one of us protests vigorously against the demand. We defend ourselves by arguing: There certainly should be a limit to what is demanded of me! I too have my rights! Why must I set aside all personal considerations, even very modest ones, out of consideration for someone who has nothing whatever to do with me and, strictly speaking, does not even belong to the world that I have made my own? (Ibid., 115)

In other words, the one-sidedness of the demand is challenged in the name of reciprocity. The fact of being delivered into the hands of another applies mutually to both of us, to the other and to myself. We therefore often attempt to "play it safe," which is why conventional morality puts such a high premium on reciprocity.

But if responding to the demand is not grounded in reciprocity, if it is neither a matter of inclination nor of acting out of prudence, where does its normative force come from? Why should we accept the claim it imposes upon us?

It is at this point that Løgstrup adds a further element to his explanation of the demand, namely, a "particular understanding of life" (ibid., 116). The ethical demand, he says, does not receive its content solely from the fact of the person-to-person relationship. That fact can be demonstrated empirically, but the second element—the understanding of life—is quite different. It is the belief that a person's life is "an ongoing gift" (ibid., 123). This belief cannot be justified in the same way as the first element: "That life has been given to us is something that cannot be demonstrated empirically; *it can only be accepted in faith*—or else denied" (ibid., emphasis added). By acknowledging the gift of life, one understands that there is no basis for claiming that one's response to the demand deserves to be reciprocated, "so that we will never be in a position to demand in return for what we do" (ibid.). Believing that one's life has been given, one accepts being under an obligation not to demand anything for oneself in return.

THE ELEMENT OF FAITH

What can we make of this appeal to an element of faith? More precisely, what can we make of it given Løgstrup's claim that his account of the ethical demand does not presuppose a religious point of view? Note in this connection that, earlier in his book, Løgstrup explicitly combines gift language with the language of creation: "Life has been given to us. We have not ourselves created it" (Løgstrup 1997, 19). The fact of basic trust with which one person approaches another is a "fact of creation" (ibid., 21). What does this language mean if not that the demand can only be adequately explained from a religious point of view? To pursue this question, we should look again at how Løgstrup responds to his critics.

The fact that the radicality and one-sidedness of the demand involve the understanding of one's life as a gift, says Løgstrup, "belongs to the human sphere" (R, 10). He concedes, however, that one can speak of this in terms of a belief, but if one does, it does not commit one to a particularly Christian belief: "If one calls it 'religiousness,' it is not a particularly Christian religiousness but a human one" (R, 10). I am not at all sure what to make of a "human religiousness," but Løgstrup appears to be serious about using the phrase.

> At all events, what I intended to say is that . . . "the religious truth that life is a gift" and my "religiously colored ontology," or . . . the questions of creation and of an absolute authority, do not belong within the realm of the particularly Christian, but within the realm of the human—they belong to a philosophical ethics. (R, 11)

190   In this connection Løgstrup admits that it was misleading in the introductory chapter of *The Ethical Demand* to distinguish between "human"
and "religious." Instead, he should have made the distinction between
"human" and "Christian" (R, 11).

Here is, then, a further concession regarding the second element in
the explanation of the demand. Understanding one's life as a gift is not
simply a matter of faith. It is also a matter of religious faith. One won-
ders, of course, what Løgstrup may have had in mind when he asserts
that "religious truth," "creation," and "absolute authority" are notions
that belong to philosophical ethics, but this remains obscure. Instead he
indicates that it would have taken "another decade" to elaborate the religious belief of life as a gift "phenomenologically" (R, 11).

Whatever he may have had in mind, however, there is clearly a remaining problem. Løgstrup claims that he could have shown that a religious perspective on life can be identified as a human perspective. But
what he needs to make his argument work is a claim that establishes the
connection the other way around. That is to say, what he needs to show is
why a human perspective must be identified as a religious perspective.
The demand depends on what he claims to be a religious belief. But why
assume that people who do not consider themselves to be religious accept this belief? How can belief in the notion of creation be warranted
without inferring the notion of a Creator? How can the religious belief in
the gift of life be warranted without referring to the notion of a Giver?
What Løgstrup needs to show is how a philosophical account of the belief in the gift of life might include these notions. I fail to see how that can
be done, unless one assumes that the philosophy one is talking about is a
religious philosophy that proceeds, right from the start, from a religious
perspective. But of course, that assumption renders Løgstrup's argument,
in its entirety, question-begging. At any rate, proceeding from a religious
perspective is not what philosophical ethics does.

THE GIVENNESS OF LIFE OR THE GIFT OF LIFE

Let us now turn to the objection voiced by Fink and MacIntyre, which
is that to avoid the charge of covertly presupposing theological commitments derived from his faith, Løgstrup would have to show that "the

gift of life" can be read in terms of the givenness of life. Thus interpreted, these authors assert, Løgstrup's claim would be that life is given in the ordinary sense of being a precondition of all we can possibly think and do.

My aim here is to show that if this were all there is to the language of the gift of life, it would seriously undermine some of Løgstrup's basic claims. For one thing, it does not seem to be true that "givenness" in this sense cannot be demonstrated empirically.[8] A few linguistic and sociological facts explaining how our thoughts and actions are dependent on preceding structures seem to be all that is needed for such demonstration. Similarly, if one were to take "givenness" to refer to the spontaneous expressions of life that appear in Løgstrup's later work, these expressions can also be accounted for without depending on a particular belief.

More important, however, is the fact that "givenness" in the philosophical sense seriously undermines Løgstrup's claim as to the one-sidedness of the demand. The mere givenness of our lives in no way warrants the claim that we are never in a position to demand anything in return for what we do, as he insists. When my life is given in the sense of being a precondition for my thinking and acting, it does not require any particular attitude or response on my part. The point at issue is Løgstrup's rejection of reciprocity.

The rejection of the claim to a reciprocal demand is grounded in Løgstrup's rejection of moral atomism. Moral atomism mistakenly assumes that when I engage in a relationship with the other by taking responsibility for his or her life, I have a rightful claim that this other person will do the same for me. This is a mistake, according to Løgstrup, because I am already part of such a relationship before I am aware of the fact. Taking responsibility for the other is not a matter of taking an initiative, but rather of *responding to* what I have already received. When, in the same connection, Løgstrup asserts that "[a] person is a debtor not because he or she has committed some wrong but simply because he or she exists and has received his or her life as a gift" (Løgstrup 1997, 116), this shows that indebtedness is not a matter of owing something to the other person. But at the same time being a debtor "simply because one exists" does not make much sense, at least not to the secular mind—or so I would argue. To be indebted is to be indebted to someone. So the question is: indebted to whom?

192   To suggest an answer to this question, let us consider the fact that, regarding the notion of indebtedness, Løgstrup brings back the thought of reciprocity once again, but now in a different guise. To explain, I invoke a similar discussion by Paul Ricoeur (Ricoeur 1989). Ricoeur proposes reading the meaning of Jesus' teaching of the so-called Golden Rule in terms of a new "economy of gift." The true meaning of that rule is not the conditional reciprocity of *do ut des.* Instead it teaches a consecutive reciprocity: "Give because you have been given."[9] Now, the interesting thing is that Løgstrup, in his later work, denies that the Golden Rule is a rule of reciprocity and claims that it is the equivalent of the radical demand.[10] This implies, I suggest, that reciprocity is suspect in Løgstrup's thought when read in the context of moral atomism, but this does not exclude the possibility of reading it differently. We are indebted for the gift of life we have received, which—as we have seen—Løgstrup can also state in terms of our createdness. This suggests that the notion of indebtedness that he invokes only makes sense if we assume that it refers to our indebtedness to our Creator. Why else would Løgstrup concede the religious nature of his gift language? Consequently, to neutralize the language of the gift and switch to *datum* instead of *donum*—from "gift" to "givenness"—is tantamount to losing the ground on which the one-sidedness of the demand can be defended. We have no debts towards "the given," which implies that the one-sidedness of the demand cannot be explained that way.

Let me add one further observation with regard to the question of indebtedness. The demand ordinarily does not address us, according to Løgstrup, in our relationships with those to whom we are most clearly indebted, namely our loved ones: parents, siblings, family, and friends. Those relationships, he explains, are governed by "natural love." These are the relationships in which the understanding of life as a gift is most evident. Natural love takes for granted the one-sided demand without the demand itself (Løgstrup 1997, 127). The demand does not address us in those relationships.

When, then, does the one-sided demand address us? When the other person whose life we are to care for is *not* a part of our own life which we have received—or, more correctly stated, *when we do not wish him or her to be a part of it.* It is when we regard him or her as something

entirely other than a gift because he or she is a bother and an incon-
venience to us. The demand that we nevertheless take care of his or
her life is therefore directed to us on the presupposition that our own
life has been given to us as a gift. . . . In other words, because we do
not want the other person to be a part of our life, the demand puts
our own understanding of life to the test. (Ibid., emphasis added)

So, the demand addresses me when a relationship arising out of natural
love does not exist and I regard the other as an intruder into my world.
But why should I consider myself to be a debtor in that situation unless
my debt is not at all dependent upon that situation? The simple fact that
the other person exists does not make me a "debtor" to that person any
more than the existence of numerous other people, at other times and in
other places, make me a debtor to them. The only reason why Løgstrup
can speak of our indebtedness in this unqualified sense is that he regards
all human beings as God's creatures. Only the belief that we all are God's
children explains why the many *different* relationships between ourselves
and others do nothing to qualify the demand. Upon this belief, there is no
reason that they should. Since we all stand in the same relation to our
Creator, the understanding of our life as a gift from God is sufficient to
acknowledge the demand to care for the other—any other.

THE UNSPOKENNESS OF THE DEMAND

The argument in the previous section was intended to show that down-
playing the importance of gift language in Løgstrup's argument undermines the claim as to the one-sidedness of the demand. Still, the argument
for the appropriateness of gift language may be taken one step further. As
we have seen, Løgstrup conceded that he presupposed a religious point of
view, but that is as far as the concession goes. He explicitly denies that this
religious point of view is a Christian point of view. But to understand
Løgstrup's account, it is highly implausible *not* to interpret the belief that
life is an ongoing gift in terms of the Christian religion, as I will attempt
to demonstrate.

To sustain this claim, I offer two further observations regarding Løgstrup's account of the ethical demand. To begin with, there is, of course,

the fact that in returning to the question of whether there is a Christian ethics, he explicitly identifies the demand as God's demand, adding that "because it is God's demand it speaks through . . . silence" (Løgstrup 1997, 109). It is not given in the form of moral rules or principles. It is not confined by the limits of reason:

> [I]f we place limits upon the demand so that its requirements of us may be within reason, we do so — as Christianity says — because we deny that life with all of its possibilities is a gift. What we do not owe God we do not owe our neighbor either. (Ibid.)[11]

The radicality of the demand implied in this statement bars us from diverting our attention from the need of the other person when asking ourselves what we ought to do. It bars us from exulting over our own words and deeds. What we do unselfishly for the other person is what counts. "The demand is intended to insure this because exultation is incompatible with gratitude." The demand has no limits derived from what we consider to be within reason, because "God demands only that which he himself gives" (ibid.). In other words, the reasonableness of ethical injunctions based upon mutual welfare implies a denial of the possibilities that we have received from God.

My second observation takes us back to the perplexity that Løgstrup spoke of with regard to the content of the proclamation of Jesus. Given all that has been said about the primordial fact of basic trust, this perplexity arises because, as Løgstrup insists, the demand cannot be fulfilled since our nature opposes it (ibid., 108, 115). It is not merely the case that the demand cannot be fulfilled because it defies articulation of what is required from us to care for the other person. Our very nature opposes it, which is the contradiction of our lives that is our guilt (ibid., 108, 207). Clearly, this is something that Christians may be expected to know. However, it escapes me how in this connection the notion of guilt can come to make sense in a philosophical manner, as Løgstrup wants it to. It does not seem to be a fact of human experience that people feel guilty for not being radically unselfish. On the contrary, experience with human nature suggests that we take the limited capacity for unselfishness seriously by grounding moral claims in what I referred to earlier as "conditional reciprocity." From the perspective of philosophical ethics, this notion of guilt does not seem at all plausible.

The real explanation here—as previously indicated—is that Løg-strup's thought proceeds from the Lutheran conception of sin. The first thing the moral law teaches us is our failure to fulfill it. His account can only be convincing for people who confess to believe in God the Creator, who is the same as the Father of Jesus Christ, who grants us forgiveness for our sins. Without such confession, guarding against the radical one-sidedness of the demand in the name of conditional reciprocity is a much more reasonable course to choose (ibid., 115). The claim regarding contradiction and guilt for not accepting the gift of life with its radical consequences can hardly be justified on the basis of philosophical reflection. As far as I can see, speaking strictly philosophically, that claim appears to be highly unreasonable.

THE ECONOMY OF GIFT-GIVING

The language of gift-giving in Løgstrup's account of the ethical demand presupposes the religious background of his thinking, even though he wants to present that account in strictly philosophical terms. In this section I will address a further objection to gift language that has been raised by Zygmunt Bauman. Bauman takes gift language to be a residue of the philosophical ethics of modernity that was the target of Løgstrup's criticisms. As we will see, Bauman's comments reflect a philosophical critique of gift-giving according to which a true gift is impossible because it cannot be disconnected from the logic of exchange.

This claim clearly undercuts Løgstrup's use of gift language as a means to oppose the view that morality is grounded in reciprocity. Moreover, it also undercuts Christian speech of God as the One who gives—speech that Løgstrup in fact invokes when he combines gift language with the language of creation. I will therefore ask what a response from Løg-strup's point of view might look like, turning in that connection to the notion of the spontaneous expressions of life that appears in his later work. My aim will be to suggest, once again, that a Christian reading of this notion in his work answers Bauman's objection.

Zygmunt Bauman deserves credit for having reintroduced Løgstrup's thought in the Anglo-Saxon world as a powerful source for the post-modern critique of modern moral philosophy.[12] Modern moral philosophy

196 has become obsolete because its attempt to control and replace moral impulse with "universal reason" has been discredited (Bauman 1993, 1–15; 1995, 10–43). Its basic endeavor was to set out universal reason as a beacon of hope for humankind in its battle against the backwardness of unenlightened cultures and societies. The aim was to liberate human beings everywhere from historical trappings and influences. That, according to Bauman, is how "the human individual" was born. Stripped of all its particularistic features, however, the human individual came to be subject to the only remaining legitimate power: that of the nation state. Cultural spaces of intimacy and togetherness were replaced by the legal realm of distance and estrangement. To counteract this development, Bauman wants to redeem the notion of a primordial "moral impulse" that modern moral philosophy declared suspect. To find that notion, he turns to Løgstrup's work, and particularly to his understanding of the ethical demand as radical, unspoken, and one-sided.

According to Bauman, Løgstrup's characterization of the demand points to the fact that moral responsibility is unconditional. In this respect the demand is radically different from conventional morality. Conventional morality falsely suggests a comfortable moral order sustainable by means of rule-following conduct. In contrast, the demand cannot be fulfilled by conforming to society's rules.

> The 'demand', unlike the comfortable precise order, is abominably vague, confused and confusing, indeed barely audible. It forces the moral self to be her own interpreter, and—as with all interpreters—remain forever unsure of the correctness of interpretation. However radical the interpretation, one can never be fully convinced that it matched the radicality of the demand. I have done this, but could I not do more? There is no convention, no rule to draw the boundary of my duty, to offer peace of mind in exchange for my consent never to trespass. (Bauman 1993, 80)

Rule-following conduct, according to Bauman, is a form of exchange within which my obedience is rewarded with esteem and peace of mind for being a respected member of society.

It is at this point that Bauman confronts the notion of "the gift of life." Justifying the demand in terms of the gift takes us back to conventional morality, because it puts reciprocity back at the center, thereby reiterating all the problems of modern moral philosophy (Bauman 1995, 61–62). Acknowledging life as a gift implies that we are indebted. "Gifts are expected to be reciprocated," Bauman argues (Bauman 1993, 57). Since reciprocity is what Løgstrup tells us he wants to get away from (Løgstrup 1997, 115–118, 124), he is caught in a contradiction (Bauman, ibid.). In justifying the demand in terms of the gift of life, Løgstrup implies that responding appropriately is a matter of recognizing our indebtedness as a way of returning the gift. Consequently, responding to the demand is grounded in the logic of reciprocal exchange.

Before we consider a potential response to Bauman's objection from Løgstrup's point of view, it is worthwhile to consider first how this objection reflects a skeptical view about gift-giving that seems endemic to our moral culture. Gift-giving has entered the world of "big business." Gifts have become a normal feature in business transactions to the effect that the production of appropriate gifts for business associates has itself turned into a profitable industry. At the same time, gifts given between relative strangers in the world of business risk being seen as bribes, which is why there is a demand for "codes of conduct" within that world. Gifts, in other words, are seen as eliciting the obligation to return them, which speaks against their nature as gifts. Next, there is the skepticism about gift-giving, as expressed particularly clearly in the rejection of charity. Charity has become suspect because it is seen as degrading. It makes people dependent on others to whom they owe a debt of gratitude. Hence the claim that charity must be replaced by justice. All these observations suggest that gift-giving *as such* has become suspect because gift-giving never seems to be what it suggests, namely, an act of pure generosity.

Gift-giving has recently been analyzed along these lines by Pierre Bourdieu and Jacques Derrida, among others.[13] In his *Outline of a Theory of Practice* Bourdieu argues that gift-giving is nothing but another part of economic production that fails to be recognized as such. It underwrites relationships of domination by prescribing rules for appropriate gratitude, courtesy, and civility between givers and receivers. Gift-giving, according to Bourdieu, is actually economic labor in disguise:

> In the work of reproducing established relations—through feasts, ceremonies, exchanges of gifts, visits or courtesies, and, above all,

198   marriages—which is no less vital to the existence of the group
than the reproduction of the economic base of existence, the labor
required to conceal the function of the exchanges is as important an
element as the labor needed to carry out the function. (Bourdieu
1977, 171)

In Bourdieu's view, gift-giving is a practice within which economic relationships governed by interest are dramatized in such a way that the
"overt domination" of economic power is "transmuted" into "socially
recognized domination" (ibid., 192).

In a sense, this apparently Marxist critique of gift-giving is but another example of sociological reductionism in that it attempts to unmask
a given social practice by showing that it is "really" the manifestation of
another underlying and, presumably, more basic practice. In this respect
Jacques Derrida's strategy of deconstruction of the gift is different. His
question is not what gift-giving conceals, but whether gift-giving is possible at all. According to Derrida, the notion of "a gift" is self-refuting.
The reason is that there is no gift *to begin with*. If what is given must be
returned, then gift-giving is enclosed in the circle of reciprocity. Given
this circle there must be a first gift for any gift to be possible. But a first
gift is only possible when it goes unrecognized as such. Hence the paradox that once the gift is recognized *as such*, it is no longer a gift.

> If the other gives me back or owes me or has to give me back what I
> give him or her, *there will not have been a gift*, whether the restitution
> is immediate or whether it is programmed by a complex circulation
> of a long-term deferral or difference. (Derrida 1992, 8, emphasis
> added)

Gift-giving is, inescapably, a form of exchange. According to Derrida,
the very fact that we are capable of "thinking" the gift marks a way of
receiving and returning it. By recognizing the gift as a gift we have already returned it in the sense of having identified the source from whence
it came as a giver. If there is to be a gift at all, there cannot be a debt, not
even the debt of recognition that one has received a gift. The purity of
gift-giving requires its absolute gratuity. Without it, giving is necessarily receiving. Hence the paradoxical conclusion: the gift cannot be re-

ceived as a gift. As Derrida puts it: "The simple identification of the gift seems to destroy it."[14]

Furthermore, as there can be no recognized gift to begin with, there can also be no purpose. If the gift is to have a purpose, it repays the giver. The gift cannot aim at doing something good for someone without immediately identifying the receiver as being the beneficiary of a benefactor, which, according to Derrida, abolishes the gift.[15] The very fact of identifying someone's act as a gift already rewards the giver with the knowledge that he or she is a giver.

What, then, is the difference between giving and exchanging? The difference, according to Derrida, is excess. True gift-giving knows no measure of propriety, neither with regard to what is given, when it is given, by whom, or to whom. The true gift is outrageously excessive (Webb 1996, 73). Accordingly, Derrida asks himself:

> What would a gift be in which I gave without wanting to give and without knowing that I am giving, without the explicit intention of giving, or even in spite of myself? This is the paradox in which we have been engaged from the beginning. (Derrida 1992, 123)

The consequence of the Derridian purification of the gift has been characterized by John Milbank as saying that if there were to be a pure gift, it would have to be "a gift without a donating subject, a receiving object, and no gift-object transferred" (Milbank 1995, 130). Milbank seeks to defend the possibility of the gift by denying that the true gift must be unilateral. However, one cannot respond effectively to Derrida's view by reiterating that gift-giving presupposes a preceding relationality, as Milbank seems to do.[16] That response appears as question-begging in the light of Bauman's objection that to argue on the basis of a gift relationship is to loose the unconditionality of the demand.

THE GOD WHO GIVES

What might a more effective response from Løgstrup's point of view look like? In this final section I can only offer some thoughts on how to answer this question. In this connection I will turn to the notion of the sovereign

200 expressions of life that appeared in Løgstrup's later work and ask how this notion is related to his understanding of the gift of life.[17]

It is clear that if there is to be any effective response to Derrida at all, we must assume that, in Løgstrup's understanding of the gift of life, the gift cannot be of the same kind as our gifts, the kinds of gifts that are recognized within sets of rules for appropriate giving. The gift of life cannot be explained by saying, for example, that we received our childhood from our parents, who went through all the trouble of raising us, that we received the opportunity of education from the community that provided us with schools, that we received our language and culture from our nation, and so on. The gift of life cannot be explained in this way, because to explain it in this way would be to underwrite both Bauman's and Derrida's views. If it were explained in such terms, the gift would dissolve into many different gifts given by many different agents, implying many different kinds of relationships, each of which would be tied to its own set of rules. We would be justified in concluding that we owe our lives to some people rather than to others, and that we therefore do not have the same moral relationship to all people. Consequently, to underscore the one-sided demand, the gift of life cannot be explained by differentiating between what we owe to whom. Løgstrup could not but agree that in understanding the gift of life we must save it from the link between gift-giving and social convention. It must be understood as something preceding social convention.

To explore this question, let us consider the possibility that here Løgstrup's notion of the sovereign expressions of life may provide a clue. In the background of this notion lies Løgstrup's lively interest in spontaneity which he inherited from the *Lebensphilosophie*, particularly in the form he learned it in his early years through the work of a Danish author, Vilhelm Grønbech.[18] Grønbech's ideal for the good life was "living immediately," which he characterized as "a life of giving." This ideal as a life of giving was further characterized as "giving unconditionally" and opposed to the life shaped by culture and morality. With regard to this ideal, it is striking how closely Løgstrup emulates this view. He distinguishes between "cultural life, which is purposive and methodical and calculating—and life itself, the life of the moment, which is forgiving and giving and merciful, in which there is, precisely, no purpose, no plan, no task, because it is not culture" (Løgstrup 1942, 103, quoted by Niekerk in this volume). This statement is striking because it has all the elements that Derrida lays out as necessary to disconnect gift-giving from social convention: "life itself," which is the "life of the moment," serves no calculated purpose, no plan, no task. For Løgstrup, "life itself" is "something definite, because it is created life" (ibid., 90). That is not just a mere phrase, as I will argue, because for Løgstrup "created life" signals the gratuitous generosity of God's gift that is creation. "Created life" as "life itself" is a manifestation that precedes all social convention.

In his later years Løgstrup develops the notion of the sovereign expressions of life to account for what he earlier called "life itself." These sovereign expressions are acts of mercy, of solidarity, and of fidelity—acts that are spontaneous in the sense of not being elicited by the recognition of moral duty. Furthermore, the sovereign expressions of life are not products of the will in the sense that they are not grounded in our self-governance. They are spontaneous expressions that present themselves to us in the given situation.[19] They are not willful decisions and do not respond to our command. In that sense they are not at our disposal.

The distinction between the sovereignty of the expressions and the will is important because it enables Løgstrup to indicate how moral life is possible despite the fallenness of human beings.[20] The sovereign expressions of life assert themselves. "Were that not so, we would not come off as well as we do in our common life. That we do so can only be because we live off something that we cannot credit to ourselves. The sovereign expressions of life are not the achievement of the will" (SEL, 67).

So here, again, the notion of creation crops up, albeit implicitly. The sovereign expressions are not tainted by conventional morality, because we do not possess them. This refers us back, I take it, to the gift of life. The possibility of "life itself" is grounded is God's gift of creation, which is gratuitous precisely because it is what God gives, not what He owes us. We have no claim to it.

The Christian way of arguing this point is, of course, to say that God remains faithful to His creation, regardless of the fact that human failure threatens to ruin it. The gratuity of divine generosity asserts itself through the sovereign expressions of life. God remains faithful to what He gives, regardless of what we do with it. Accordingly, Løgstrup argues that there are no limits to human selfishness, although there are limits to the devastation it is able to effect. These limits "are evidenced by our inability to prevent the sovereign expressions of life from forcing their way through and realizing themselves" (SEL, 69). I daresay it is no mere coincidence that immediately following this quote, Løgstrup talks of "the grace of existence." The grace of existence manifests God's undeserved trust in us, which is manifest in the sovereign expressions of mercy, fidelity, and human solidarity and kindness.

This account of Løgstrup's notion of the sovereign expressions may raise some doubts as to how the sovereignty of our createdness relates to our moral agency. The sovereign expressions reveal what creation offers, but we remain responsible for measured actualizations, given the reality of evil. We cannot act upon these actualizations, one may argue, in an unreflective manner.[21] Fair enough. But what Løgstrup is looking for at this stage is not reasons that justify action, but ontology. He wants to identify "the basic conditions of life prior to cultivation" (Christoffersen, in this volume). The sovereign expressions are unconditioned. As such they are not under our control, but they have to be shaped. As Christoffersen puts it, citing Løgstrup's *Metaphysics*: "The sovereign expressions do not belong to me, but shaping them is up to me." The expressions as such belong to created life.

I suggest, therefore, that if we read the notion of the sovereign expressions of life within a theological rather than an ethical frame of reference, then such a reading underwrites what Løgstrup has been saying all along about our lives as gifts. The sovereign expressions do not force themselves upon us, but in acting upon them we find ourselves as human beings. Of course it is true that the possibility of actualizing these expressions entails the possibility of not acting upon them. It is also true that there may be good reasons not to actualize these expressions, but if we do not, we can never deal with them by simply ignoring them. Sovereignty neither implies overpowering nor forecloses ethical reflection. I would like to suggest that it is, instead, a religious warrant for our hopes of the possibility of a tolerably humane world. The beacon of that hope lies not in morality but in the expressions of life.[22]

What I am suggesting, then, is the possibility of understanding Løgstrup's notion of the sovereign expressions of life as embodying the gift of life that God gives in creation. The gift of life consists not so much in the various gifts that we have received from various people—the kind of gifts that occur within conventional morality. Instead it consists in acts of mercy, of solidarity, of fidelity—the kind of sympathetic acts that human beings cannot prevent themselves from doing towards others, oftentimes regardless of who these others are. In the sovereign and spontaneous expressions of life we may recognize that "life" is a continuing possibility, even, or perhaps especially, at times when the world does not appear to be a very hospitable place.

It is my hope that these reflections indicate the direction in which the response to Derrida's and Bauman's critique of gift language might go from Løgstrup's point of view. They imply, ultimately, that this response must develop Løgstrup's theological presuppositions. For the gift to be a true gift, it can neither have a beginning nor an end, which for Derrida was sufficient reason to assume that a true gift is impossible. The divine gift of creation is such a gift, however, because its beginning does not establish a circle of reciprocity. God creates the world and brings it to life. But when His work is corrupted, He does not abandon it but restores it by sending His Son into the world to fulfill the demand. Giving is what God does in excess, in that He ultimately gives Himself in Christ.

Because God's gift does not establish a circle of reciprocity, it is also without end. Whether or not we respond does not determine His will to give, because God *is* what he does, which is giving. Note in this connection that the crucial notion in a Christian conception of the gift, namely the notion of grace, has no place in Derrida's account. In his view, the true gift must be both unilateral and indifferent. The nature of grace, however, is such that it transcends the opposition between interest and indifference. God is not indifferent to what happens with His gift, but the continuation of it—what theology knows as *creatio continua*—is not dependent upon that.

Finally, the true gift must be excessive, wasteful, without measure, and without plan or purpose, according to Derrida. Again, the gift of God transcends this dichotomy as well, because God's giving diminishes neither His richness nor His freedom. From Derrida's perspective, to give excessively is to squander without regard for limited resources, which is humanly impossible. This is not true for God, however, because He gives from abundance. Even when we give the utmost of what we have to give—which is our life—we can do so only once. In contrast, God's gift of Himself does not end life but recreates it.

I am aware, of course, that these reflections go far beyond what Løg-strup believed to be appropriate as a defense of his views on ethics. I do hope, however, that they lend some plausibility to the claim that his views are best explained and defended by taking the course I have pursued, even though Løgstrup would probably be the first to disagree. When his notion of the gift of life is read as the givenness of life, the radical nature of the one-sided demand is lost. That gift must be truly a gift. If there is to be that true gift, however—the gift that is unconditional, unspoken, radical, and one-sided—it must be God's gift.

NOTES

1. The term "foundational relation" is found in his response to critics published in *Beyond the Ethical Demand* (2007) as "Rejoinder."

2. Hans Fink and Alasdair MacIntyre, "Introduction" to Knud Ejler Løgstrup, *The Ethical Demand* (Løgstrup 1997), xxix.

3. This I take to be an implicit reference to the commandments as given by Moses in Lev. 19:18 and Deut. 6:5.

4. It is striking that in his Rejoinder, Løgstrup identifies the ethical demand with "the law" without further explanation (R, sections 3 and 8). This usage evokes the long-standing debate in German theology on "Gesetz und Evangelium" (law and gospel), which I think must have been in the back of his mind.

5. On the Lutheran background of Løgstrup's views on ethics, see Kees van Kooten Niekerk's essay "The Genesis of K. E. Løgstrup's View of Morality as a Substitute" in this volume.

6. Løgstrup already addressed this point in *The Ethical Demand* (Løgstrup 1997, 18 n. 6), however, by acknowledging that there is a gap between the fact and the demand. There he suggests that the intimate connection between the two follows from "man's creatureliness."

7. Later in *The Ethical Demand* Løgstrup argues quite strongly that the demand is unfulfillable given our human nature. "We disregard the silent, radical, and one-sided demand. It is resisted by our self-assertion and will to power, by our ceaseless concern about what we ourselves will get out of what we do. This resistance is so real that often our falling short of the demand is not so much a matter of our failing to live up to it as of our inability to live up to it except at the expense of our nature" (Løgstrup 1997, 164).

8. Here I refer to Løgstrup's claim that belief in the gift of life is a belief that cannot be empirically demonstrated (Løgstrup 1997, 123).

9. See my discussion in Reinders 1996.

10. Løgstrup writes: "The demand comes to expression in, for instance, the Golden Rule: Do unto others as you would have them do unto you. This is anything but a tepid rule of reciprocity, even if, taken literally, it might seem to be such. . . . Clearly, it is as radical as anything could be" (SGCN, 85–86).

11. Note that the last sentence, "What we do not owe God we do not owe our neighbor either," is an indirect confirmation that Løgstrup had in mind something similar to Ricoeur's explanation of the Golden Rule.

12. For Bauman's interpretation of modern moral philosophy (i.e. "ethics") and the importance of Løgstrup's work for attacking it, see his *Postmodern Ethics* (Bauman 1993) and *Life in Fragments: Essays in Postmodern Morality* (Bauman 1995).

13. For what follows I am very much indebted to Stephen H. Webb, *The Gifting God* (Webb 1996).

14. Derrida 1992, 14. That gift-giving must remain unnoticed in order not to be corrupted by the intention of receiving public esteem is a theme that occurs in the Gospel of Matthew, where Jesus teaches us that God will only reward alms-giving by revealing what has been given unnoticed (Mt 6:1–4). The teaching implies that when the motive of being rewarded corrupts the gift, then the motive of receiving a divine reward does so all the more. True generosity does not intend to oblige, and definitely not to oblige God.

15. See Derrida 1995: "On what condition does goodness exist beyond all calculation? On the condition that goodness forgets itself, that the movement be a movement of the gift that renounces itself, hence a movement of infinite love" (50–51).

16. Milbank 1995, 145. That the giver's interest in the gift should cancel the gift as such—as Derrida would have it—betrays a Kantian concern that makes the goodness of the gift dependent upon the purity of motivation.

17. Here I depend on what I learned from the essays of Anne Marie Pahuus and, especially, Svein Aage Christoffersen now included in this volume.

18. See the section on Vilhelm Grønbech in Niekerk's essay in this volume.

19. See Pahuus's essay in this volume.

20. As Niekerk points out in his essay in this volume, Løgstrup's view of morality in the book *Norm and Spontaneity*, where he develops the notion of the sovereign expressions of life, is more positive in contrast to *The Ethical Demand* because it leaves aside the problem of sin.

21. This concern is the main subject of MacIntyre's reading of Løgstrup's work from a Thomist point of view. See MacIntyre's essay in this volume.

22. When our will—in the sense of practical reason—takes over, the expressions are subdued by moral claims. This is why I take Niekerk's notion of "morality as a substitute" to be a very adequate phrase to characterize the drift of Løgstrup's ethical thinking.

206   REFERENCES

Bauman, Zygmunt. 1993. *Postmodern Ethics.* Oxford: Blackwell.

———. 1995. *Life in Fragments: Essays in Postmodern Morality.* Oxford: Blackwell.

Bourdieu, P. 1977. *Outline of a Theory of Practice.* Cambridge: Cambridge University Press.

Derrida, J. 1992. *Given Time.* Chicago: University of Chicago Press.

———. 1995. *The Gift of Death.* Chicago: University of Chicago Press.

Løgstrup, K. E. 1997. *The Ethical Demand.* Notre Dame: University of Notre Dame Press. [Danish original: *Den etiske fordring.* 1956. Copenhagen: Gyldendal.]

———. 2007. *Beyond the Ethical Demand.* Notre Dame: University of Notre Dame Press.

Milbank, John 1995. "Can a Gift Be Given?" In *Rethinking Metaphysics,* ed. L. Gregory Jones and Stephen E. Fowl, 119–161. Directions in Modern Theology. Oxford: Blackwell Publishers.

Reinders, Hans. 1996. "The Golden Rule between Philosophy and Theology." In *Ethics, Reason, and Rationality,* ed. Alberto Bondolfi, Stefan Grotefeld, and Rudi Neuberth, 145–168. Münster: LIT Verlag.

Ricoeur, Paul. 1989. "Entre Philosophie et Théologie: La Règle d'Or en question." *Revue d'Histoire et de Philosophie Religieuse* 69: 3–9.

Webb, Stephen H. 1996. *The Gifting God: A Trinitarian Ethics of Excess.* New York and Oxford: Oxford University Press.

CHAPTER ELEVEN

A Response to Hans Reinders's "Donum or Datum?"

Jakob Wolf

Hans Reinders makes three points in his essay in this volume:

1. K. E. Løgstrup's ethical views are grounded in a theological perspective to the effect that his philosophical argument does not work unless that perspective is adopted.
2. One cannot defend Løgstrup's view by replacing "the gift" with "the given," as Hans Fink and Alasdair MacIntyre suggest, without seriously undermining the force of Løgstrup's account.
3. Baumann's objection to gift language ignores the theological background of this language in Løgstrup's work. The notion of "gift" is crucial to Løgstrup's ethical position, and his position can be adequately defended only on theological grounds.

I will comment here on all three points. The first is *the* central point in Reinders's essay, and I discuss it at some length. Does Løgstrup's ethical view presuppose that one adopts a theological perspective? Reinders says it does. I, like Løgstrup, maintain that it does not.

Reinders claims that Løgstrup "was much more of a Christian thinker in his ethics than he himself was prepared to acknowledge." He bases his claim on Løgstrup's description of the ethical demand as dependent on the assumption that life is

208   a gift. This assumption, according to Reinders, is a theological assumption, not a philosophical one. Reinders, of course, is not the first to criticize Løgstrup on this point. Soon after the publication of *The Ethical Demand*, critics, such as Henrik Stangerup, objected to Løgstrup's statement that the one-sidedness of the demand is grounded in the belief that a person's life is an ongoing gift, which implies that we will never be in a position to demand anything in return for what we do. Stangerup, for instance, derided it as sermonizing of the worst and most commonplace kind.

Løgstrup initially responded to that criticism in his book *Kunst og etik* (Art and Ethics). There Løgstrup admitted that he had not sufficiently clarified the relationship between philosophy and theology in *The Ethical Demand* when speaking of life as a gift. The statement that life is a gift appears as a sheer assertion, and one that is not illuminated phenomenologically, like the assertion about interdependency. Løgstrup regrets this omission, observing as his only defense that "were the understanding of life presumed by the radicality of the demand to have been as phenomenologically well elaborated as the fact from which the demand gains its content, another decade would have passed before I could have published my book. The reason is that the phenomenological analyses required to do so are of an altogether different nature" (R, 11).

Løgstrup provided these analyses in his *Metafysik I–IV* (Metaphysics, 4 vols.).[1] Here we find Løgstrup's arguments that the statement "life is an ongoing gift" is a philosophical assertion rather than a theological one. These arguments are also the response to Reinders's criticism, and are very helpful in clearing up the question of Løgstrup's view of the relationship between philosophy and theology.

Løgstrup's view is that philosophy does not contrast with a religious interpretation of life and existence; it contrasts with the Christian gospel. A great deal of anti-metaphysical philosophy does, of course, contrast with a religious interpretation of life and existence, but Løgstrup criticizes this philosophy. It is wrong, he maintains, not for theological reasons but for philosophical reasons: it is bad philosophy. The difference between philosophy and theology lies in a difference in the grounding of one's assertions. Philosophical assertions are grounded in phenomenological descriptions, an argument everyone must concede whatever their other thoughts or beliefs. Theological assertions are grounded in the faith that God has revealed himself in Jesus of Nazareth. This means that specific theological assertions are convincing only to believers. Philosophical assertions come in many varieties, but they can include assertions such as "God exists," "the universe is created," "we are faced with a radical, unconditional ethical demand," "life is an ongoing gift," and "we are guilty." Examples of theological assertions are "God's forgiveness is unconditional" and "the coming of the Kingdom of God will bring the the resurrection of life and the elimination of evil and death."

Løgstrup is, in fact, traditionally Lutheran on this point—which does not mean, however, that he makes or presupposes any Lutheran confessions. He states in his rejoinder in *Kunst og etik*: "The law, or the ethical demand, is given with life as it happens to be. The gospel, the message of God's forgiveness, is given historically with Jesus of Nazareth. A confrontation cannot be arranged unless one has a common cause, and philosophy and theology have that with regard to the law and to creation, but not with regard to the gospel" (R, 13). He continues, in his own way, the Lutheran distinction between the law and the gospel.

It would also be fair to say that Løgstrup's distinction is parallel to Thomas Aquinas's distinction between natural theology and revealed theology. His disagreement with Thomas lies in the fact that Thomas regards natural theology as *rational* theology, whereas Løgstrup regards natural theology as *phenomenology*. A finite being such as man is not able to deduce God's existence from his experience of a finite world, but it is possible that God makes himself known in the finite phenomena of the world. For instance, an unconditional ethical demand is not the result of a deduction. Rather, it is a fact that meets us when we describe the phenomenon of life as an interdependent activity. The unconditionality of the demand means that it is without any immanent cause, just as the spontaneity of trust means that it is without any immanent cause. The phenomenon thereby becomes open to a religious interpretation. It is possible to see the phenomenon as a manifestation of transcendence. That is one possible interpretation, and, according to Løgstrup, it is a very good interpretation. The question is, can anyone provide a better one? Yet it is still not a proof; it is not a result of a rational deduction, as is, for instance, the cosmological proof of God by Thomas. Kant criticized Thomas on that point, and Løgstrup agrees with Kant in this respect. From a theological point of view, the ethical demand belongs within the sphere of the law and creation, which in turn belongs within the sphere of philosophy. It does not presuppose any faith in the revelation of God in Jesus of Nazareth.

But still, does the ethical demand not presuppose Christianity? In the final analysis, is the ethical demand not grounded in the teachings of Jesus of Nazareth? Løgstrup is not blind to the fact that there exists a relationship between living in a Christian tradition and recognizing the ethical demand. But what *is* this relationship? It is not one in which the ethical demand is grounded in the "proclamation" of Jesus of Nazareth, but rather one in which the recognition of the ethical demand is *inspired* by the teaching of Jesus of Nazareth. As Løgstrup says in *The Ethical Demand*, once this demand is proclaimed and out in the open, "we are then able to recognize it ourselves without recourse to the proclamation itself." The ethical demand is a universal fact that anyone may recognize. The Gentiles, too, know the law, as Paul says in his letter to the Romans. Jesus recognized the demand with exceptional clarity, but anyone might have done that. One could draw a parallel to such an event as Newton's discovery of the law of gravity. Anyone might have discovered this law, but Newton did so with exceptional skill. And now, after his discovery, any schoolboy or schoolgirl can easily recognize this law on their own. The same goes for the proclamation of Jesus where the ethical demand is concerned, though not where the coming of the Kingdom of God is concerned. No one is able to recognize the latter proclamation on their own, either before or after the proclamation of Jesus. The coming of the Kingdom of God is not a natural, recognizable fact. It is grounded in the faith that God has revealed himself in this proclamation of Jesus. It is not based on phenomenology, although it is not without a relationship to a phenomenologically based religious ontology. The ethical demand and creation constitute a horizon of understanding, a hermeneutical horizon, to the proclamation of the coming of the Kingdom of God. We are not able to recognize and understand this proclamation on our own, but we are able to recognize and understand that this proclamation is not an impossibility.

Now for Reinders's second point, which I treat briefly. I completely agree with Reinders: Fink and MacIntyre's suggestion that one can avoid the religious connotations in Løgstrup by replacing the concept of "the gift" with that of "the given" is futile. Løgstrup's language of gift-giving is open to a religious interpretation, which does not mean, however, that it presupposes theology. From Løgstrup's point of view, the idea that there are only two alternatives, nonreligious philosophy or revealed theology, is a fallacy. Religious philosophy—that is, phenomenological description and religious interpretation of phenomena—bridges philosophy and theology.

As for Reinders's third point concerning the rejection of gift language, Reinders argues that when Løgstrup tells us about the radical demand in connection with human nature, it becomes clear that the assertion about life being a gift presupposes Christianity. Løgstrup tells us that the demand cannot be fulfilled because our nature opposes it. We decline to respond to the radical demand for selfish reasons. Our very nature opposes it, which is the contradiction of our lives—therein lies our guilt. To Reinders, this way of reasoning presupposes the Christian or, more precisely, the Lutheran confession of human sinfulness. He argues, "It does not seem to be a fact of human experience that people feel guilty for not being radically unselfish. On the contrary, experience with human nature suggests that we take the limited capacity for unselfishness seriously by grounding moral claims in what I referred to earlier as 'conditional reciprocity.' From the perspective of philosophical ethics, this notion of guilt does not seem at all plausible."

Does this argument substantiate the conclusion that the assertions about life being a gift and human guilt are based on a Lutheran confession, rather than on philosophical grounds? I do not think so. I do not agree that it is not a fact of human experience that people feel guilty for not being radically unselfish. It certainly is a fact that many people feel no such guilt, but I do not believe it is true of all people. This feeling of guilt has been expressed by various writers, including poets. The Danish writer and Nobel Prize-winner Henrik Pontoppidan—who certainly made no Christian (let alone Lutheran) confessions, but on the contrary, made numerous anti-Christian and atheistic confessions—recognized that life is nothing but an ongoing gift and that therefore he was guilty. Furthermore, whether many, some, or no people feel guilty for not being radically unselfish, it may still be true that they are guilty. The assertion that life is a gift and that human nature seems to contradict the ethical demand is not based on what people feel. It is a phenomenologically based assertion, and phenomenology can reveal things that people are loath to recognize and try with all their might to suppress.

Since the phenomenology on which the assertion is based is not presented in *The Ethical Demand*, as mentioned above in my comments on Reinders's first point, I should present it here. Unfortunately, that task would exceed the limits of this response. I can, however, give the briefest possible outline of it. It is fairly easy to agree on the fact that we have not created the universe. This leaves us with two options: either the universe was created by chance, or it is a gift. Scientific theory holds that it was created by chance, which has to do with the definition of science. The project of science is to attribute immanent causes to everything. This project becomes precarious, however, when confronting the question of the cause of the universe as such. But this problem is conveniently solved by the notion of chance. Actually, this is not a solution but a way to avoid religious interpretation. From a phenomenological point of view, however, no one experiences life as a series of meaningless chance events. Everyone lives in the expectation that life will be generous. People may experience accidents, times when life seems meaningless or absurd chance, but we are only able to experience this feeling because we presuppose life to be a generous gift. Some might argue that chance, the accidental, reveals the truth about life: our expectations are illusions. But from a phenomenological perspective, this ranking is impossible. Phenomenologically, the expectation that life is generous is ontologically primary to all experiences that contradict this expectation. I shall go no further here, but simply refer to Løgstrup's *Metafysik*, in which Løgstrup elaborates this phenomenology with his usual profoundness.

If life is a gift in the sense that we expect it to be generous, and if it is generous (or even if it is not experienced as a gift, it is somehow primarily generous anyway), then we are guilty if we are not radically unselfish. Why? Because if life is a gift, a person cannot make any conditions and demand more gifts. One cannot demand anything from the other. One must be unselfish, because one cannot live together with other people without either giving and taking. A person never lives in isolation, but always lives in interdependency. It is a contradiction in terms to demand a gift. If anyone does that, they contradict life, and that is what Løgstrup means by being guilty. Consequently, since we are all inclined to demand something from others, to demand reciprocity, we are all guilty.

The circumstance that one cannot exhaustively discuss the notion of "the gift of life" in purely immanent terms does not prove that the notion is not philosophical. One could say, however, that this proves it is not a scientific notion, but that is already clear from the fact that it is a phenomenologically based notion. The phenomenological description of life as a gift is open to a religious interpretation. The gift of life is given to us by someone—whom we do not know. We are guilty in the face of someone—whom we do not know. God is not a revealed God; he is a hidden God in the philosophical recognition. The notions of "gift" and "guilt" exclude chance, but they do not presuppose a Christian confession.

Incidentally, it is not only the one-sidedness of the ethical demand that makes it open to a religious interpretation. The description of it as *silent* is also open to a religious interpretation. It is silent because it is not articulated—either in the claims of the other or in social norms and duties. The demand is silent. Silence refers to someone who is able to speak, but who refrains from doing so. The demand is not mute. By refraining from speaking, transcendence leaves it to us to find out what to do in the concrete situation. It does not take the responsibility away from us.

I add one more observation about the philosophical recognition of our guilt: Løgstrup's favorite way of expressing this recognition is not by using gift-giving language, but by pointing to the fact that the ethical demand is unfulfillable in the sense that it demands to be superfluous. Once we hear the demand as a demand, it is too late. The demand tells us what we ought to have done but did not do spontaneously. It tells us that we ought to have been good, but that we were not good. The demand judges us.

According to Bauman, gift language should be rejected as a residue of what Løgstrup was trying to get away from, namely, the idea that moral responsibility is grounded in reciprocity. Gift language presupposes a social system of mutual expectations in the service of equity and fairness. Gifts are expected to be reciprocated.

I agree with Reinders's criticism of Bauman, but I would put it a little differently. My question to Bauman is: Is this not a sociological description of the gift, rather than a phenomenological description? A true gift is given without conditions. My father, for example, was once offered a painting by the well-known Danish painter and satirist Fritz Jürgensen. It was offered to him by his aunt (Fritz Jürgensen's grandchild) as a "gift" but with the condition attached that I, and not my brothers or sister, should eventually inherit it. He rejected the gift, for he wanted a

214 gift and nothing else. I admire his moral standing in the matter, although I selfishly regret his decision. If a gift is conditional, then it is not a gift but a deal. If Bauman, Bourdieu, or Derrida claim there is no such phenomenon as gift-giving, that there is only conditional gift-giving, then they hypostasize the material economy as the ultimate reality. The fact that business and society as a whole pervert the notion of the gift and the language of gift-giving does not mean that the phenomenon does not exist. Must we not say: Of course there is such a phenomenon? Haven't many of us received unconditional gifts in our lives?

The next question is whether Løgstrup perverts the language of gift-giving. One must admit that a statement such as "A person is a debtor not because he or she has committed some wrong but simply because he or she exists and has received his or her life as a gift" (Løgstrup 1997, 116) is prone to misunderstanding. If guilt is connected to the gift, it sounds as if the gift is a conditional gift. I think the criticism is justified when applied to such statements. We can defend Løgstrup, however, if we regard his use of gift-giving language in his own broader context. Løgstrup does not say that the demand is grounded in the fact that life is a gift. It is only the one-sidedness that is grounded in the fact that life is a gift. The demand is grounded in the interdependency. But interdependency does not rule out my making claims on the other, which is, however, ruled out if life is a gift. If life is a gift, I cannot make any claims to it. That life is a gift does not mean that the giver makes conditions, but means that the receiver cannot make conditions and demand more gifts.

Perhaps one could also defend Løgstrup with the following reflection: It is right to describe life as a gift in the sense that everything we have, we have received from something or someone else; or, if we ourselves have contributed to what we have, then we have done so on the basis of what we have received. If one receives a gift, the only natural response is to be thankful and pass on gifts to others. This is what happens in natural love. We pass on gifts to our children, for instance. There is a general consensus that we ought not to use up all the resources of our planet and leave a polluted and desolate planet to our children. It is not considered natural to keep all the gifts of the Earth to ourselves. This example shows us that when we do not pass on gifts, we experience a demand to do so. But that means it is only when we do not understand life as a gift that we experience the ethical demand. Thus, the connection between the idea of life as a gift and the ethical demand is not direct but 215 indirect—and delicate. It is too simplistic—and thus misleading—to say that accepting a connection between life being a gift and guilt means that life is a conditional gift, and therefore not a gift. In my view, such criticism of gift-giving language uses a kind of bulldozer logic that indiscriminately flattens everything.

NOTE

1. An anthology compiled from *Metafysik I–IV* has been translated into English and published in two volumes (Løgstrup 1995).

REFERENCES

Løgstrup, K. E. 1995. *Metaphysics.* 2 vols. Milwaukee: Marquette University Press.
———. 1997. *The Ethical Demand.* Notre Dame: University of Notre Dame Press.
———. 2007. *Beyond the Ethical Demand.* Notre Dame: University of Notre Dame Press.

Contributors

Brenda Almond, Emeritus Professor of Moral and Social Philosophy, University of Hull

Svend Andersen, Professor of Ethics and Philosophy of Religion, University of Aarhus

Zygmunt Bauman, Emeritus Professor of Sociology, University of Leeds

Svein Aage Christoffersen, Professor of Ethics and Philosophy of Religion, University of Oslo

Hans Fink, Senior Associate Professor of Philosophy, University of Aarhus

Kees van Kooten Niekerk, Associate Research Professor of Ethics, University of Aarhus

Øjvind Larsen, Associate Professor of Philosophy and Sociology, Copenhagen Business School

Alasdair MacIntyre, Research Professor of Philosophy, University of Notre Dame

Anne Marie Pahuus, Assistant Professor of Philosophy, University of Aarhus

Hans S. Reinders, Professor of Ethics, Vrije Universiteit, Amsterdam

Jakob Wolf, Associate Professor of Systematic Theology, University of Copenhagen

Index